Shades of Citizenship

RACE AND THE CENSUS IN
MODERN POLITICS

Melissa Nobles

Stanford University Press
Stanford, California
2000

Stanford University Press
Stanford, California
© 2000 by the Board of Trustees of the
Leland Stanford Junior University
Printed in the United States of America
CIP data appear at the end of the book

Library of Congress Cataloging-in-Publication Data

Nobles, Melissa
    Shades of citizenship : race and the census in modern politics /
Melissa Nobles.
        p.   cm.
    Includes bibliographical references and index.
    ISBN 0-8047-4013-5 (cloth : alk. paper) —
    ISBN 0-8047-4059-3 (paper : alk. paper)
    1. Race. 2. Group identity. 3. Census. 4. United States—
Census. 5. Brazil—Census. I. Title.

HT1523.N63   2000
305.8'007'2—dc21   00-026707

This book is printed on acid-free, archival-quality paper.

Original printing 2000
Last figure below indicates year of this printing:
09   08   07   06   05   04   03   02   01   00

Typeset by John Feneron in 10/13 Sabon

Contents

Tables

Preface

In January 1999, the U.S. Supreme Court ruled that the Bureau of the Census may not use sampling techniques in determining representational apportionment. The Court's ruling rejected the Census Bureau's announced intention of introducing statistical sampling in order to reduce the undercount of racial minorities, especially blacks and Hispanics, in the 2000 census. The House of Representatives (including the District of Columbia) and residents of thirteen states had all filed separate suits challenging the constitutionality and legality of the Census Bureau's plans. Support and opposition divided largely along party lines, at least in the matter of apportionment. Democrats favored sampling because they expected to benefit from it electorally. Republicans opposed sampling because they expected to be disadvantaged. Yet the possibility of increasing accuracy through sampling is, in many ways, beside the point. With or without it, both Democratic and Republican state and local politicians remain keenly interested in ensuring the most accurate counts for their localities. More bodies mean more dollars, because numerous federal, state, and local funding formulas, as well as the business strategies of private enterprises, are based on population data. State and municipal governments throughout the country are gearing up for the 2000 census with the kind of fanfare that usually accompanies election campaigns. Making sure all bodies are counted is as important, if not more important, than getting out the vote.

Another important decision about the census did not, however, receive as much public attention, although it was just as politically and socially significant. In 1997, the Office of Management and Budget (OMB) announced that for the first time in the history of U.S. census-taking, Americans would be allowed to check more than one racial category on their census schedules. U.S. censuses have always asked a race question, have always required Americans to be so categorized (either by an enumerator or by self-selection), and have always offered a list of categories from which only one race was to be chosen. Sampling and racial undercounts presume the legitimacy and coherence of racial categorization. Only if the categories are themselves taken for granted can the task at hand become simply to count more accurately.

The fleeting attention given to OMB's decision is illustrative and symptomatic of the presumptions this book challenges. My intention has been to confront the presumed transparency and political neutrality of racial categorization on censuses directly. Even a brief survey of U.S. census schedules, past and present, raises questions that require answers: What do the terms *octoroon* and *quadroon* mean, and what were they doing in the 1890 census? How does one explain the seeming explosion of racial categories since 1970? More basically, why does race even appear in the census, and why have the categories changed from nearly one census to the next? How have Census Bureau officials thought about race? And how should we think about race? How has census categorization mattered to our political, intellectual, and social life? Inasmuch as bureaucratic procedures and demographic techniques provide few answers, I turned to history and politics for an explanation.

In writing this book, I first examined the assumptions that characterize most scholarly and popular treatments of censuses and census bureaus, and then assumed the opposite. In my view, census bureaus are not innocent bystanders in the arena of politics; census data are never merely demographic data. But the convention of technical objectivity and political disinterest is so jealously guarded and pervasive that it is difficult to isolate the supporters of this view. Confidence in census-taking and its success in capturing truth is so thoroughly embedded that the process has taken on what might be called a "Teflon" quality. One can criticize census bureaus and census methods without seriously damaging them. In the end, the view seems to be that if census categories are counting something and census data are telling us something, does it much matter where the categories come from? This book demonstrates that it matters enormously. Unraveling the origins of racial categories requires us to think differently about race. Racial census categories are not self-evidently right or natural, because race itself is not. Race is a complex and often internally contradictory set of ideas about human similarity and difference. Racial membership and racial boundaries are actively created and recreated through language, thought, social interactions, and institutional processes. Census-taking is one of the institutional mechanisms by which racial boundaries are set.

My claim that census bureaus and their products are politically implicated does not usually give rise to much disagreement (nor does it shake confidence in them). The myriad uses of census data, especially racial data, in public life expose the political stakes that accompany census methods and census-taking. But my argument goes further, because I also claim that racial enumeration itself creates and advances concepts of race, bringing into being the racial reality that census officials presume is already there, waiting to be counted. Ideas of race, in turn, shape public policies. In this book, I identify precisely how censuses do this and then explore its political consequences in two societies, the United States and Brazil.

This book seeks to advance theorizing about race and its political significance through comparative study. Until the mid twentieth century, American political scientists approached racial politics as the study of the problem that the treatment of the "Negro" (if not the very presence of "Negroes") presented to American democracy. Since then, political scientists have focused on the Civil Rights Movement and the political, legal, economic, and social gains that African Americans have managed to secure and struggle to protect. The equation of the study of "race" with the study of "blacks" is only the most obvious of the problems characteristic of most conventional approaches. That "white" has served as a fundamental racial category anchoring American political, economic, and social life is mostly taken for granted. That "black" and other "nonwhite" categories are made meaningful because of their relationship to "white" is at once acknowledged and largely dismissed.

The book also challenges the assumption that state institutions only manage "race relations" and have nothing to do with the creation of race itself—the nature of which is taken for granted. It seeks to insert the discipline of political science into a conversation about the constitution of race in which social theorists, historians, legal scholars, philosophers, anthropologists, and sociologists have long been engaged. In an unfortunate if predictable way, American political scientists are the "Johnny-come-latelys" on the issue.

The problem of how to approach race is even more acute among Brazilian social scientists, because in Brazil there is supposed to be nothing to study. Brazil has no race problems, because Brazilians are racially mixed and there has been neither racial segregation nor apparent racial animus. Foreign and Brazilian scholarship has finally laid this image of a racially democratic and harmonious Brazil to rest. Yet scholarly thinking about race in Brazil remains muddled. Like American social scientists, Brazilians (and many Americans studying Brazil) have measured the significance of race in Brazilian society and politics according to how blacks are treated and the ways in which racial concerns drive institutional and party politics. Using the United States as an external referent, Brazilians have judged race to be of low political salience, and its absence from institutional politics—no racial segregation laws, no affirmative action policies, no racial bloc voting—has sustained this assessment. However, equating the study of race with blacks and discrimination has obscured the central significance of race and the role played by one state institution, the Census Bureau, in upholding it. Race is important precisely because Brazilians have viewed themselves as forming a single "new" race, composed of three original races. Understanding race in Brazil is far from marginal to understanding Brazilian politics. Indeed, race goes to the heart of Brazilian national identity and politics. In the national development of the United States and Brazil, the idea of race has mattered profoundly. Their censuses show us how.

This book grew out of my doctoral dissertation, which focused on Brazil, and made only passing references to the United States. In reconceptualizing and expanding the book's scope to include both countries, I have benefited enormously from the suggestions, comments, criticisms, and support of many people. I have presented this research in various stages of development, and at each stage, exchange has been fruitful and edifying. With the generous financial support of the Alfred P. Sloan Foundation and MIT, I organized a two-day workshop on censuses in 1996. Participants included historians, demographers, sociologists, legal scholars, and officials from the U.S. Bureau of the Census and Statistics Canada. I thank Anita Allen, Margo Anderson, Rogers Brubaker, Joan Bryant, Stephen Feinberg, David Theo Goldberg, Joshua Goldstein, Francine Hirsch, John Kralt, Clara Rodriguez, Sharon Russell Stanton, Ibrahim Sundiata, Michael Teitelbaum, and Clyde Tucker for their participation. Although unable to attend the conference, Nathan Glazer read an earlier draft of the manuscript and provided useful comments. In 1997, I gave a talk at Brown University's Watson Center for International Studies to an interested and receptive audience. Its seminar series "Politics, Culture, and Identity" eventually culminated in a two-day conference on racial, ethnic, and language categorization in national censuses. Here, I was introduced to an even larger group of scholars, all interested in issues of categorization, from a variety of disciplines and with a range of regional expertise. The conference felt like a homecoming of sorts, as I realized that an exciting area of scholarly investigation was taking on new life through another generation of scholars. I have especially profited from my continuing collaboration with the conference organizers, David I. Kertzer and Dominique Arel.

My experiences with Brazilian scholars and student audiences have also been productive and enhancing. In 1998, I presented my research at the Centro de Estudos Afro-Asiáticos (Center of Afro-Asian Studies) at the Candido Mendes University in Rio de Janeiro and at the Centro Brasileiro de Analise e Planejamento (CEBRAP) in São Paulo. My conversations with Livio Sansone of the Center of Afro-Asian Studies, Giralda Seiferth of the Federal University of Rio de Janeiro, and Elza Berquó and Luiz Filipe de Alencastro of CE-

BRAP were especially helpful. Lucila Bandeira Beato, of the Instituto Brasileiro de Geográfia e Estatística (IBGE), Wania Sant'Anna of the Federação de Órgão para Assistência Social e Educacional (FASE), and Regina Domingues have incalculably deepened my understanding of Brazilian racial politics. Closer to home, my colleagues at MIT have contributed directly and indirectly to my thinking and writing; I thank Suzanne Berger, Margaret Burnham, Josh Cohen, Dan Kryder, Richard Locke, and Judith Tendler. Anani Dzidzienyo and Thomas Skidmore, both of Brown University, have supported my research and encouraged its development from dissertation to book by reading and commenting on successive drafts.

When I began research on the history of American racial categorization, there were few secondary sources that were of any use. My research assistant, Julie Lorinc, and I quickly turned to primary sources to learn anything at all. Julie possesses an impressive ability to negotiate the labyrinth of government documents efficiently and productively, and her assistance is greatly appreciated. The staff of Harvard's University Lamont Library (the depository of government documents) are to be especially commended for their help and services. Phil Creech, civil records librarian of the U.S. National Archives, David Pemberton of the History Staff of the Policy Office of the U.S. Bureau of the Census, and Justin Murray, reference librarian of the Bureau of the Census Library, provided invaluable assistance and advice. My secretary, Peter Kubaska, competently assisted in every stage of the book's development.

Stanford University Press has been encouraging and enormously helpful from the very beginning. I want to especially thank executive editor Muriel Bell, production editor and desktop-publishing specialist John Feneron, and copyeditor Peter Dreyer.

Finally, I thank most deeply my family and the many friends who have patiently endured this project along with me and have managed to remain interested in it.

Shades of Citizenship

CHAPTER I

Race, Censuses, and Citizenship

Obtaining racial data would seem to be a straightforward process: the census asks a question; statisticians, demographers, and other properly trained professionals tabulate the responses. To count by race presumes, however, that there is "something" there to be counted—but what exactly is it? Nor does counting by race necessarily reveal how racial data will be tabulated or what purposes they will serve. The answers to these questions are found in the actions of politicians, scientists, public-policy makers, organized advocates, and in particular political and historical circumstances. Counting by race is as much a political act as it is an enumerative one. Census bureaus are not simply producers of racial statistical data; they are also political actors.

This book analyzes the mutually reinforcing dynamic between concepts of race, censuses, and citizenship. It argues that censuses help form racial discourse, which in turn affects the public policies that either vitiate or protect the rights, privileges, and experiences commonly associated with citizenship. To support this argument, it makes four basic and related claims. The first is that race is not an objective category, which censuses simply count, but a fluid and internally contradicting discourse, partly created by and embedded in institutional processes, including those of the census itself. The second is that census bureaus are not politically neutral institutions, employing impartial methods, but state agencies that use census methods and data as instruments of governance. Third, racial discourse influences both the rationales for public policy and its outcomes. Public policies not only use racial census data; these data assist in the development of public policy. Fourth, and finally, individuals and groups seek to alter the terms of racial discourse in order to advance political and social aims, and have targeted censuses precisely because they help to make and sustain such discourse. At its broadest level, this book examines the interaction between ideas and institutions: ideas about race are partly created and enlivened by census bureaus, which thus structure political outcomes.

I should clarify at the outset what this book does *not* argue: that racial ideas and discourse are entirely reducible to more fundamental material interests and political power, or that they are wholly independent of larger political and economic arrangements. The same is true of census bureaus. Rather, this book contends that racial discourse is itself consequential, and that the existence of accompanying interests and power neither diminishes its power nor exhausts its meanings.[1] Similarly, census bureaus do not operate in a vacuum but within broad political and economic contexts.[2] The statement that racial ideas and discourse matter would seem to need little defense. Yet stating *that* they matter is not the same as showing *how* they matter or explaining *why* they matter. This book takes up that task and does so by way of census-taking. Finally, although census-taking is the focus of the book, this does not mean that census bureaus are the only or the most important places where concepts of race are made and remade. The point is that census bureaus are typically overlooked as participants in the creation and perpetuation of race. This book seeks to remove the cloak of neutrality and social scientific objectivity to reveal their insider status.

It is no surprise that politics infuses census-taking. Public distrust of statistics is long-standing, a sentiment captured in a quip by Benjamin Disraeli: "[T]here are three kinds of lies: lies, damned lies, and statistics." Yet this distrust exists uneasily alongside a deep reliance on statistics and a strong belief in statistical methods, if not in any specific set of numbers.[3] This reliance is obvious; statistical data are used everywhere, in countless ways and for all conceivable purposes. Demographic and medical statistics provide information on virtually all stages of human existence: life expectancy, fecundity, morbidity, nutrition, and mortality. Economic statistics furnish similarly comprehensive information. Statistics provide a powerful and useful way of knowing the world. But we also come to know the world, in part, through the order that statistics and statistical methodology impose. Our dependence on numbers is linked to our "trust in numbers" and their ability to reveal truth, if not *the* truth.[4] The force of statistics in public life is not derived solely from their methods and truth claims, however. It is also derived from state authority. States have long relied on census statistics.[5] In the past, rulers have used censuses to spy on inhabitants, to conscript them into military service, and to levy taxes on them. Today, states more often use censuses to assess a country's population and resources, the enumerated being considered citizens to be served, not simply subjects to be watched, conscripted, or taxed. The state's production and use of census statistics enhance their influence in public life precisely because they thus become "official." The pall that state involvement casts over census-taking, however, extends beyond the political uses of this information to the political origins of certain categories. One of these is race.

Our thinking about race is conflicted. On the one hand, we are confused about it—is it a biological or a social construct?—and about what it means to be of "one race" or of "mixed race." On the other hand, we are convinced that there is something there, that we can know an individual's race by looking at him or her or by asking questions. Science has shaped our thinking on race in profound ways. Yet science has also raised as many questions about race as it has purported to answer. As historians of scientific racial thought have shown, ideas about what groups were or could be properly defined as "races" have changed over time, as have methods of determining racial membership. People with religious, linguistic, or physical characteristics in common, or who have simply shared geographical space, have at various times been defined as constituting a race.[6] Moreover, scientific determinants of racial membership have ranged from simple observation of skin complexion to elaborate and precise measurement of skull size (craniology and phrenology), shape of face and facial features, and body stature (anthropometry).[7] Today, many scientists and anthropologists call for the abandonment of the idea of discrete raçes.[8] Science's new stance on race is not that of census bureaus, however, which still count by race. In recent years, as in the past, census definitions of race have differed from scientific definitions, however much science has influenced census-taking. The interests of science and of social science in knowing about race differ too. The questions nonetheless remain, what are censuses counting today and why; what have they counted historically and why? Through examining census methods and policies, we come closer to understanding what race is and what it is not.

If race is a vexing but salient social identification, citizenship is the most fundamental political identification. A citizen is formally a member of a nation-state, but citizenship is more than a mere formality; it entitles a person to a set of rights, imposes obligations, and engenders lived experiences. To be sure, the road to the civil, political, and economic rights described by T. H. Marshall as the hallmarks of citizenship has always been a rocky and winding one.[9] Deciding who enjoys these rights has often been as contentious as establishing the rights themselves. As important as citizen status is, then, it does not stand alone. Other identifications, such as race, gender, class, and nativity, have often qualified citizenship, if not defined it explicitly. Across nations and historical epochs, political communities have included groups and excluded groups according to different, often shifting, criteria. In the United States, for example, race has been a fundamental qualifier of citizenship. During the antebellum period, citizenship depended on group membership: whites were citizens; slaves were not.[10] Free blacks were legally citizens until the Dred Scott Decision of 1857, "when the Supreme Court ruled that they were not citizens after all."[11] Yet, even as citizens, free blacks did not enjoy the same rights and privileges as whites. The passage of the Thirteenth, Fourteenth, and Fifteenth amendments after the Civil War formally extended citizenship and the franchise to black Americans, but it would be another 100 years before all black Americans could hope to enjoy the rights described and guaranteed in the Fourteenth and Fifteenth. To be a black in apartheid South Africa or a Jew in Nazi Germany was to be a noncitizen.[12] To be Brazilian, in contrast, has turned on an elastic notion of race in which all Brazilians are regarded as racially mixed and all are becoming "whiter." Yet whatever the extent of racial mixture among Brazilians, the majority have lacked the basic rights associated with citizenship for most of the twentieth century and for all of the country's earlier history.

A discussion of citizenship and race would seem a far remove from census-taking, but it is not. Most simply, censuses register and reinforce the racial identifications germane to citizenship through the process of categorization itself. But their involvement goes much deeper. Justifications for racial exclusion in the United States have relied heavily on racial census data. As we shall see, nineteenth-century politicians and scientists marshaled racial census data as incontrovertible proof of the racial inferiority of black Americans and their unsuitability for full citizenship. Of course, political and economic forces more powerful than the census were ultimately responsible for undermining full citizenship for blacks, but racial ideas were essential to these justifications, and census data in turn became crucial to sustaining and advancing these ideas. Today, U.S. racial data are vital to a range of public policies and laws designed to address racial disadvantage and discrimination; indeed, the successful remedying of such disadvantage is viewed as essential in deepening the meanings and experiences of American citizenship. In Brazil, census data have sustained the linked ideas of Brazilians as "racially mixed" and of Brazil as a "racial democracy," even when there was no political democracy. As Brazilians seek to strengthen democracy and enrich the meanings of their citizenship, they have begun to demand a change in census-taking methods and in interpretations of census color data.

The story of censuses, race, and citizenship is larger than the sum of its parts. After all, censuses are conducted only once every ten years; and the census schedule is a form, albeit an official one. Taken together, however, census schedules have been used as the building blocks of social knowledge. State officials, scientists, politicians, and citizens have assigned great weight to censuses, with great political consequences. Racial categorization likewise tells us much and yet obscures much about the societies in which racial thought is prevalent. Censuses provide a lens for examining at close range how race is constructed. National citizenship is often taken for granted by everyone—except those who are excluded or disallowed from enjoying its full benefits. Who is considered a first-class citizen and what it means depends on who is considered a second-class citizen and what it means. Race has qualified citizenship. Examining race, censuses, and dimensions of citizenship together enhances our understanding of all three as separate components and as a working whole. The United States and Brazil provide the evidence for my argument, and it is to the reasons behind this comparison that we now turn.

Comparing the United States and Brazil

Along key dimensions of political and economic analysis, the United States and Brazil hardly seem comparable. America's history of democratic and constitutional governance (albeit with long-restricted electoral participation for nonwhites and women and racial subordination) and twentieth-century economic and military world dominance contrasts starkly with that of Brazil. Brazilian political history is a story of highly concentrated elite governance: nineteenth-century monarchical rule followed by twentieth-century oligarchical and military rule, with periodic disruptions in the twentieth century by competitive party politics and elections, first from 1945 through 1963, and then from 1985 to the present. Brazil's economy is now the world's eighth largest, but its income distribution is among the most unequal in the world. Brazil has yet to contend in a sustained manner with this maldistribution of income and its accompanying crushing poverty, or with the crisis of public education, the necessity of land reform, or the absence of efficacious social policies for the poor and working classes. Politics largely takes place on the state and municipal levels, making it difficult for federal legislators and the president to develop and sustain national policy goals. Indeed, in terms of political economy and politics, the United States and Brazil occupy two discrete, if connected, universes. On the axis of race, however, comparison has been unavoidable and has seemed utterly appropriate. It is also a comparison that scholars have judged Brazil to have "won" in this respect, in that Brazilian race relations appear far more harmonious and less rigidly stratified than those of the United States. The basis for this comparative scholarship is slavery and its aftermath. The economies of both countries were rooted in African enslavement and European settlement. Brazil was dominant among Latin American and Caribbean sugar producers in the nineteenth century[13] and was also the "largest single participant in the transatlantic slave trade, accounting for 41 percent of the approximately ten million people transported."[14] The United States, by comparison, imported approximately 693,000 slaves, 7 percent of the ten million. But if it imported far fewer slaves proportionally than Brazil or English colonists in Jamaica, the United States came to have the largest slave population in the Western Hemisphere owing partly to the fostering of slave reproduction by American slaveowners and partly to the extremely brutal slave-labor conditions in Brazil and Jamaica.[15] American slavery was finally abolished in 1865 by way of a bloody civil war. In Brazil, the parliament and Princess-Regent Isabel abolished slavery peacefully by decree in 1888, making it the last country in the hemisphere to do away with the institution. The idea of "races" and strict boundaries between them, created and sustained until the mid twentieth century by U.S. law and custom, were absent in Brazil.

Their shared histories of slavery, coupled with the postslavery experiences of U.S. racial segregation and the absence of such experiences in Brazil, have been grist for the scholarly mill. Scholars have provided a range of explanations to account for the differences between these societies during and after slavery. According to these explanations, Brazil and the United States are polar opposites: the former a "racial democracy" and the latter a racial tyranny.

However, this book contends that the hidden similarities between the two countries are as important as their evident differences. Unlike most comparative scholarship, this study does not equate race with "black" or define racial politics or race relations as the existence or absence of racial segregation against blacks. Rather, it treats racial discourse, which pertains to everybody, as a fundamental organizing principle of politics and society in both countries. Its comparative focus on racial discourse is significant precisely because it makes race the object to be explained and compared. The concept of race itself has usually been overlooked, even as scholars have stressed the dissimilarities between the societal formulations of racial membership in both countries. A brief review of conventional scholarship shows that racial discourse, the most fundamental similarity, has been obscured by studies committed to the divergent fates of "the Negro," erroneously conflated to mean the study of race.

According to earlier scholarship, the differences were rooted in founding traditions.[16] American traditions were said to have developed from English legal and political thought, with its emphasis on individual liberty, from Protestantism with its accompanying work ethic, and from a profound negrophobia.[17] Brazilian traditions, in contrast, developed from Portuguese legal and political thought, Catholicism, and an apparently relaxed attitude toward blacks, owing to Portugal's contact with the Moors.[18] Slavery presented profound philosophical as well as constitutional and institutional problems for both societies, but more especially for American political development.[19] Scholars, most prominently Frank Tannenbaum, argued that these contrasting traditions account for the differences in the institutions of slavery and in postabolition race relations.[20]

American slavery was thought to be harsher because of lower manumission rates and rigid color lines that corresponded closely, if not exactly, to civil status: "whites" were free and "blacks" (broadly defined) were not. Brazilian slavery, in contrast, was thought to be less harsh because of higher manumission rates, the religious protections provided by Catholicism, and a sizable class of persons known as "free people of color," whose free status made a strict correspondence between color and slave status impossible. Postabolition relations also bore the stamp of these traditions. American society was socially, and in the South legally, segregated by race. Racial identification was rigid and consequential in either positive or negative ways, depending upon one's racial identification. Brazilian society lacked such rigid racial distinctions, and their absence was supposedly the creator and the guarantor of racial integration. Finally, interracial sex was not prohibited in Brazil, whereas it was closely monitored and proscribed in the United States. The Brazilian anthropologist Gilberto Freyre added another crucial element to this generally sanguine view when he called Brazil a "racial democracy"; in sharp contrast to the racial tyranny of the United States, racial mixture had led in Brazil to a type of society unknown elsewhere in the New World.[21]

Scholars have since drastically reduced the explanatory weight accorded to founding traditions and to the differences between the American and the Brazilian slave systems. They now emphasize economic, political, and social explanations rather than ideational ones,[22] and focus on more contemporary factors, rather than on slavery's long shadow, to explain both the differences and the emerging similarities in social relations between the two countries.[23]

Most important for our purposes, however, is the fact that the very coherence of these comparisons hinges on racial categorization. Scholars have handled the issue of defining race in seemingly contradictory ways. On the one hand, much of this scholarship has necessarily focused on shifting ideas about race and on different ways of categorizing people according to race. It is impossible to understand nineteenth- and early twentieth-century America or Brazil without taking into account competing views of race in science, law, and religion.[24] At the same time, this scholarship has considered the race categories of "white," "black," and "mixed," or "mulatto," as self-evident, assuming that however differently these racial labels have been applied, they ultimately corresponded to a natural reality. Much of the comparative scholarship of the 1930s through the 1970s stressed the variations in racial classification in explaining the differences between American and Brazilian societal relations.

Today, scholars are less interested in highlighting variations in black racial categorization than in dismissing them. According to these views, Brazil's racial categorization more closely resembles America's, in consequence if not in form, than was previously thought. Because the "mixed race" category in Brazil offers no significant material advantage over "black," they claim, the "mixed race," or "brown," and "black" categories can reasonably be grouped together in scholarly work and demographic analyses, if not in common parlance. This view is advanced by both Brazilian and North American scholars. A second view generally imposes a North American construction of "black" without explicitly calling it that: Brazil is described, for example, as having the largest "black" or "African origin" population outside of Nigeria, although how such a description is appropriate is not explained.[25] Other scholars discuss "Afro-Brazilians" and compare them to "black Americans," when the evident frailty of a corporate black racial identity in Brazil is precisely what these same scholars are motivated to explain.[26] Chapter 4 considers how Brazilian activists are attempting to create a black identity that can be applied to Brazilians and that will be widely asserted by them. Likewise, in the United States, the creation and recreation of corporate racial identities remain ongoing political and social projects, undertaken by state institutions, intellectuals, organized groups, and individual citizens.

The United States and Brazil are comparable, not simply because of historical slavery and the presence today in each country of large populations descended from African slaves, but because of shared functions of racial discourse. Indeed, racial discourse has existed in societies without plantation slavery or Africans. In colonial Malaysia, for example, race was used to describe the broad groupings of Europeans, Malays, Chinese, Indians, and others, and by 1901, the term *race* appeared in colonial censuses.[27] Modern racial thought, which had its beginnings in the Enlightenment,[28] marked not only the establishment of European colonies in Africa and Asia but

European settlement of North and South America, South Africa, and Australia.[29] Although scholars have generally treated racial thinking as a distinctly Western phenomenon, recent scholarship argues that racial thought has been the foundation of national identities in China and Japan too and is not simply a Western import there.[30] In all of these cases, race has been an ensemble of ideas that make up a language of inclusion and engender experiences of membership.

Race as Discourse

Counting by race is hardly a transparent process, because of the very conceptual ambiguities that surround race itself and the political stakes attached to it. These ambiguities are neither trivial nor simple, given the place of race in economic, political, and social life. Although the scholarship that refers to race in one way or another is vast, the portion of it that explains the concept of race is noticeably less so, albeit still substantial. The intellectual consensus today is that race has no objective existence. In the wake of this revelation, itself largely the result of scientific decree, scholars have set themselves the task of defining, explaining, describing, and analyzing race. Thus, according to the sociologists Michael Omi and Howard Winant, race is "a concept which signifies and symbolizes social conflicts and interests referring to different types of human bodies."[31] The historian Evelyn Brooks Higginbotham understands race to have various "faces"; it is at once a "social construction," "a highly contested representation of relations of power between social categories by which individuals are identified and identify themselves," "a myth," "a global sign," and a "metalanguage."[32] The philosopher David Theo Goldberg argues that race is an "irreducibly *political* category," in that "racial creation and management acquire import in framing and giving specificity to the body politic."[33] According to Ian Haney Lopez, the law constructs race legally by fixing the boundaries of races, by defining the content of racial identities, and by specifying their relative disadvantages and privileges in American society.[34] The literary critic Henry

Louis Gates sees race as the "ultimate trope of difference because it is so very arbitrary in its application."[35] Historians of ideas have traced ideas of race and racial thought in various countries and different historical epochs.[36]

Scholars are a long way indeed from seeing race as fixed or objective, and, in significant ways, as deriving its existence from human bodies at all. Instead, its existence derives from and rests in language, in social practices, in legal definitions, in ideas, in structural arrangements, in the distribution of political and economic power, and in contests over such distribution. On these views, taken together, race is at once an empty category and a powerful instrument. Yet theoretical formulations that stress the radical plasticity of race, mostly correctly, I think, risk obscuring its concrete manifestations and the institutional sites of its construction and maintenance. These scholars may view race as political in some fundamental way, but they pay little close attention to state institutions and political processes.[37]

Building on this theoretical work, this book also interprets race as discourse. That is, race is not something that language simply describes, it is something that is created through language and institutional practices. As discourse, race creates and organizes human differences in politically consequential ways. The book advances this understanding of race by analyzing how census bureaus help to develop and maintain it.

Race has many, although not equally formative, sources. Science, religion, moral philosophy, law, politics, and economics have all contributed to a greater, and internally contradictory, discourse of race. Christianity, for example, has long nurtured belief in a cosmic order to which every race belongs and in which it is hierarchically ranked. God created human races, and the observable differences in appearance and in political, economic, and social standing are God's will.[38] National laws have also at times provided explicit definitions of racial membership. Slavery was, of course, a prime contributor to the entrenchment of racial thought in the Americas. Racial thought has accompanied, if not preceded, and been used to justify a range of economically exploitative arrangements. In both the United States and Brazil, the ongoing material consequences of racial memberships complicate how class inequalities are viewed and politically addressed.

The power of racial discourse derives from the mutually reinforcing dynamic among these separate foundations, with science, law, economics, religion, and politics coming together on a macro level to reinforce the positive consequences of some racial memberships and the negative consequences of others. Just as all these sources have not made equal contributions to racial discourse, the influence of each has also been unequal. The weight of scientific thought in racial discourse can hardly be overestimated. As the historian Nancy Stepan observes, during the period from 1800 to 1960, European and American scientists especially were "preoccupied by race," which was viewed as a principal determinant of human affairs.[39] It would be a mistake, too, to regard this science simply as "pseudo-science." Race science was not perceived as "pseudo" in its own time, and far from being regarded as "quacks," its practitioners were highly regarded and respected. Today, although scientists reject race as a scientifically meaningful concept, whether race was (or is) viewed as "natural" is, in certain ways, quite beside the point. Scientific racial thought has never simply meant "proving" the biological reality of race. Equally important has been the role of scientific ideas in shaping political discourse and public policies. As we shall see, the nineteenth-century scientist Josiah Nott's interest in race was inextricably connected with his ideas about slavery, Negro citizenship, and the propriety of white economic, political, and social supremacy.

This formulation of race as discourse sets out to clarify what race is, but just as important and illuminating is what race is not. "Racial discourse," as referred to here, is not synonymous with racism. This distinction is a fine one, and it is intended to capture differences in degree, not in kind. Once dominant and still highly influential variants of racial discourse have themselves been profoundly racist. Yet there are also variants that attempt to define race in nonhierarchical ways, that purport merely to acknowledge human differences without according them undue significance.

Whatever their impulses, however, these two broad variants constitute a discourse that variously creates race and imparts to it political and social salience.

Ethnicity is sometimes defined in terms of race, as well as of culture, language, ancestry, and religion, but racial discourse is not ethnic discourse.[40] Scholars treat ethnic categorization as a benignly descriptive marker—albeit one sometimes used for politically objectionable ends—but race has always had political meanings and uses. Nonetheless, whether ethnic identity is a matter of birth, of choice, or of some other factor, ethnicity indisputably resembles race in that it points to human similarities and differences. Ethnicity is a fluid designation, however, and, unlike race, it has never had the imprimatur of science: scholars have regarded it as socially made and subjective, and race as naturally created and objective. This book takes the opposite view, treating race as artificial, although not arbitrary, and subjective, although not inconsequential.

Census Bureaus and Race

Bureaucracies are not necessarily monolithic, omnipotent organizations; nor need they be entirely beholden to other, more powerful political bodies, such as legislatures, courts, or chief executives.[41] Their organization and their culture, as well as the motivations of bureaucrats and the capacities of leaders, are important in explaining their behavior and efficacy. The larger institutional and political context in which bureaucracies operate is also of great significance. This is as true for statistical bureaucracies as for any other kind. Yet, however obvious the claim, census bureaus are not always viewed as political bureaucracies. Rather, scholars present them as embattled state institutions that attempt to shield themselves (usually unsuccessfully) from political pressures that may impede their ability to produce impartial numbers. Somehow statistical methods are expected to cleanse the census-taking process of politics. History and politics cannot, however, be expunged from census-taking. Numbers without categories are useless, and the origins of categories require explanation. This view of census-taking as political in origin and consequence competes with concerted efforts by international bodies and national governments to ensure and demonstrate its political impartiality.

Most national census bureaus employ similar statistical methods and administrative procedures, and international guidelines have advanced this uniformity. Since 1946, the United Nations has sponsored four world population programs whose express purpose is to improve and standardize national censuses.[42] The push for standardization entrenches the view that census-taking methods, and, by extension, census bureaus, can transcend particular political and economic environments. Thus, census-taking can, in theory at least, be methodologically the same in democratic states and in authoritarian ones, in rich countries and in poor ones, in homogeneous and heterogeneous societies. Indeed, when censuses have been overtly tied to political regimes, they have been seen as the exceptions that prove the rule of impartiality. Soviet census data were completely suppressed in 1937, for example, because they revealed the unusually high mortality rates that resulted from the 1932–33 famine, brought on by forced collectivization.[43] Senior statisticians who had supervised the census were arrested and shot. The appearance of political noninvolvement is crucially important to the legitimacy of census bureaus and censuses, both domestically and internationally. Soviet census data were mistrusted internationally precisely because of their obviously close connection to the regime's political goals.[44] At the same time, this Soviet example reveals, albeit in an extreme way, the enduring connection between census-taking and statecraft in all countries. State officials have long used censuses to fulfill basic state "behavioral imperatives" to know and control their populations, consolidate political and economic power, and present national bills of health and wealth.[45] Today, state officials and international organizations consider census-taking an indispensable component of responsible governance. Yet censuses remain instruments at a state's disposal, not simply registers of performance and population.

Census bureau statisticians treat racial enumeration as the task of devising appropriate categories and counting by them. Race and its use as a counter have been regarded as self-evident in a way that belies the conceptual and political wrangling surrounding the production of racial data. Most scholarly and popular books on censuses present racial categorization as a technical procedure in need of little explanation. An institutional history of the U.S. Census Bureau written by a former bureau director never mentions racial categorization's contentious history.[46] Similarly, unpublished histories of the Instituto Brasileiro de Geográfia e Estatística (IBGE), the Brazilian statistical institute, recount political decrees and administrative acts, but make no mention of the checkered past of color categorization in Brazil.[47] Until very recently, census officials and statisticians of both countries have offered no clear public explanations of the racial categories employed and their definitions. Current explanations raise as many questions as they answer.

According to Sally Katzen, director of the Office of Information and Regulatory Affairs at the Office of Management and Budget, "[W]hen the OMB got into the business of establishing categories, it was purely statistical, not programmatic. . . . It was certainly never meant to *define* a race."[48] However, OMB's Statistical Directive No. 15 explicitly defines races, making her statement inconsistent with practice. Her point, however, is that races are out there in the world, waiting to be counted. Government officials reject any notion that OMB plays any role in creating race through categorization. Similarly, in explaining the rationale for a 1976 household survey, the IBGE statistician and demographer Valeria Motta Leite implicitly claimed impartiality for her agency by saying that it had "tried to verify the best way of discovering the color of the Brazilian population."[49] In thus seeking to distance census methods of racial and color categorization from politics, these two responses achieve the very opposite: they raise more questions than they answer, prompting demands for even fuller disclosure of census methods and purposes.

It would be inaccurate to suggest, however, that those most closely connected to census-taking are the only ones who insist on the political disinterest of census bureaus and objectivity of statistical methods. Social scientists, who have long recognized the role of other state institutions in shaping racial politics, have all but ignored census bureaus and censuses. Instead, they have emphasized the ways in which state institutions distribute public goods along racial lines and/or manage racially based demands from civil society. The actions and policies of public institutions such as schools, courts, and social service agencies have been examined extensively, and the role of electoral systems in shaping racial politics has been analyzed. However, scholars have usually treated state agencies as managers of racial issues or referents for racial demands, not as places where race is constituted. An important exception is the work of critical race theorists in the United States, who examine, not only the ways in which the law treats persons categorized into different races differently, but how the law creates the racial categories themselves.[50]

When social scientists mention censuses, they refer to contention over numbers and over the distribution of political power, public goods, and rhetorical claims that hang in the balance. Census politics are, according to one scholar, an "entitlement" issue, where an ethnic group's anxiety about its own fecundity vis-à-vis that of another group combines with fear of political domination.[51] Majority group status effectively determines which group is entitled to political, economic, and social power. Much of the scholarly and public reaction to potential changes in race categories in the 2000 U.S. census has focused on the efforts of organized groups to protect their numbers and the benefits and protections that attach to racial categorization.[52] Undoubtedly, census politics overlap with racial/ethnic politics in matters of distribution, but the connection between race and censuses goes deeper. The Census Bureau has escaped inquiry both as a state institution that determines the benefits and penalties of racial memberships through the data it collects and as a place where racial categories themselves are constructed. The perception that census agencies and census categories are at some remove from politics ensures that a deeper theoretical appreciation of how the census supports racial discourse and how census racial data serve public policy is blunted.

Public Policy and the Census

Public policies give citizenship its fullest meaning. In the United States, a range of public policies and laws turn on racial distinctions. In contrast, in Brazil, public policies are said to be explained by and reflected in the supposed absence of racial distinctions. Moreover, public policies employ extensive statistical data, including racial data, linking them with censuses in an obvious and important way. Racial data are the basis of public policies, and public policies generate and justify the need for racial data. Certainly, in the United States, public policies designed to address past and present racial discrimination rely heavily on census racial data, fueling charges that the U.S. census has become politicized. In Brazil, the push for census racial data is driven, in part, by the desire to develop such public policies and legislation.

But there is more: in both the United States and Brazil, racial and color categories have served larger discourses about race. Some politicians and bureau officials have viewed censuses as a means of testing and proving various theories about race, making the "self-evident" presence of race categories in censuses not so self-evident at all. Scientists used censuses to test and prove racial theories as much as to simply count by race. The "mulatto" category appeared in seven U.S. censuses in order to provide answers to scientific questions about race. These answers would be employed to develop and justify policies of racial preservation, that is, legal segregation. In Brazil, scientists and officials postulated that through racial mixture, white Brazilians would become stronger, and black and brown Brazilians "whiter" and "better." Turning race science on its head, Brazilians accepted the existence of races and their hierarchical ranking and argued that racial mixing led to racial cleansing and regeneration, not degeneration. "Whites" would remain "whites," only stronger and better equipped for life in the tropics, while "blacks" and those of "mixed race" would eventually become "white" through cleansing. The 1920 census text was the first to describe and predict the inevitable "mixing" and "whitening" of the Brazilian people, which reflected the reality of racial democracy. Racial democracy, in turn, resulted from the absence of state-sponsored segregation. The racial democracy ideal, in other words, did not require racially segregatory public policies and, indeed, found them repellent.

Equally important, IBGE has resisted cross-tabulating color categories with socioeconomic variables and released color data slowly. Without such data, activists and scholars have been stymied in their efforts to test claims that color is inconsequential and to push for policy interventions. Whereas in the United States, racial data are the raw material for civil rights legislation and policies, in Brazil, activists seek to recast the census as the destroyer, not the sustainer, of the racial democracy idea. In so doing, they seek to create a rationale for generating data for positive public policies. The racial democracy idea has disallowed positive policies by proclaiming them unnecessary. The move from the discourse of a racially mixed and hence racially democratic society to that of a multiracial and racially stratified society today justifies the very affirmative action policies long deemed unwarranted.

Social Movements and the Census

It is not surprising that state institutions should be referents for organized collective action. As generators and possessors of political power, state agencies create channels for nondisruptive or acceptable expressions of political action. The state is both "target and mediator" of collective action.[53] State institutions order political action both by setting the rules of the game and by providing incentives and disincentives for organized action. As one particular type of state agency, census bureaus function in these general ways.

That the census bureau itself may be the target and arena of collective action, however, still does not fully explain why it has been so identified at a particular historical moment. Here, an explanation based in the concept of "political opportunity structures" is most useful.[54] Sidney Tarrow defines a political opportunity structure as "consistent—but not necessarily formal, permanent or national—dimensions of the political environment which either encourage or discourage people from using collective action."[55] This conception offers both dynamic and static views of political arrangements: political opportunity structures are channels for political action that may open wider or close more firmly at key moments, such as changes in legislation and administrative rules, shifts in ruling alliances, splits between ruling elites, and reformulations of the terms of public debate.[56] When organized groups take advantage of these available openings, they often pave the way for other such opportunities.

In the United States, the Civil Rights Movement transformed the structure of political opportunities. Civil rights legislation and social policies extensively use census data: the Voting Rights Act, for example, requires population tabulations by race at the city-block level for redistricting plans.[57] Such legislation and policies have, in turn, led some groups to protect and defend the census categories and the data upon which these laws and policies depend. The Office of Management and Budget's Statistical Directive No. 15, issued in 1977, represents an even more specific shift in political and institutional arrangements. Directive No. 15 systematically codified racial classifications and disclosed their political rationale. In creating and subsequently recognizing four official races and two official ethnicities, the Directive thus acts as a "gatekeeper" to their official statistical existence.[58] Invested with this power and this visibility, the directive has become a referent for groups seeking official recognition. OMB's public review of Directive No. 15, initiated in 1993, gave the multiracial movement the most immediate impetus for its efforts to have "multiracial" made the fifth official racial classification.

Even without immediate and easily identifiable institutional precipitants, Brazilian democratization was itself a necessary precondition for the 1991 census campaign. This democratization did not generate legislation or social policies stipulating the use of racial census data, however, as had U.S. civil rights legislation: in fact, the constitutional and legislative initiatives to combat racism were broad, even vague, and there was no public review like OMB's of the rationale and methods of IBGE color classification. Brazilian activists targeted the census, in part, because the full economic and political benefits of Brazilian democratization for nonwhite Brazilians rested, in significant measure, both on accurate socioeconomic data and on political claims pressed on behalf of Brazil's black population. Using the "proper" methods, it was held, the census would show that population to be the majority.

New political opportunities can encourage (or discourage) collective action, and they can also influence the specific tactics and overall strategies of collective actors. The specific actions and inactions of the U.S. Census Bureau and IBGE have had a direct bearing on the actions of the American multiracial movement and the Brazilian *movimento negro*, although those actions are neither entirely reactive to, nor intelligible in terms of, institutional triggers. These movements have aims that ultimately cannot be wholly satisfied by changes in the census, or even by institutionally derived policies and remedies.

Both movements seek to alter the ways in which their followers self-identify and associate socially and politically. The desired result is the emergence, or, some would say, reemergence, of America's "mixed race" population and the awakening of Brazil's "black" majority. But their demands are not devoid of material concerns. Multiracial activists contend that by virtue of their noncategorization, multiracial persons can neither benefit fully from existing public policies nor advocate for more suitable policies. Brazil's black movement argues that new census terms and resulting numbers will advance demands for a redistribution of political power and economic resources in ways that would benefit Brazil's black majority. However, it would be a misreading of both movements to attribute their motivations solely to material advancement. They are motivated as much by the desire for recognition in and of itself.

The American multiracial and Brazilian black movements have identified the census as a vehicle for their larger political ambition: to refigure and reconstitute racial identities through categorization.

In an important way, these movements invite reexamination of a basic premise of social movements theory, which presumes a pre-existent group identity that guides organized action. Rather than simply organizing on the basis of a shared and widely assumed identity, what these two movements are shaping is a discourse about identity. Their tactics and strategies may have been influenced by political and institutional changes, but their motivations are derived in part from prevailing racial discourse and their desire to change it. Multiracial activists in the United States seek to challenge the mutual exclusivity and conceptual coherence of existing racial categories (both in society and on the census) by advancing an idea of multiraciality. This multiracial discourse gives content to a multiracial identity. Similarly, in Brazil, black activists attempt to disrupt the commensurability between images of whiteness, national identity, and racial harmony by advocating the idea of distinct races instead of one mixed Brazilian race. If Brazil is a country with distinct races, it would then be possible to construct a discourse about blackness and the political obligations of black racial membership. As these activists rightly see it, the censuses that have upheld ideas of distinct races in the United States and of one mixed race in Brazil can also be used to undermine those ideas.

Organization

The evidence presented in following chapters bears out this book's central claims that census bureaus are political actors that help to make race a political reality and do not simply count by it. Race, in turn, is not a self-evidently meaningful and objective marker. It is rather a shifting set of ideas that themselves create boundaries of membership, assign meaning and value to such memberships, and invariably shape the distribution of political power and the experiences of national citizenship. Although race and census-taking at present occupy two discrete fields of study, this book seeks to unite them. In so doing, it shows that the disciplinary boundaries that scholarship has managed to erect at once impoverish our understanding of both and bear very little resemblance to the very real and complex connections between race and censuses in political life and history.

Chapter 2 reconstructs and analyzes the history of racial categorization in U.S. censuses from 1790 to the present. It demonstrates that at different periods in American history, census-taking has contributed directly to the formation of racial ideas, and that throughout the nation's history, census categories and data have been part of larger political processes and policies, both negative (slavery, racial segregation, and nonwhite racial subordination) and positive (civil rights legislation). This chapter draws heavily on primary documents in uncovering and reconstructing the political origins of the categories. The main sources for nineteenth-century censuses are the *Congressional Globe* (now known as the *Congressional Record*) and other congressional and executive branch documents. I have also consulted secondary sources on broader political, economic, legal, and social developments. My analysis of twentieth-century censuses draws on internal Census Bureau documents and scholarly sources.

Chapter 3 turns to Brazil and examines the policies of color classification and the Brazilian Statistical Institute's interpretations of census data from the first modern Brazilian census of 1872 to the present. The chapter argues that the idea of "whitening" and the "myth of racial democracy" have hinged on color categories, color data, and the interpretation of such data. This chapter also draws heavily on primary sources, most of which are twentieth-century IBGE documents, and a range of scholarly sources. My analysis of nineteenth-century census-taking necessarily relies on secondary sources.

Chapter 4 analyzes recent attempts by the multiracial movement in the United States and the black movement in Brazil to challenge methods of racial and color categorization in the two countries, respectively. It argues that both movements used census-taking to create new racial identities and not simply to activate old ones. This chapter's primary sources are the range of publications and Internet sites established by U.S. multiracial organizations since the early 1990s. Analysis of the Brazilian census campaign also draws on primary sources, such as internal campaign documents and field-work in Brazil, which allowed for personal interviews with campaign organizers.

Finally, Chapter 5 examines the latest OMB and IBGE decisions in light of historical racial/color categorization. It concludes by considering whether the United States and Brazil are unique cases of racial categorization and judges that they are. Yet it is their exceptionalism that richly illuminates the sinuous and profoundly consequential dynamic that links racial ideas, censuses, and citizenship. More broadly, both cases show the central role that the state plays in creating and perpetuating the categories of political existence.

CHAPTER 2

"The Tables present plain matters of fact"

Race Categories in U.S. Censuses

The slave schedules of the 1850 census occasioned particularly contentious debate in the U.S. Senate. One issue was whether the (slave) schedules should contain a query asking the "degree of removal from pure white and black races." In a move to silence criticism of this inquiry, Senator Joseph Underwood (Whig–Ky.) declared: "The Tables present plain matters of fact." Underwood's invocation of facts in order to advance his political agenda prefigured contemporary appeals to the neutrality of census-taking. Like Underwood, social scientists, lawmakers, and Census Bureau officials have routinely touted the data's objectivity, even as they have deliberately used censuses to further (social) scientific thought and political aims. As the history of racial categorization shows, the Census Bureau has always been entrenched in politics: it partly creates the racial facts it tabulates.

This chapter analyzes the history of racial categorization in the United States and the U.S. census from the first census in 1790 to the 2000 census. It argues that census-taking has supported, and at times has directly shaped, a shifting racial discourse. During two periods, 1790–1840 and 1930–60, the census largely reflected racial thinking. During two others, 1850–1930 and 1970 to the present, the census has contributed directly to the formation of racial ideas. American racial ideologies have shown a certain rigidity as well as a certain plasticity. The census has been most closely involved in developing ideas about race when (social) scientific thinking on race itself has been most unstable. American (social) scientists have always sought out knowledge about race and treated it with particular care and interest. They have long held the presupposition that such knowledge, properly applied, should be the basis of public policy. Proceeding chronologically, the chapter necessarily addresses the larger political, social, and economic developments to which census officials and (social) scientists responded and that they attempted to control. Its main aim, however, is to examine the long-overlooked theoretical and political significance of racial categorization in censuses.

The First Censuses: 1790–1830

The race question and race categories have appeared on every decennial U.S. census.[1] Why is not self-evidently—or transparently—connected to demographic concerns, since the initial impetus for census-taking was political. The U.S. Constitution mandated that "an actual enumeration" be conducted every ten years to allow for representational apportionment. How slaves would be counted was especially contentious, but in fact, the issue of representation was itself contentious. Delegates had to decide how representatives would be apportioned, on the basis of population or of wealth? Should the Articles of Confederation system of equal congressional representation for all states be retained? And, if apportionment was based on population, should slaves be counted, and how? Once the majority of delegates had agreed on population-based representation and the fears of the small states had been addressed in the "Great Compromise," which ensured an equal number of representatives in the Senate, the question of slaves and representation remained.[2] The debates emerged most forcefully after the Convention's initial acceptance of the three-fifths clause and divided along sectional lines. Southern delegates advocated full representation for slaves in the federal legislature and begrudgingly accepted counting a slave as three-fifths of a person. Not surprisingly, slaves were not represented in the legislatures of southern colonies. Northern delegates opposed any representation of slaves because of the undue numerical advantage it would afford the South and because of the apparent contradiction involved in counting them in the same way as free white persons. Slaves were both persons and property, "being considered by our laws, in some respects, as persons, and in other respects, as property," as James Madison wrote.[3] They could not live as full persons, and therefore should not count as such. Second, counting slaves as full persons diminished the value of being counted as free men and women. In the end, the delegates decided to count slaves as three-fifths of a person in determining apportionment and in direct taxation. As Madison put it: "[T]he Federal Constitution therefore, decides with great propriety on the case of our slaves, when it views them in the mixt character of persons and property. This is in fact their true character."[4]

How do we understand the reasons for asking about race in the census? The three-fifths compromise in and of itself does not provide an explanation. Representation depended on civil status—whether one was slave or free—and if free, on whether one was taxed or not. It did not depend on racial status. The race question was included (and combined with civil status) because race was a salient social and political category (see Table 1). In keeping with Enlightenment thought, eighteenth-century political elites regarded race as a natural, self-evident component of human identity. Observed differences in physical appearance and cultural practices were the result of differences in natural environments. Mankind was one species and all were capable of infinite improvement.[5] These ideas, most robust in the years immediately preceding and following the American Revolution, were gradually subordinated to theories of polygenesis and the innate and permanent superiority or inferiority of races. It is important to emphasize, however, that the egalitarian ideas emerging from the European Enlightenment in general and the American Revolution in particular com-

TABLE I

U.S. Census Race Categories, 1790–1840

1790	1800	1810
Free White Males, Free White Females All Other Free Persons Slaves	Free White Males, Free White Females All Other Free Persons, except Indians Not Taxed Slaves	Free White Males, Free White Females All Other Free Persons, except Indians Not Taxed Slaves

1820	1830	1840
Free White Males, Free White Females Free Colored Persons All Other Persons, except Indians Not Taxed Slaves	Free White Persons Free Colored Persons Slaves	Free White Persons Free Colored Persons Slaves

Source: United States Bureau of the Census.

peted with others claiming natural hierarchies and limitations. Just as significant, the deepening entrenchment of slavery in U.S. economic and political life rendered abstract commitments to universal equality and liberty moot. To underscore why the census would ask questions about race and not only civil status, it is useful to examine the citizenship status of free blacks and to compare the race inquiry with the proposed inquiry on occupation.

Racial identification mattered because citizenship status and the nature of participation in the political community depended on it. To be free and white and to be free and black were distinct political experiences. Free whites were presumptively citizens. In the early years of the Republic, in the absence of federal statutory definition, they became citizens by choosing to support the republican cause and, by the early nineteenth century, by birthright. As citizens, they enjoyed the full benefits of political membership (including the franchise). The citizenship status of free blacks remained unclear throughout the antebellum period. As the historian

James Kettner explains, beginning with the Missouri debates of 1820, state courts generally approached black citizenship from two opposing directions. On the one hand, "many northern and at first some southern courts defended the idea that free native born blacks were citizens entitled to the general benefits of membership."[6] These same courts also upheld discriminatory practices that effectively canceled such benefits. On the other hand, "the courts of slave states increasingly . . . rejected the contention that Negroes could be citizens." The federal government finally resolved the question when the Supreme Court settled the Dred Scott Decision in 1857, deciding that blacks were not citizens because in the words of Chief Justice Taney, they were "not intended to be included, and formed no part of the people who framed and adopted" the Declaration of Independence and the Constitution.[7] Yet however ambiguous the citizenship status of free blacks was, the constraints and burdens on their participation in political life were clear. Although free blacks were taxed like whites, they did not in any way enjoy the same rights and entitlements as whites. In most states, free blacks were restrained, and commonly prohibited forthrightly, from voting, owning property, working in certain occupations, attending public schools, serving on juries, testifying against whites, and exercising personal liberties, including freedom of movement. The census counted by race because the census reflected the belief that race was constitutive of human identity. It also so counted because race was constitutive of American political identity.

The roles played by the census become even clearer when one juxtaposes the uncontroversial inclusion of the race question against the founders' initial refusal to classify the population by occupation. A question on occupations was first proposed by James Madison of Virginia for the 1790 census. As a member of the House committee that drafted the enumeration bill, Madison presented the House with a more detailed census schedule than apportionment required.[8] It included the categories "free white males," subdivided into those over and under the age of sixteen, free white females, free blacks, slaves, and occupation (agriculture, manufactures, commerce) for all working persons.[9] The House approved Madison's schedule, but the Senate rejected the occupations inquiry category, for reasons unknown. But the debate over an occupations inquiry for the next census, in 1800, reveals two competing visions of census-taking and the public good. Proponents argued that facts like these would allow the government to chart the country's progress and make improvements based on wider knowledge of the population. Opponents held that classifying by occupation artificially—and unnecessarily—divided the white population into classes.[10] Most Americans, they argued, were engaged in all three of Madison's occupational categories; why should they be forced to choose only one? Critics also charged that such categories undermined the notion of the common good, because they would inevitably encourage competition between groups. The social cleavage the first three national censuses needed to measure, for constitutional, philosophical, and social reasons, was that of race, and not the occupational divisions among whites. The 1820 schedule was the first to require that a household belong to only one sector of the economy.

The censuses from the years 1790 through 1840 asked few questions beyond those related to population. They counted free white males and free white females, subdivided into age groups; slaves; and all other free persons, except Indians not taxed. Race was considered a natural fact, but its political and social significance was still being sorted out. Were Anglo-Saxons, for example, a superior race, destined to "bring good government, commercial prosperity and Christianity" to America?[11] Even more disconcerting were the obvious contradictions in ideas about the black race and its place among other races. If all humankind belonged to the same human race, how could one part of it justifiably be enslaved? To be sure, colonial racial discourse had long regarded Africans as different from and inferior to the English, whatever their common humanity. Yet white political elites did not regard these differences, which they judged to be black deficiencies, as permanent. By the mid nineteenth century, racial discourse would change dramatically in this respect. So too would the role of census categorization. The earliest censuses registered race as it was then understood. By the 1840 census, census-taking was doing much more.

The 1840 Census and Slavery

In the 1840s and 1850s, thinking about race changed significantly. Scientific explanations of race and racial differences gained credibility and assumed authority over prevailing religious and philosophical explanations to become an important point of departure in the ongoing discussion about slavery.[12] Whether science could prove or disprove the Negro's inherent inferiority mattered as greatly to proponents of slavery as to opponents. According to the "American School of Ethnology," which emerged in the 1840s and would remain influential until the end of the century, the human race comprised not one species (monogenism) but several unequal species (polygenism). Samuel George Morton and Josiah C. Nott, both medical doctors, and the Egyptologist George R. Gliddon were the school's main spokesmen and practitioners and sought data to substantiate their claims of polygenism. By 1850, Nott hoped to enlist the census itself in generating the necessary data. The 1840 census was the first instance in which the emerging sciences of race and statistics would converge to shape public debate and political maneuvering over slavery.

Political and public attitudes toward numeracy and the nascent science of statistics were also changing. The idea that statistics could help to chart the nation's progress and address its social problems, and that it could reveal underlying natural laws, was increasingly accepted. Lawmakers now envisioned uses for the census extending far beyond its constitutionally mandated function. Doubts evident in earlier congressional debates were subsumed, but not completely quelled, by a new faith in the positive societal applications of census-taking. In 1839, the American Statistical Association was founded in Boston. In the almanacs long popular among Americans, statistical tables figured prominently. Several commercial journals that relied on statistics were established at this time, the most important being Freeman Hunt's *Merchants' Magazine and Commercial Review* (1839) and *De Bow's Review*, which served as the voice of southern economic interests. The work of almost every major antebellum statistician appeared in one of these two journals.[13] Nascent statisticians and legislators perceived statistics as powerful and practical tools in addressing immediate social and political concerns. The addition of such categories as "deaf" and "blind" to the 1830 census schedule, and of "illiteracy," "insanity," and "feeblemindedness" to the 1840 census reflected the influence of the new statistical thinking.

The heated controversy surrounding the 1840 census reveals the depth of sectional divisions and the new importance of census data in buttressing conflicting positions on slavery. More important for our purposes, however, is not simply the role played by racial discourse in shaping the slavery debate, but the role played by the census in reinforcing the scientific valence of racial discourse. The results of the 1840 census were immediately and explosively controversial, because they seemed to show a higher insanity rate among free blacks than among slaves. The rate of insanity among free blacks in northern states was one in every 144.5, while the rate of insanity among slaves in southern states was one in every 1,558.[14] More incredibly, the frequency of insanity decreased in nearly exact mathematical proportion from north to south. As the historian Leon Litwack writes: "In Maine, for example, every 14th black person was insane; in New Hampshire every 28th; in Massachusetts every 43rd; in Connecticut every 184th; in New York every 257th; and in New Jersey every 297th."[15] But in states from the upper to the deep South, insanity rates decreased: one in 1,299 black persons was insane in Virginia, one in 2,477 in South Carolina, and one in 4,310 in Louisiana.[16]

The conclusion to be drawn from these numbers was unmistakable: freedom drove black people insane. The high insanity rates quickly became part of the larger racial discourse, confirming the view that Negroes were naturally inferior and thus uniquely suited for servitude and subjugation. Southern representatives spoke glowingly on the floor of the House about the evidently salutary effects of slavery, and for a brief period, the results went unchallenged. In fact, Dr. Edward Jarvis, a physician and a founding member of the American Statistical Association, wrote in an article in the *Boston Medical and Surgical Journal* of 1842 that slavery must have "a wonderful influence upon the development of moral faculties and the intellectual powers," for in "refusing many of the hopes and responsibilities which the free, self-thinking and self-acting enjoy and sustain, of course it saves him [the slave] from some of the liabilities and dangers of self-direction."[17] Jarvis quickly changed his opinion, however, once he had examined the returns of several northern states more closely. On several census returns, he found that the number of insane black people equaled the number of townspeople. In other cases, insane black people were counted in towns where no black people lived. Jarvis wrote a second article in the *American Journal of the Medical Sciences* in which he refuted the census and called for its correction. The American Statistical Association sent a petition, or memorial, as it was then known, to the Congress. Congressman John Quincy Adams of Massachusetts several times demanded a correction as well.

In 1844, under a motion directed by Adams, the House asked Secretary of State Abel Upshur, under whose jurisdiction the census had been conducted, to confirm or disconfirm whether the census was erroneous. Unfortunately, Upshur died two days later, and his successor, John C. Calhoun of South Carolina, did not intend to have the census invalidated. In fact, Calhoun used the census data to assuage the British foreign secretary's concern about slavery in the recently annexed territory of Texas. In a letter that same year, Calhoun argued that slavery in Texas was a local concern, not one for the U.S. federal government or the British. Calhoun's letter not only defended slavery in Texas but argued that slavery reflected the natural order: blacks had always been and would always be inferior to whites and in need of subjugation by them. The 1840 census data provided solid proof. His letter read in part: "[T]he census and other authentic documents show that, in all instances in which the States have changed the former relation between the two races, the condition of the African, instead of being improved, has become worse."[18] In the north, Africans had "invariably sunk into vice and pauperism, accompanied by the bodily and mental afflictions incident thereto—deafness, blindness, insanity and idiocy—to a degree without example."[19] In contrast, in southern states, where the "ancient relation" between blacks and whites had been preserved, blacks had "improved in every respect—in number, comfort, intelligence, and morals."[20] This "ancient relation" had been proven by the preeminent race scientists Gliddon and Morton, who in their studies of the origins of races had found proof, in Gliddon's words, of "the antiquity of niggers" and their servile status. Calhoun met privately with Gliddon once in Washington and maintained correspondences with him and with Morton.[21]

To the House's inquiry to Secretary Calhoun on the soundness of the 1840 census, Calhoun responded evasively, sidestepping the issue by capitalizing on a technical mistake in the resolution. Nonetheless, his report endorsed the census. In June, a House committee on the census received the American Statistical Association's memorial and again called for a reexamination of the census results. A second House resolution was passed. According to a private conversation with Calhoun recorded by Adams in his diary, Calhoun argued that "there were so many errors that they balanced one another, and led to the same conclusion as if they were all correct."[22] The House moved a third time, under Adams's motion, that the secretary should inform the House if there were mistakes in the 1840 census and, if so, to identify the origins of the errors and show how they had been corrected. At this point, Calhoun assigned William A. Weaver, superintendent of the census, the task of investigating the census he had supervised. Not surprisingly, Weaver concluded, and Calhoun reported, that the census was correct: the errors identified by the memorialists were not errors at all. Calhoun went on to suggest that census detractors were motivated by a desire to discredit the census because it revealed the true conditions of free blacks. The fact of high insanity rates among free blacks remained "unimpeachable," according to Calhoun.[23] The results of the embattled 1840 census stood. Confidence in census-taking itself had, however, been badly damaged in many quarters.

The direct political fallout of the census controversy for free northern blacks has been little studied. Dr. James McCune Smith, a prominent black physician, wrote a series of articles published in the *New York Tribune* in which he challenged the proslavery claims of southern politicians and spokesmen, and the 1840 census data used to support them.[24] Smith's efforts, of which the *Tribune* articles formed only a part, were directed at refuting the claims of race scientists. At the time of the crisis, a group of free black people in New York met "to consider the calumnies recently uttered against free people of color by John C. Calhoun," and submitted a memorial to Congress calling for a reexamination of the census results.[25] Yet even in the absence of direct evidence of harm to free blacks, it is clear that the results would not help alter their degraded social and economic status or clarify their ambiguous political status.

The 1850 Census and Race Science

The 1850 census marked a watershed in census-taking, and its significance is multifaceted. First, it was designed in a more developed institutional context and with greater input from social scientists and more financial resources than previous censuses. For the first time, a Census Board was impaneled by Congress to discuss all matters pertaining to census-taking, including which inquiries should be included in the schedules and how the information should be collected and eventually reported.[26] In the past, Congress had made these decisions, usually through enumeration committees. Congress still authorized the census schedules, but now it deliberately solicited outside advice and assistance. Second, this collaboration resulted in census schedules that were far more extensive in scope than those of earlier censuses. The Census Board recommended, and the Congress eventually approved, with changes, six separate schedules: Schedule 1 for the free population, Schedule 2 for the slave population, Schedule 3 for mortality, Schedule 4 for agriculture, Schedule 5 for manufacture (or products of industry), and Schedule 6 for social statistics (such as estate values, schools, annual taxes, newspapers and periodicals, religion, pauperism, crime, wages).[27] It is also important to note that the enumeration of all Native Americans (and not only "Indians Taxed") was authorized under a clause of an Indian Appropriation Act in 1846.[28] The results of this special Indian census were reported with those of the 1850 census. Third, and finally, the census was conducted just as the sectional crisis over slavery deepened and sharpened. This census, legislators hoped, might allow them to assess, in the words of Congressman James Thompson (D–Penn.), the country in its "unity and beauty" and not in its "fragments, weak and distracted."[29] Nevertheless, congressional debates about the census were heated, and those about the slave schedule quite contentious.

A heretofore underappreciated but crucially important aspect of the 1850 census was the influence of race science in the development and justification of race inquiries. The category "mulatto" was added under color. Historical texts have assumed that the mulatto category was added to better measure racial intermixture.[30] Historians have undoubtedly based their assumptions on official Census Bureau documents, which provide no explicit explanation, giving the impression that its introduction was driven by demographic changes, but they are wrong. The mulatto category was added and other race queries debated because of the lobbying efforts of race scientists and the willingness of certain legislators to do their bidding. The mulatto category signaled the ascendance of race science.

Polygenist thought gave rise to interest in the "mulatto" and attempts to measure "[d]egree of removal from pure white and black races." Built on the idea of racial essence, polygenism presumed "that there is some hereditary essence expressing itself in a number of visible peculiarities that mark every member of a 'pure' race and distinguish it from other races, . . . since the only process which could significantly modify a race was racial mixture."[31] The "American School of Ethnology" distinguished itself from prevailing European racial thought by its adherence to polygenism.[32] Polygenist conclusions directly contradicted a basic tenet of Christianity, that mankind shared a common origin. Although most monogenist thinkers were not racial egalitarians, they were unwilling to accept claims of separate origins, permanent racial differences, and the infertility of racial mixtures.[33] Yet the hard facts generated by scientific investigation would override religious doctrine. Racial scientists sought such hard facts, specifically statistical ones. Josiah Nott, who sided with polygeny, set out to prove that mulattoes, as hybrids of different racial species, were less fertile than their parents of pure races, and hence lived shorter lives. Since most nineteenth-century biologists thought that human races belonged to one species, it was necessary for polygenists to show that the "apparent infertility of human races was not real."[34] To this end, Nott published a short article in the *American Journal of the Medical Sciences* in 1843 aptly titled "The Mulatto a Hybrid—Probable Extermination of the Two Races if the Whites and Blacks Are Allowed to Intermarry,"[35] in which he asserted the general fragility of mulatto bodies and their lower fertility. He drew his evidence from a variety of sources, including scientific journal articles, scholarly works, and his own personal observations, yet warned readers of the article's speculative nature: "I will here attempt nothing more than to throw out some materials for reflection.—I am well aware that my assertions would have much greater weight, *if they were supported by statistics*" (italics added).[36] Four years later, in an 1847 letter to *De Bow's Review*, a journal to which he had frequently contributed, Nott again called for greater and more accurate statistics:

> I hope I have said enough to make apparent the paramount importance of *negro statistics* [italics in original]. If the blacks are intellectually inferior to the whites—if the whites are deteriorated by amalgamation with the blacks—if the longevity and physical perfection of the mixed race is below that of either of the pure races, and if the negro is by nature unfit for self-government, these are grave matters for consideration.[37]

Here, Nott's concerns explicitly disclose the political issues upon which racial thought was brought to bear and from which it emerged. The connection Nott draws between Negro statistics and Negro citizenship is clear: statistics would reveal whether blacks were fit or, more precisely, unfit for freedom by proving that they were inferior. Given the natural and political truths that Nott insisted "negro statistics" would bring to light, it is no wonder that he turned to the 1850 census to generate them.

The 1849 Congressional Debates:
"Mulatto" and "Pure Races"

The 1850 schedules were the first to include the category "mulatto" under color, and on both the "free" and "slave" schedules. With some modifications, the Senate and House select committees on the census adopted the schedules devised by the Census Board, and the decision to add "mulatto" did not command much congressional attention. However, these same draft schedules also contained an inquiry into "Degree of removal from pure white and black races."[38] This inquiry generated a great deal of discussion, in which prevailing ideas and questions about "mulatto-ness" figure prominently. Discussions on the congressional floor, as recorded in the *Congressional Globe*, especially in the Senate, are quite revealing. The section that follows, then, draws heavily from these debates.

After a delay of nearly two months, the Senate took up the Census Bill on April 9, 1850.[39] Of the four census schedules (free population, slave population, mortality, and manufactures) the senators were to approve, the slave schedule was the most fiercely contested and "became the target of opposition to the bill as a whole."[40] Opponents, all Southerners, focused on its inquiries: there were too many. They ranged from the names of slaves, to their birthplaces, to the number of children born and number known to be dead or alive, to "removal from pure race."[41] Why Southerners would object to these inquiries is clear: the less information collected (and hence distributed) on slaves, the better. Why some of these inquiries would have a southern advocate is not as clear. Yet, as the discussion unfolded, Joseph Underwood of Kentucky emerged as a point man for the scientific projects of the South's most prominent racial theorist, Josiah C. Nott. Nott's name, however, is never mentioned.

He is referred to instead as "the distinguished gentleman" or "a very distinguished physician at Mobile."[42]

After opening remarks by John Davis of Massachusetts, Andrew Butler (States Rights Democrat–S.C.) voiced his objections. He wanted slaves' names removed from the schedule, leaving only an inquiry about the number of slaves. In past censuses, he argued, only the number had been required, and he saw no good use, and only extra labor for enumerators, in recording names. However, Joseph Underwood saw no harm in collecting names, inasmuch as the census-taker would already be inquiring about the sex and age of each slave. To Underwood's remark, George Badger (Whig–N.C.) responded: "What do you want of such names as Big Cuff and Little Cuff?" "Or of little Jonah and Big Jonah?" Butler added, amid laughter in the Senate chamber.[43] Underwood's desire for as much information on slaves as possible was first revealed here.

The senators voted to remove the inquiry on slave names. William King (D–Ala.) then moved to have the inquiries about the birthplace of slaves, the number of children borne to slave women, and the number of children known to be dead or alive stricken from the schedule. All three were eventually removed. But at this point, both Davis and Underwood protested against further deletions. Davis countered that such information about children borne was important insofar as it increased the enumeration's, and hence representational, accuracy. Underwood's justifications went far beyond accuracy. In a lengthy exchange with his colleagues, Underwood eventually revealed the sources and proposed uses of many of the inquiries.

"[T]hese tables, in reference to the slave population, which were adopted by the committee, were adopted in compliance with the wishes of southern gentlemen," Underwood said.[44] The Committee was in pursuit of "a number of philosophical inquiries" having to do with "the effect of various localities on health and longevity; to the effect of climate, on the condition of the colored race, and all matters of importance in reference to the contemplated object."[45] Underwood then called his colleagues' attention to the tables and referred indirectly to Josiah Nott.

You will find in these tables that we require not only the age and sex, but the color of the person; and we find in another column the degree of removal from pure blood is required to be stated; and this inquiry, in reference to the number of children which each woman may have had, I can inform my honorable friend, was inserted, as far as I know, at the instance of a southern gentleman [Nott], with a view to ascertain certain facts which he told me, but which I do not think necessary to go into here.[46]

According to Underwood, a practical justification for retaining the inquiries was life insurance. Insurance tables depended, after all, on knowledge about rates of longevity among racial groups over time. Nott had written an article on the importance of slave statistics for the development of insurance policies, published in 1847 in *De Bow's Review*.[47]

Solon Borland (D–Ark.) responded that such inquiries on racial characteristics were properly taken up by the "scientific men of the country." Underwood's inquiries, Borland charged, demanded that enumerators become natural scientists. The government should not be involved in the "investigation of great natural truths."[48] Underwood replied that no such extraordinary skill or scientific knowledge was required of enumerators. "It is not a matter of scientific investigation at all," he argued, "but a mere inquiry as to facts whether an individual is a quadroon, a mulatto, or any other proportion of blood."[49] After a sharp exchange between William Seward of New York and William King of Alabama over slavery, Underwood finally disclosed the reason for the "removal from pure race" inquiry. He explained:

The gentleman [Nott] in conversation with me said that he believed that a certain class of colored people had fewer children than a certain other class; and he believed that the average duration of the lives of the darker class was longer than that of the lighter colored class, or mixed. And it was for the purpose of ascertaining the physiological fact, that he wanted the inquiry made. This was the motive for its insertion, and it was never dreamed, so far as I know, that out of this census bill we were to get up a discussion on this slavery question. I never dreamed of such a thing. But I have now told you the motive which led to the adoption of his table; it was to illustrate the truth or falsity of the theory on this subject.[50]

William Dayton (Whig–N.J.) supported the value of such racial inquiry, but George Badger (Whig–N.C.) expressed skepticism about its usefulness. William Butler (D–S.C.) summarized the negative reactions of his fellow southern senators to the "removal from pure race" inquiry:

> I know, sir, that there is a discussion going on at this time in the southern portion of the United States—perhaps in the northern portion too—on this very subject. A very philosophical discussion is being carried on by a very distinguished physician at Mobile, and others involving the very information, or connected with the information that may be obtained in this way. I am utterly opposed, however, to using our proceedings here, as a vehicle for information of a philosophical kind for other persons.[51]

The inquiry on "Degree of removal from pure white and black races" was removed from the schedule along with four others: slave names, birthplace of slaves, number of children borne by slave women, and number of children known to be dead or alive. The final slave schedule (Schedule 2) contained only seven columns: "Names of slave owners," "Number of slaves," "Age," "Sex," "Color," "Deaf and dumb, blind, insane, or idiotic," and "Remarks." The instructions to enumerators read as follows: "Under heading 5, entitled 'Color,' insert in all cases, when the slave is black, the letter B; when he or she is a mulatto, insert M. The color of all slaves should be noted."[52] For the free population schedule (Schedule 1), instructions were slightly different: "Under heading 6, entitled 'Color,' in all cases where the person is white, leave the space blank; in all cases where the person is black, insert the letter B; if mulatto, insert M. It is very desirable that these particulars be carefully regarded."[53]

In an apparently ironic twist, the aims of a slave-owning southern physician and ardent supporter of slavery were thus pitted against southern legislators. Nott wanted additional inquiries about slaves put on the census schedule; southern senators did not. But the collision was more apparent than real. As a racial theorist and scientist, Nott's support for slavery was derived from his study of the origins of the black and white races. He argued that the enslavement of blacks required no defense: blacks were naturally slaves and had been slaves since antiquity. Thus, as Underwood explained, no doubt disingenuously, by revealing Nott's motives, he did not intend to spark an argument over slavery. Nott's arose from his long-standing interest in the "hybridity of mulattoes" and his argument that the black and white races belonged to separate species. If census data showed that persons of "mixed blood" (hence the question on "removal from pure races") and their children (hence the question of number known dead or alive) lived shorter lives, it would be proof of their weakness of bodily constitution, owing, Nott theorized, to mixing races of different species. That such persons of "mixed blood" survived at all had led many racial theorists in Europe to abandon the ideas of "hybridity" and polygenesis. Nott, however, was undaunted. He wanted to use the census to gather information in order to better theorize about race itself. While many of his census inquiries were rejected, the category "mulatto" was not. It would remain on U.S. schedules through the 1920 census.

By mid-decade, census data from the 1850 census had been published. The largely successful efforts of southern legislators to restrict inquiries about slaves did not constrain public use of the data in the increasingly contentious debates over slavery.[54] Abolitionists and proslavery advocates combed the data looking for support for their positions, and social scientists insisted on future improvements. In a twenty-page letter to Superintendent James De Bow (Joseph Kennedy's successor), Edward Jarvis urged that the distinction between "pure blacks" and mulattoes be extended throughout the census in order to determine whether mulattoes were more susceptible than either "pure blacks" or whites to disease.[55] The 1850 census proved to be a watershed, not only because (social) scientists were marshaled in its service, but because they brought with them, as scientists, their thinking about race. This census boldly ushered in the inextricable and enduring link between census categorization, racial scientific thought, and public policy in the United States. Despite fundamental political, social, and economic changes in the country as a whole between 1850 and 1930, the agenda of the consulting (social) scientists and census administrators remained essentially unchanged. A better theoretical understanding of race gave credence to the development of segregationist public policy.

The 1860 Census: The Fate of Colored People

Whereas the 1850 census shaped political debate about slavery, the 1860 census informed discussion of abolition. Like its predecessor, the 1860 census was deeply implicated in maintaining racial discourse, its data providing the racial statistics sought by race scientists. Census officials interpreted these data and offered their assessment of the Negro's natural state and of his ability to live as a free person among other free people, inserting racial statistics into the debates precisely because of their growing authority as truth bearers about race in general and the Negro in particular.

The 1860 census was administered under the same law that had governed the 1850 census: the inquiries were the same with a few additions. Schedule 1, the free population schedule, now contained an inquiry into "the profession, occupation, or trade of each person, male and female, over 15 years of age."[56] An inquiry into the number of slave houses was added to Schedule 2, the slave population schedule. The inquiries into "color" and the instructions to enumerators were also slightly different. Although "Indian" was not listed on Schedule 1, the instructions under "Indians" read: "Indians *not taxed* are not to be enumerated. The families of Indians who have renounced tribal rule, and who under State or Territorial laws exercise the rights of citizens are to be enumerated. In all such cases write 'Ind.' opposite their names, in column 6, under heading 'Color.'"[57] Under "Color," the instructions stated: "in all cases where the person is white leave the space blank; in all cases where the person is black without admixture insert the letter 'B'; if a mulatto, or of mixed blood, write 'M'; if an Indian, write 'Ind.' It is very desirable to have these directions carefully observed."[58] The 1860 census schedule discussions were calm in comparison to 1850.

TABLE 2

U.S. Census Race Categories, 1850–1990

		1850–1920—"The Mulatto Category" and Race Science					
1850	1860[a]	1870	1880	1890	1900	1910	1920
[b]	[b]	White	White	White	White	White	White
Black	Black	Black	Black	Black	Black	Black	Black
Mulatto	Mulatto	Mulatto	Mulatto	Mulatto	Chinese	Mulatto	Mulatto
	(Indian)	Chinese	Chinese	Quadroon	Japanese	Chinese	Indian
		Indian	Indian	Octoroon	Indian	Japanese	Chinese
				Chinese		Indian	Japanese
				Japanese		Other (+	Filipino
				Indian		write in)	Hindu
							Korean
							Other (+
							write in)

	1930–1960 "The One-Drop Rule"			1970 Post Civil Rights	1980–1990 Post Statistical Directive #15	
1930	1940	1950	1960	1970	1980	1990
White	White	White	White	White	White	White
Negro	Negro	Negro	Negro	Negro or	Negro or	Black or
Mexican	Indian	Indian	American-	Black	Black	Negro
Indian	Chinese	Japanese	Indian	Indian	Japanese	Indian
Chinese	Japanese	Chinese	Japanese	(Amer.)	Chinese	(Amer.)
Japanese	Filipino	Filipino	Chinese	Japanese	Filipino	Eskimo
Filipino	Hindu	(Other	Filipino	Chinese	Korean	Aleut
Hindu	Korean	race—	Hawaiian	Filipino	Vietnamese	Chinese
Korean	(Other	spell out)	Part-	Hawaiian	Indian	Filipino
(Other	races,		Hawaiian	Korean	(Amer.)	Hawaiian
races,	spell out		Aleut	Other	Asian	Korean
spell out	in full)		Eskimo	(print race)	Indian	Vietnamese
in full)			etc.		Hawaiian	Japanese
					Guama-	Asian
					nian	Indian
					Samoan	Samoan
					Eskimo	Guama-
					Aleut	nian
					Other	Other API
					(specify)	(Asian or
						Pacific
						Islander)
						Other race

SOURCE: United States Bureau of the Census.

[a]Although "Indian" was not listed on the census schedule, the instructions read:

5. *Indians.*—Indians *not taxed* are not to be enumerated. The families of Indians who have renounced tribal rule, and who under State or Territorial laws exercise the rights of citizens, are to be enumerated. In all such cases write "Ind." opposite their names, in column 6, under heading "Color."

[b]"White" did not actually appear on the census schedule. Instead, enumerators were instructed: ". . . in all cases where the person is white leave the space blank."

However, statisticians and social scientists maintained their interest in improvements. In August 1859, Edward Jarvis, on behalf of the American Statistical Association, sent a memorial to the secretary of the interior on the upcoming census. Jarvis also sent a letter to Superintendent Joseph Kennedy in which he detailed the short-comings of the 1850 census.[59]

The political context of the 1860 census was, of course, the Civil War. According to the official census volume, the actual count was completed before the war began. The Census Office was an active participant on the Union's behalf, providing crucial data on the military strength of the Confederacy, its terrain, and its agricultural products. In 1862, in a joint resolution on "war statistics," Congress authorized Census Superintendent Joseph Kennedy to report census data directly to the War Department.[60] Kennedy was also called upon to provide data on the black population. The abolition of slavery was recognized as a probable outcome of the war, given the Union's anticipated victory, yet the likely fate of freed slaves was unknown. The mass removal of emancipated slaves to another country was seriously considered. In 1860–61, President Lincoln actively pursued colonization plans in negotiations with the Panamanian and Haitian governments to accept emancipated American slaves.[61] He also asked that Congress appropriate money for government-sponsored colonization. In 1862, a House committee issued a report on emancipation and colonization. In it, the committee members, mostly Republicans, declared: "[T]he Anglo-American looks upon every acre of our present domain as intended for him and not for the negro."[62] The large number of slaves, however, four million according to the 1860 census, made state-sponsored colonization efforts improbable. That the Union forces were prepared to end slavery did not mean that they were prepared to accept freed slaves either as citizens or as human beings equal to whites. What, then, would eventually become of the Union, with its large population of newly freed but unwanted colored people?

In a Preliminary Report in 1862, Superintendent Kennedy assured northern whites that the future of the Union would not include Negroes. The introductory chapter of the final 1860 census volume, published in 1864, repeated his Preliminary Report's predictions: of approximately nine million "colored" people in the United States, a great percentage would be of "mixed descent,"[63] and the eventual predominance of mulattoes did not bode well for the colored race as a whole. The condition of free colored people in the North, the majority of whom were "mulatto," showed clearly, according to Kennedy, that moral and physical decline accompanied racial mixture. For him, as for Josiah Nott, the issue was not simply how many colored people there were, but what kind of persons (let alone citizens) they would be, or, indeed, could be, given their racial origins. Census data provided the answers:

> That corruption of morals progresses with greater admixture of races, and that the product of vice stimulates the propensity to immorality, is as evident to observation as it is natural to circumstances. These developments of the census, to a good degree, explain the slow progress of the free colored population in the northern States and indicate, with unerring certainty, the gradual extinction of that people the more rapidly as, whether free or slave, they become diffused among the dominant race.[64]

The "great excess of deaths over births" among the free colored, he added, might also be partly explained by an inhospitable natural environment and the "exposures and hardships which accompany a people of lower caste." Nonetheless, these factors were not "sufficient" in and of themselves to account for the high mortality rate.

Superintendent Kennedy attached a caveat to his certain predictions: the census had only twice distinguished between blacks and mulattoes (1850 and 1860), and thus "it is not yet easy to determine how far the admixture of races affects their vital power."[65] The continued inclusion of "black" and "mulatto" categories on subsequent census schedules is thus given a rationale: the presumed differences in "vital" power could be measured more easily with more data about blacks and mulattoes collected over time. Kennedy's final prognosis was that the colored race would be unable to compete, as free laborers, with whites, and that "rapid" racial mixture would result in a physically weaker and immoral race:

[T]he colored population in America, where ever, either free or slave, it must in number and condition be greatly subordinate to the white race, is doomed to comparatively rapid absorption or extinction. How this result is to be averted, partially at least, we leave to the determination of others, feeling our duty accomplished in developing the facts, as the figures of the census reveal them respecting the past.[66]

Here again the census is used to buttress racial theory and not simply to count by race. Racial theory, in turn, provides a rationale for the proper political, social, and economic treatment of blacks.

Kennedy's reports did not find approval in all quarters. Edward Jarvis, for one, thought the preliminary volume "hastily written and imperfectly digested."[67] In 1863, Kennedy appointed Jarvis to write the commentary for the final volume on mortality statistics. Jarvis would base his comments on the raw data Kennedy sent him. Jarvis's assessment of the data he received was, however, largely unfavorable. There were serious discrepancies, and mortality data had not been aggregated according to color or to country of birth.[68] Jarvis demanded that the data be reaggregated "to show the mortality of blacks, mulattoes & whites separately," presumably to see if such data revealed significant differences between the three groups.[69] Kennedy did not respond. The data were never reaggregated for the official volume, but the lack of such mortality data did not effect Kennedy's written interpretations of the overall census data.

Josiah Nott's ideas about "hybridity" and the fragility of mulattoes were alive and well in this census document. This time, they were enlisted to explain the Negro's place in a radically different political, economic, and social context. Before the war, Nott and others had argued that blacks were uniquely suited for slavery, and that weak mulattoes were living testaments to the dangers of racial mixing. With emancipation, it was predicted, blacks and mulattoes would eventually disappear through extinction or absorption. Nature would eventually provide the solution to the political and social problem posed by the presence in the nation of millions of negroes. In the meantime, abolition and the end of the Civil War demanded immediate efforts to reunite the Union and to reconstruct southern society.

Kennedy's prediction of the rapid diffusion and absorption of blacks was partly premised on the continued sexual encounters between blacks and whites. Lawmakers in the reconstructing South, however, moved quickly to outlaw interracial marriage between whites and newly freed blacks through Black Codes, the first efforts of southern whites to construct the South's new racial order. South Carolina's Black Code, passed in 1865, for example, contained the state's first law prohibiting marriages between blacks and whites.[70] Alabama's Constitution made such unions null and void, and Mississippi's Black Codes sentenced a violator of its anti-interracial marriage law to a life sentence in the state penitentiary.[71] Yet these same states did not pass distinct laws explicitly prohibiting interracial sex outside of marriage. There were, however, many other laws governing fornication, lewd and immoral behavior, and cohabitation through which interracial sex could be punished.

"Anti-miscegenation" laws were justified because of concern for the racial preservation of blacks and whites guaranteed by racial purity. "The progress of either [race] does not depend upon admixture of blood," the Tennessee Supreme Court advised in 1871.[72] According to southern lawmakers, the future of blacks and mulattoes in the South might well lead to extinction, as Kennedy predicted, but it would not lead to absorption. Southern laws ensured that the road to extinction would be a segregated one.

Post–Civil War Censuses: Race Science Renewed and Racial Domination Reconstituted

The successes and failures of congressional Reconstruction in challenging white racial domination are well known. The passage of the Thirteenth, Fourteenth, and Fifteenth Amendments to the Constitution and the Civil Rights Acts of 1866, 1870, 1871, and 1875 fundamentally altered the legal foundations of U.S. citizenship.[73] Slavery was abolished. The rights and privileges of citizenship emanated from national sovereign power, not individual states, and were protected by it. Newly freed slaves and formerly free blacks were now American citizens formally entitled to the rights, privileges, and immunities of such status. Black men were given the right to vote. These fundamental legal changes reflected—and engendered—profound shifts in political arrangements. Ultimately, however, what it meant for blacks to be citizens was settled by political, social, and economic processes, not only legal alterations. The steadfast resistance of southern whites to accepting blacks as full participants in political life and the weakening resolve of northern whites to protect black political rights resulted in Reconstruction's failure. In addition, there was no fundamental restructuring of the southern economy: it remained a system of elite white planters, masses of white workers, some of whom were small property owners, and a large ex-slave population without property. In accounting for the failings of Reconstruction, scholars have rightly identified the convergence of northern capitalist and southern planter economic interests in maintaining cotton cultivation, the desire of white laborers to rebuff competition, and an ideological commitment to laissez-faire capitalism and private property as underlying, if not determinative, factors.[74]

Racial discourse also played a pivotal role in the demise of Reconstruction and the reconstitution of white supremacy. It did not merely reflect—or obscure—the underlying political and economic interests of northern and southern elites, it helped to shape political outcomes. Predictably, the ideas race scientists and proslavery advocates had marshaled to defend slavery were used to oppose the recognition of black political rights. Blacks were naturally inferior to whites, whether as slaves or free people; if blacks were fit to be slaves, they were as surely unfit to exercise their rights as citizens and were thereby disqualified from full participation in American economic, political, and social life. On the issue of black inferiority and white superiority, southern Democrats and northern Republicans agreed. To the claim that black inferiority demanded black disqualification, white defenders responded weakly that such inferiority did not justify the deprivation of rights.[75] But claims of black inferiority and white superiority were supported and advanced by science, and science was a formidable opponent. As the historian

Thomas F. Gossett observes, "[A] striking feature of the literature of racism . . . is the patient way in which the racists explain 'scientific fact' to their opponents."[76] Race science left proponents of black rights with two basic options: to accept the premise of black inferiority and appeal to natural rights and the moral equality of blacks (white Radical Republicans most often chose this option) or to reject the premises of inherent inequality and disqualify race as the basis of civic participation (black thinkers chose this option).[77]

Although ideas about race and the political applications of these ideas were inextricably linked, it is necessary to consider them separately in order to understand the role of the census. The political and educated white elite based their opinions on prevailing scientific wisdom, and race science continued in its basic task of investigating racial origins. Darwinism presented a challenge to the still dominant polygenism. The mulatto category retained its significance. Josiah Nott had earlier theorized that if blacks and whites were different racial species, mulattoes would live shorter lives, and both the 1870 and 1880 censuses were designed to accumulate proof for this theory, as the enumerators' instructions reveal. Once again, the census was neither a neutral political bystander nor simply a mirror of contemporary racial ideas. Census officials used the 1870, 1880, and 1890 censuses, as they had those of 1850 and 1860, to advance race science in basic ways.

The 1870 census was authorized by the Census Law of 1850. This was not the outcome intended, however, by Congressman James A. Garfield, the leading member of a special select committee on the census that drafted the new census bill, or by the social scientists whose advice he solicited. In March 1869, the committee on the Ninth Census, headed by Garfield, presented a census bill that, after substantial amendments, passed the House but was rejected by the Senate.[78] Although the first bill died, the House charged a special committee with issuing a report on the census and drafting new legislation. Garfield was appointed head of this new committee. While Congress was out of session, the committee prepared a detailed report on the ninth (1870) census. Garfield himself was genuinely interested in improving the census and actively sought outside advice. In January 1869, before the first attempt at a 1870 census bill, Garfield had contacted Edward Jarvis of the American Statistical Association. In a series of letters between the two men, Jarvis spelled out his many suggestions. The most germane, for our purposes, was his insistence that the census distinguish between blacks and mulattoes.[79]

The select committee's report was comprehensive and wide-ranging. It began with a historical discussion of census-taking over time and in several European countries and then addressed the history of U.S. census-taking. Much of the report detailed proposed changes in the census apparatus and in schedule inquiries, yet for all of its breadth, it made no mention of the enumeration of whites, blacks, and mulattoes, and offered an opaque explanation for the addition of the "Chinese" category ("that [inquiry] relating to color has been made to include distinctively the Chinese, so as to throw some light on the grave questions which the arrival of the Celestials among us has raised").[80]

When Congress reconvened, Garfield presented the committee's report and the census bill. The proposed census bill "required an automatic reduction in representation to those states that refused blacks the right to vote,"[81] but this apportionment penalty was ultimately removed from the bill and reintroduced separately. With this amendment, Congress voted on the remainder, which proposed significant changes in the census apparatus. The House passed the amended bill, but the Senate defeated it. According to historians, most senators considered Garfield's suggestions on census reorganization unnecessary, while others objected to Garfield's proposal to take responsibility for field enumeration away from U.S. marshals.[82] Senators appointed federal marshals, and the bill threatened a form of senatorial patronage. Worse yet, the proposed bill transferred enumerative responsibility to supervisors along congressional district lines, thus shifting patronage goodies to the House. Yet this baldly political move should not overshadow the bill's ambitious desire to radically modernize the census, its aggressive measures to enable enforcement of Section 2 of the Fourteenth Amendment, or its few telling words about Chinese enumeration. In the end, after all the effort, the 1870 census was conducted according to the 1850 Census law.

However, the 1870 schedules and enumerator instructions were significantly different from those in 1850 and 1860. The slave schedule was eliminated. On the population schedule, two inquiries under "Constitutional Relations" were added. There were five "Color" response categories, four from previous censuses: "White (W)," "Black (B)," "Mulatto (M)," and "Indian (I)"), along with an additional one, "Chinese (C)." In the "Personal Description" section of their instructions, enumerators were sternly reminded that "[C]olumns 4, 5, and 6 must in every case be filled with the age, sex, or color of the person enumerated. No return will be accepted when these spaces are left blank."[83] Under "Color," the instructions read:

> It must be assumed that, where nothing is written in this column, "White" is to be understood. The column is always to be filled. Be particularly careful in reporting the class *Mulatto* [italics in original]. The word is here generic, and includes quadroons, octoroons, and all persons having any perceptible trace of African blood. Important scientific results depend upon the correct determination of this class in schedules 1 and 2.[84]

Schedule 1 was for population, Schedule 2 for mortality. There were no instructions for enumerating blacks, Indians, or Chinese, only for mulattoes. If a space was left blank, the person was white. The 1880 instructions for "Color" were the same, with one small exception, and the schedule for mortality was Schedule 5, not Schedule 2.

Neither the census committee report nor congressional floor debates disclose who wrote the enumerators' instructions for the 1870 and 1880 censuses. However, it is clear why "important scientific results" rested on the accurate count of mulattoes in the population and mortality schedules: the results were needed to prove the presumed inferiority and distinctiveness of the mulatto. Polygenist ideas and their derivatives survived Darwinism's arrival. For decades after the publication of Darwin's *On the Origin of Species* in 1859, American scientists remained deeply committed to the distinctness of races, their separate origins, and their hierarchical ordering. How was it possible for polygenism to persist after Darwinism's claim that all humankind had descended from a common evolutionary ancestor? It was possible because Darwin's main claim left unattended two of polygenism's central concerns: the effects of racial mixture and the capacities of races. Moreover, "Darwinism was not even logically incompatible" with the basic polygenist claims that blacks and whites were fundamentally different or that blacks were a permanently inferior race, if not species.[85] The evolution of humankind from one ancestor through a process of natural selection did not mean that the evolutionary process for blacks and whites was similar or even comparable. Indeed, whites and blacks had evolved so differently, so far in the past, that it rendered their common ancestry practically meaningless. For polygenists, political practicalities were always of the utmost concern. As Josiah Nott perceived it, Darwin's "refinements of science" changed little about the reality of Negro (or mulatto) inferiority. For Nott, the efforts of the Freedman's Bureau to uplift ex-slaves were futile, since the bureau would not have "enough vitality to see the negro experiment through many hundred generations, and to direct the imperfect plans of Providence."[86]

Just as the polygenist idea of the permanence of races initially withstood Darwinism, so too did the tenet about "racial hybridity," although not without modifications. Common ancestry neither erased the evident fact of human diversity nor explained the content of those differences or the effects of racial intermixture. That whites and blacks could mate did not mean that they should. More information was needed about the physical and psychological effects of racial mixture on whites, blacks, and their "mulatto" offspring. Darwinism did not replace polygenist thought about race and racial mixture, it combined with it. By the 1890s, race scientists and social theorists were convinced, according to their interpretation of Darwin, that all races were engaged in a struggle for survival. They translated Darwin's idea of natural selection into a social theory of racial struggle. Yet in keeping with their polygenist preoccupation with "mulattoes," these same scientists and social theorists considered mulattoes to be at a distinct disadvantage and thought that they would die off. If earlier polygenist thought had posited that "mulatto frailty" was proof that whites and blacks were different species, later polygenism held that such frailty proved that racial mixture engendered racial disadvantage and would result in eventual disappearance or reversion back to the "dominant type."[87] The "dominant type" was of course presumed to be black; at no point before or since had "mulattoes" been considered "mixed whites." Blacks and other nonwhites were mixed; whites were not. These ideas emerged powerfully in the 1890 census, and certain of them persist today.

The 1890 Census: Social Darwinism
Meets Polygenism

By the late 1880s and early 1890s, nearly all the political gains made by southern blacks were being reversed. Radical Republicans had begun to retreat in the early 1870s from Reconstruction's core commitments to the protection of black political rights in the South. The compromise of 1877 resulted in the election of President Rutherford B. Hayes and the withdrawal of federal troops from the South. As Republicans abandoned the South, Negro rights largely ceased to be a paramount national issue. White Southerners were free to reconfigure social, political, and economic arrangements in ways that vitiated any notion of equal citizenship for blacks. At century's end, blacks were largely disenfranchised, despite the Fifteenth Amendment, and subject to pervasive public and private segregation, discrimination, and violence, despite the Fourteenth Amendment and the Civil Rights Acts. Supreme Court decisions played a crucial role in this state of affairs. By interpreting the Fourteenth Amendment narrowly in cases dealing with racial segregation, violence, and exclusion, the justices reduced it to little more than a definition of citizenship for blacks.[88] White political and economic interests were pursued and black interests thwarted without apparent regard for the idea of race as such. Whiteness and nonwhiteness were given meaning by the presence of economic, political, and social liberties or by the absence of these liberties, which societal categorization reflected and reinforced. Yet, racial ideas were insinuated throughout and provided a rationale for political decisions. Racial discourse continued to explain what race itself was, and social scientists again used the census to further theorize about race. This time, their aims were to determine the extent of racial mixture among blacks and whether the race was becoming more "purely Negro." To this end, the categories of "quadroon," and "octoroon" were added to the census schedule and enumerator instructions were changed accordingly. In 1896, the Supreme Court decided the case of Homer Plessy, a New Orleans "octoroon," who challenged Louisiana's separate train car law.[89] Although there is no direct connection between the 1890 census process and the Plessy case, the pivotal role racial mixture played in both provides a useful way of highlighting the divergent approaches of census-taking and law. How the 1890 census helped to advance racial theory is shown through a close examination of the census-taking process. How the census and the law diverged is illustrated through a comparison of the assumptions of census-taking and those of the Supreme Court in the Plessy case.

"TO DISTINGUISH BETWEEN QUADROONS AND OCTOROONS"

The central question that had driven polygenist race science since the 1850s still had not been satisfactorily answered: Were there differences in the life spans of members of "pure" races and of "mixed races"? Like its predecessors after 1850, the 1890 census would include inquiries designed to generate the desired data. On July 30, 1888, Congressman Joseph Wheeler (D–Ala.) introduced the following bill:

To ascertain and exhibit the physical effects upon offspring resulting from the amalgamation of human species. Be it enacted by the *Senate and House of Representatives of the United States of America in Congress assembled*, That the Superintendent, or officer in charge of the Eleventh Census be, and he is hereby, authorized and directed, in making the enumeration provided for by law, to take such steps as may be necessary to ascertain, report, and publish the birth rate and death rate among pure whites, and among negroes, Chinamen, Indians, and half-breeds or hybrids of any description or character of the human race who are found in the United States, as well as of mulattoes, quadroons, and octoroons.[90]

This bill was read twice, referred to the House Select Committee on the Eleventh Census, and ordered printed. Nothing in congressional records discloses Wheeler's motivations. Unlike in the cases of the 1850, 1860, and 1870 censuses, neither the floor debates nor the published text of the 1890 census reveal much about color enumeration. Yet even without a fuller knowledge of Wheeler's motivations, his bill, on its face, warrants attention. Its fixation on ascertaining the results of "amalgamation" mirrors censuses past. Since the 1850 census, instructions had demanded the accurate count of mulattoes, while laws and social customs had aggressively monitored social interactions. Moreover, the bill's use of the term *species* is ambiguous, because the word is spelled the same in both its singular and plural forms. If used in its plural form, polygenist thought is at work, but if used in the singular, Darwinist thought. The requirement that birth and death rates be ascertained requires explanation. Mortality schedules devised for 1850 and included in every subsequent census contained the same color inquiries as the population schedules. The bill's insistence on these tables would seem unnecessary, if not for prevailing racial thought. When concerns about "amalgamation" and birth and death rates are considered in tandem, the gist of the bill is clear: to determine whether there was a difference between members of "pure" racial groups compared to those of mixed groups.

On March 1, 1889, the bill governing the 1890 census was made law. Although close to that of the 1880 census, this law included significant differences, at least in terms of enumeration. The 1890 bill required that "quadroons" and "octoroons" be counted in addition to "mulattoes," "blacks," "whites," "Indians," "Chinese," and "Japanese." Commissioner of Labor Carroll D. Wright, in a December 1888 letter to the Senate committee on the census, suggested how the committee should amend the House bill and why the categories "octoroon" and "quadroon" were necessary. Wright was a powerful and influential advocate for the establishment of a permanent Census Bureau, and as acting superintendent, he finished the work of the 1890 census when Robert Porter resigned from the superintendent's post in 1893.

In a section entitled "Statistics relating to the Negro Race," Wright declared that "[c]omprehensive information relating to the negro is absolutely demanded by the present condition of affairs,"[91] and that the addition of new categories would be neither administratively nor fiscally onerous. "To secure the information relative to quadroons and octoroons," he assured, "would simply require another check-mark on the schedule."[92] Although such assurances also applied to the enumeration of "half-breeds of different races," Wright was most concerned about "negro statistics" and "the present condition of affairs." At issue were two diametrically opposed views of the Negro population's size and prospects: Was it growing at a more rapid pace than the white population (as was seemingly shown by 1880 census data)? Or was it reverting back to a "purer" Negro race because mixed Negroes were unable to compete in the racial struggle for survival? It then followed that if white southerners would soon be outnumbered by blacks, they were justified in their enactment of repressive measures, designed to preserve white dominance. If, on the other hand, the data showed that blacks were dying off, such repressive measures might not be necessary, since blacks could not ever seriously challenge such domination. Given all that was at stake in the production of these "negro statistics," Wright stressed the importance of careful enumeration since only statistical data could reveal the truth.

> The very greatest care should be exercised in the Eleventh Census to secure accurate information—as full as possible with the limitations of an enumeration—regarding the Negro race. So many questions are

arising that can only be answered by statistical information that this becomes a necessity. Whether the mulattoes, quadroons, and octoroons are disappearing and the race becoming more purely Negro, is a question which can not be settled by observation. It must be settled by statistics, and the sooner the statistics are collected the better.[93]

Wright concluded by suggesting that the 1890 census "be the starting point for a series of comparisons through subsequent decades." He envisioned that census data could be used to compare birth and death rates among "pure whites" and "negroes." Echoing the words of earlier census advisors, most recently those of Congressman Wheeler, Wright stressed the need to tabulate mortality data according to race.

The Senate's report to the House incorporated Wright's suggestions as well as his reasoning, stating: "[A]nother Senate amendment provides that the population schedule shall include an inquiry as to the number of negroes, mulattoes, quadroons, and octoroons. This seems to be an inexpensive inquiry, to be accomplished by a check mark in the schedule, and *is desired by scientists*"[94] (italics added). The House approved this and several other Senate amendments to the census bill. In the end, the following eight categories appeared on Schedule 1, the schedule of population and social statistics: white, black, mulatto, quadroon, octoroon, Chinese, Japanese, or Indian. The instructions to enumerators read:

> Write *white, black, mulatto, quadroon, octoroon, Chinese, Japanese, or Indian* [italics in original], according to the color or race of the person enumerated. Be particularly careful to distinguish between blacks, mulattoes, quadroons, and octoroons. The word "black" should be used to describe those persons who have three-fourths or more black blood; "mulatto," those persons who have from three-eighths to five-eighths black blood; "quadroon," those persons who have one-fourth black blood; and "octoroons," those persons who have one-eighth or any trace of black blood.[95]

The collection of vital statistics, so crucial to race scientists, was handled by Dr. John Billings, a retired U.S. Army surgeon and a leading authority in the field. He served as the Census Board's "expert special agent" on vital statistics, statistics of special classes, and social statistics for the 1890 census. The consistent inability to obtain accurate color mortality data was largely because of how the collection of vital statistics data was organized. Although mortality schedules had been a part of federal census-taking since 1850, they were not uniformly distributed during the actual enumerations. Federal agents enumerated mortality data only in those states and cities that did not have their own local systems of birth and death registrations. Where local systems of registration existed, such information was forwarded to the superintendent of the census.[96] Billings sought to improve this method by including more sources of data. He asked physicians from numerous cities to keep registers of their patients' deaths. He also made special efforts to improve data on "colored people" by requesting that black clergymen keep birth and death registers of their congregants.[97] In both cases, his office sent out blank forms with a color inquiry and a list of recommended categories: "White, black (negro and mixed), Chinese, Japanese, and Indian."

The 1890 vital statistics were compiled and analyzed by Billings in the Census Office's 1896 *Report on Vital and Social Statistics in the United States at the Eleventh Census*.[98] Curiously, for all of the evident concern to obtain mortality tables for each group to allow comparisons between them, Billings's tables only distinguished between "Native born whites," "Foreign born whites," "Colored" (including Chinese), and "Indian." There were no separate tables for blacks and mulattoes. According to the report, taking the nation as a whole, death rates for colored people were higher than for whites. In the South, where the majority of black people lived, they were likely to be higher still. Poor recordkeeping, especially of deaths among colored people, made underreportage highly probable, Billings explained.

1890 census data, once produced, were used by scholars and policymakers to answer the burning question of the day: was the black population destined to increase or disappear? The general consensus was that blacks were headed toward extinction. Billings concluded, even with mortality data he judged inaccurate, that blacks were dying at a higher rate than whites. In 1896, Frederick

Hoffman's influential *Race Traits and Tendencies of the American Negro* was published by the American Economic Association. Hoffman, a statistician for the Prudential Insurance Company, thought that he, as a foreigner from Germany, was uniquely suited to study the Negro race. Although extensive data existed, little, he claimed, was "free from the taint of prejudice or sentimentality." His aim, then, was to show through a "concise tabular statement of the facts" the true condition—the traits and tendencies—of the colored race. Hoffman argued that census data from 1800 to 1890 revealed that the death rates among blacks consistently exceeded their birthrates. Death rates in excess of birthrates among blacks strongly suggested that freedom had vitiated their "vital force" and jeopardized the race's future. "Of all the races for which statistics are obtainable . . . the negro shows the least power of resistance in the struggle for life," Hoffman wrote. Mulattoes, unsurprisingly, fared worse still. Referring to the work of Josiah Nott and others, Hoffman claimed that the mulatto was in every way "inferior to the black, and of all races the one possessed of the least vital force."[99] Francis A. Walker, the superintendent in charge of the 1860 and 1870 censuses and president of MIT, also analyzed 1890 census data, but reached less dramatic conclusions than Hoffman and others. According to Walker, blacks would continue to be concentrated in the lower South, where they were best suited to its climate and agricultural work. He also predicted that black birth- and death rates would continue to be higher than white rates. The Census Board itself regarded the "mulatto, quadroon, and octoroon" data as useless. The Eleventh Census Report stated only that "these figures are of little value. Indeed as an indication of the extent to which the races have mingled, they are misleading." Indeed, the Census Board's own assessment of the "mulatto, quadroon, and octoroon" data led census officials to remove "quadroon" and "octoroon" permanently from census schedules. These two categories appeared in the 1890 census only. "Mulatto," however, would be used again in the 1910 and the 1920 censuses.

THE PLESSY DECISION: THE CENSUS VENTURES
WHERE THE SUPREME COURT WILL NOT

The law and the census both rely on categories, yet the two have at times differed in their approaches to the determination of racial categories. Indeed, as demonstrated by the Plessy case, a legal argument against the arbitrary nature of racial categorization did not in the end much matter. Racial segregation was constitutional, however arbitrary the application of racial labels or unsound the methods used to devise them. As Justice Henry Billings Brown, writing for the majority, explained, the Fourteenth Amendment "could not have been intended to abolish distinctions based upon color, or to enforce social, as distinguished from political equality, or a commingling of the two races upon terms unsatisfactory to either."[100] In census-taking, by contrast, the soundness of the methods of racial categorization mattered greatly. For census officials and social scientists, the existence of a natural racial order was a given. Part of their task was to devise categories that faithfully reflected and further revealed the workings of nature. Such knowledge could in turn be used to guide public policy. Moreover, for certain politicians, (social) scientists, and census board officials, determining racial membership was a matter of simple inquiry and visual observation. During the 1850 census debates, Senator Joseph Underwood had remarked that the race inquiry was "but a mere inquiry as to facts." But for the courts it had been an issue of review, if not consistent judgment, of the boundaries, the accuracy, and, with the passage of the Fourteenth Amendment, the constitutionality of racial distinctions. In the 1896 Plessy case, counsel for the plaintiff contested the "observation" method of determining racial classification employed by a Louisiana railway company in its compliance with Louisiana law. The state law required "equal, but separate" accommodations for blacks and whites on all passenger railways. Without providing a definition of race, the law stated, "[n]o person or persons, shall be permitted to occupy seats in coaches, other than the ones assigned to them on account of the race they belong to."[101] The law penalized, with hefty fines, train officers who incorrectly assigned passengers to the wrong coach, as well as company officers and directors of railroad companies who refused to comply with the law.[102]

In a test devised by the Citizens' Committee to Try the Constitutionality of the Separate Car Law, an organization of colored New Orleans citizens, Homer Plessy purchased a railway ticket on June 7, 1892, sat in the railway car reserved for whites, and was arrested and charged with violating the separate car law. Plessy was a fair-skinned man—an "octoroon" in Louisiana parlance—and had been picked expressly to underscore the arbitrariness of classification. His counsel claimed that his "mixture of colored blood was not discernible." This elemental point was part of a much larger and more complex argument that the separate car law violated the Thirteenth and Fourteenth Amendments.[103] In the end, the Supreme Court chose not to address directly how racial distinctions were determined (i.e., whether an individual was white or black), but to presume the existence of distinct races.[104] The justices left the defining of racial membership to state legislatures.

Where the Supreme Court chose not to venture, the census nonetheless presumed knowledge. The basis for racial distinctions was taken to be immediately accessible and knowable: individual racial identifications, even blood quanta, were assumed observable to enumerators. Had census officials confronted the argument of Plessy's counsel, they would have defended their methods as scientifically sound—even though they later considered the 1890 "mixed race" data "useless." "The mixture of [Plessy's] colored blood" was held discernible to enumerators.

Twentieth-Century Censuses: From
Jim Crow to Civil Rights

Political, economic, social, legal, and intellectual developments in the twentieth century significantly diminished the role of the census in constituting racial discourse for roughly seventy years. As we have seen, in the nineteenth century, censuses directly advanced racial science, and racial science directly informed public policy and political discourse. Twentieth-century censuses ceased to play such a prominent role in racial theory. Instead, they have mostly counted by race. The definitions of "non-white" categories became consistent with legal definitions of racial membership. For the purposes of the census, race was self-evident. Census categorization sustained racial discourse inasmuch as categorizing and counting by race gave it an official existence. Theorizing about race continued in scientific and social scientific circles, but scientists and thinkers did not deliberately enlist the census as they had in the past. The "mulatto" categorization was, however, an important exception to this overall trend. After 1970, the census once again emerged as a venue for directly enabling public policies and for shaping debate about race itself. In striking contrast to its past, the census now supports civil rights legislation. However, (social) scientists today increasingly reject the idea of counting by race at all, since they now believe that race has no natural, objective basis. Their views are a sharp reversal from those of their predecessors, for whom race was an objective reality and the census the instrument for uncovering this reality and for directing public policy. The remainder of this chapter explains and analyzes this double reversal: the sublimation of the census in configuring racial discourse for most of the twentieth century and its reemergence at century's end.

There were three fundamental and interrelated shifts in American intellectual, institutional, and political life that account for the constrained influence of the census. First, race science settled into a set of ideas that would dominate for nearly forty years, but would then be challenged for decades thereafter: discrete races existed; these races possessed distinctive intellectual, cultural, and moral capacities; and these capacities were unequally distributed within and between racial groups. Predictably, the white race was judged superior to all others, and especially to the black race. The census no longer sorted out race science's basic questions; instead, it registered the evident existence of races.

Second, the Census Bureau's gradual institutionalization changed perceptions about the purposes and limits of racial enumeration. With its methods soundly grounded in statistical science, it would eventually become a full-fledged bureaucracy, whose revised self-appointed mission was to provide racial data without explicitly advancing racial thought and without submitting to political interests. Counting by race would become an administrative task and a technical procedure, or at least be widely viewed as such. Moreover, decisions about racial categorization became even less public, and supposedly less political, because Congress deferred to the internal decision-making processes of the Census Bureau, which in 1902 became a permanent federal agency under the Department of Commerce and Labor. In 1918, to assist in the development of schedules and inquiries, including the question on race, an advisory committee was formed, which consulted the Census Bureau until the mid 1940s. By 1954, all census legislation had become Title 13 of the U.S. Code.

Third, the hardening of racial segregation and subordination, both de jure and de facto, paralleled the hardening of scientific thought. Southern law had largely settled on the "one drop of nonwhite blood" rule by 1930. The definitions of nonwhite categories as spelled out in instructions to census enumerators were identical to those of southern racial membership laws. It is important to emphasize, however, that these ideas about white and nonwhite racial membership were not limited to the South. They were assumed and imposed nationwide, which explains their appearance in the federal census. However, census categories did not simply reflect race laws, social customs, and scientific thought. The enumeration of "mulattoes" shows how census-taking followed its own path to the "one-drop rule."

On the Road to the "One-Drop" Rule:
The 1900–1930 Censuses

Although scientific thought about race reached a loose consensus in the first decades of the twentieth century, at the century's start, there were three competing and overlapping theories: polygenism, which although waning, still persisted; Lamarckian ideas about the inheritance of acquired characteristics; and Darwin's hypothesis of evolution by natural selection, especially Herbert Spencer's application of it in the form of Social Darwinism.[105] A number of (social) scientists employed these three ideas separately or in tandem, however incongruously, to explain nature's racial designs and workings. In all three uses, "the mulatto" figured prominently. For polygenists, the supposed frailty of mulattoes proved that blacks and whites were permanently different races, if not separate species. Social Darwinists judged mulattoes ill-equipped to survive life's struggle, thus proving that racial separation was necessary for racial preservation. Neo-Lamarckianism warned that because basic racial characteristics were carried, literally, in the blood, the mixing of bloods was bad, for whites especially.[106] Mulatto offspring were themselves clear proof.

The emerging intellectual agreement on race accompanied the establishment of disciplinary boundaries in the social and natural sciences.[107] By 1910, polygenism had been completely abandoned. American biological science was firmly rooted in Darwin's principles. Social Darwinism, the foundation of American sociology, was gradually replaced by progressive scientific thought, confident in its ability to know and improve the human condition. Mendel's theories on heredity led to the rapid demise of Lamarckianism. While physical anthropology was the dominant subfield within the larger discipline of American anthropology, cultural anthropology could potentially offer fresh views on race. Yet, for all the reconfiguring, the new consensus initially looked much like the old. Eugenicists claimed they could prove that human intelligence followed Mendelian rules of inheritance.[108] They soon extended their hypotheses about individuals to groups, concluding that certain races and classes were genetically inferior and others genetically superior. The tentative steps of cultural anthropology toward culture as a variable explaining differences in human expression were undercut by the way in which culture itself was conceived. Many anthropologists viewed culture as deriving from racial origins. As the historian George Stocking writes, "[F]or 'race' read 'culture' or 'civilization,' for 'racial heredity' read 'cultural heritage.'"[109] The basic idea that distinct races existed and were permanently unequal remained firmly in place. For this reason alone, scientific interest in the "mulatto" endured. What happened when superior and inferior races mated? Social and natural scientists still wanted to know.

The *Plessy* decision was singularly important to the entrenchment of legal racial segregation. Southern racial membership and segregation laws were less concerned with distinguishing between blacks, whites, and mulattoes legally than with rigidly separating their social interactions and economic productivity. The prohibition of interracial marriages, if not interracial sex, was a logical and necessary continuance of this segregating imperative. Up to forty-one states enacted "anti-miscegenation" statutes at one time or another, from the antebellum period to the mid 1960s.[110] Segregation laws did not uniformly define race. Instead, segregatory practices built upon supposedly self-evident racial distinctions and otherwise marched forward without clear or consistent definitions. When definitions were provided, three criteria were used: "ancestry, blood quanta, and appearance," alone or in some combination.[111] In the early decades of the twentieth century, legal definitions of *Negro* were broad, and those of *white* nearly nonexistent, in those states where race statutes existed. As a rule, southern laws did not recognize, and thus did not define, a separate class of persons as "mulattoes," who might thus be treated differently from Negroes. Indeed, anti-miscegenation laws were designed to prevent racial mixture entirely. The general inattentiveness of the law to mulatto status shows that it conferred the same legal disabilities as Negro status. At the same time, the law's reliance on "blood quanta" presumed a natural, scientific basis.

If science during this period was still very interested in the "mulatto," law, comparatively speaking, was not. What was the position of the U.S. census? It would continue counting mulattoes, even if such enumeration now required defending. This defense was provided by Walter Willcox, a prominent Census Bureau statistician and a Cornell University statistics professor. The Census Board had judged the final 1890 data on mulattoes, quadroons, and octoroons "of little value and misleading," thus explaining the removal of these categories from the 1900 census. Willcox argued for the accuracy and utility of the mulatto data. In a 1906 census text, *Supplementary Analysis and Derivative Tables*, Willcox wrote that the enumeration of octoroons and quadroons, as required by the 1890 census law, accounted for the data's alleged inaccuracies. A "simple" question, however, which asked only whether the respondent was of "pure or mixed blood," would generate valuable data.[112] Earlier censuses, from 1850 through 1880, used a simple query, and Willcox judged the resulting data reasonably accurate. The 1910 census included "mulatto," along with "white," "black," "Chinese," "Japanese," and "Indian." The enumerators' instructions read:

> Write "W" for white; "B" for black; "Mu" for mulatto; "Ch" for Chinese; "Jp" for Japanese; "In" for Indian. For all persons not falling within one of these classes, write "Ot" (for other), and write on the left-hand margin of the schedule the race of the person so indicated. For census purposes, the term "black" (B) includes all persons who are evidently full-blooded negroes, while the term "mulatto" (Mu) includes all persons having some proportion or perceptible trace of Negro blood.[113]

Willcox's defense here was straightforward: mulattoes existed in the American population and should be counted.[114] Like other statisticians before him, he desired an accurate count and believed that statistical data would provide the objective data needed to bolster conventional thinking about the races: blacks and mulattoes were naturally inferior to whites and were losing the struggle for racial survival.[115] In keeping with the Census Bureau's gradual professionalization and the introduction of disciplinary boundaries, censuses should simply provide racial numbers, without excessive commentary.

Yet the categories upon which these numbers were based were not free-floating: they were anchored in the idea and the language of "blood quantas," which carried scientific and legal meanings. Scientifically, this language worked in two ways: it served as an imprecise shorthand for ancestry, and it conveyed the idea that group racial traits existed and were transmitted intergenerationally. Legally, this language ensured that race was understood as unchanging, natural, and ever-present, if not always visible.[116] The exact proportion of white and nonwhite blood set the parameters of the color line. In those instances when a person's racial membership was called into question, "blood quantas" would provide the legal, if not the social, answer. By 1930, science, law, and the census had converged to accept the "one-drop" rule of nonwhite racial membership. This convergence was overdetermined by science's enduring obsession with white racial purity, on the one hand, and the deep history of political and economic subordination of nonwhites on the other. The removal of "mulatto" from the 1930 census schedule conforms to this pattern and at the same time differs from it. Enumerators' instructions employed the one-drop rule, which brought the census in line with Jim Crow and anti-miscegenation laws. The Census Bureau decided to drop "mulatto" for methodological reasons, but it did not explain its explicit adoption of the one-drop rule, because such an explanation was unneeded. The one-drop rule had served as a default, thus attesting to its acquired hegemony.

The Census Bureau's advisory committee resolution of December 1928 read:

> The principal reason for giving up the attempt to separate blacks and mulattoes was the fact that the results of the attempt in past censuses had been very imperfect. It was suggested that the increase in the percentage mulatto shown by the 1910 census figures was probably the result of the employment of large numbers of Negro enumerators and that this might explain the decrease in the percentage mulatto between

1910 and 1920. Prof. Willcox made the point that, while he felt the question ought not be permanently dropped, it was not necessary to carry it at every census.[117]

After seven censuses, social scientists, statisticians, and economists decided that the past data had been "very imperfect." The committee's stated reasons for removing "mulatto" rested on accuracy. Had they had confidence in the data's accuracy or in the ability of the census to secure better data, the category "mulatto" might well have continued to appear on census forms. Willcox's statement suggests that he, for one, thought the category's scientific and social utility had not been exhausted, however inaccurate the data. Neither this resolution nor other committee decisions explained how definitions of "Negro" or other nonwhite categories were devised. The pervasive one-drop rule obviated the need for explanation.

The 1920 census contained three new "nonwhite" categories: "Filipino," "Hindu," and "Korean." Advisory committee records neither mention these additions nor provide reasons for their introduction. Scholars have assumed that they were added in response to immigration.[118] However, the Immigration Act of 1917 expressly prohibited immigrants from the "Asiatic Barred Zone," which included, among other areas, India and most of the Polynesian Islands.[119] Like "Chinese" and "Japanese" earlier, these new categories were used to track and record Asian residents as "races." Restrictions on the naturalization of nonwhites finally ended in 1952.[120] The remaining categories on the 1920 census were those of past censuses: White, Black, Mulatto, Chinese, Japanese, Indian, and Other.

Jim Crow in the Census, 1930–1960

The instructions for the 1930 census mirrored the racial status quo in American law, society, and science. Southern statutes that had defined nonwhites in terms of specific blood quanta now defined the category "Negro" more broadly. Any person with even a trace of black blood was legally black and subject to all the disabilities the designation conferred. In Virginia, for example, where *Negro* and *colored person* were synonymous, before 1910, a person of "one-fourth or more Negro blood" was considered colored. In 1910, the blood quantum was switched to "one-sixteenth Negro blood," and by 1930, any ascertainable quantum of Negro blood made one a Negro.[121] Likewise, before 1927, a Georgia state general statute defined colored persons as those with "one-eighth or more Negro blood." After 1927, the statute read that all persons of any ascertainable Negro blood were colored. In contrast, legal definitions of *white* did not change, if they existed at all. In general, to be "white" was conceived as the complete absence of any "negro or non-white blood," down to the last drop and as far back generationally as one could go. The 1935 Georgia State Code is illustrative: "[T]he term 'white person' shall include only persons of the white and Caucasian race, who have no ascertainable trace of either Negro, African, West Indian, Asiatic Indian, Mongolian, Japanese, or Chinese blood in their veins."[122] U.S. naturalization case law functioned in a similar way: it focused not on defining the term *white person* but on defining who was, and what it meant to be, "non-white."[123] Here too the census broadly conformed to law by never providing a definition of *white*.

Legal definitions mattered enormously to the racial identification Americans bore and asserted publicly (and often privately). The interaction between laws, customs, and racial identification did not begin in the 1930s, of course. But now the "one-drop" rule marked the boundaries rigidly, as it had not done before. It settled the matter of who was white and who was not, inasmuch as the matter could be settled. The phenomenon of "passing" attests to the authority of these boundaries—*and* their incoherence. "Passing" referred to a black person who lived as a white person, and not vice versa. Passing is only intelligible in terms of racial laws, their meanings, and social customs, because if a person *passed* as white, then why was he or she still not *really* white? Well into the 1950s, popular black American magazines featured articles on passing that presented it as a small collective victory against segregation and as insider knowledge. Sociologists periodically studied passing in hopes of ascertaining reliable figures on how many Negroes had passed, were passing, and might be expected to pass.[124] With these numbers, sociologists questioned whether all Negroes could and would pass into white, over time. They concluded that they could not and would not.

During the late 1920s when the advisory committee decided to eliminate "mulatto," most scientists (both natural and social) were firmly committed to the belief in the existences of races and in their innately unequal character. Although these same scientists were unable to isolate "pure races" or to identify what their particular characteristics might be, this basic failure did not diminish the authority of race science.[125] Scientists relied on and advanced a "common-sense" notion of race, a notion that science itself had helped to create. Racial differences were real and observable. The job of science was to discern the sources and meaning of those differences. In the 1920s, the IQ test was the main instrument for proving objectively what scientists had long thought to be true: "whites" were mentally superior to "nonwhites" and to "blacks" in particular.[126] From these same IQ tests, American (social) scientists also concluded that not all whites were equal: "Anglo-Saxon" whites were superior to "non Anglo-Saxon" southern and eastern Europeans. Concern about the racial stock of these immigrants and their fitness for republican life contributed to the passage of restrictive immigration legislation in 1924. This legislation abruptly arrested the massive European immigration that had begun in the 1850s with the Irish.

The purported proof of the inferiority of certain white races mirrored the long-standing preoccupation with white racial degeneracy resulting from racial mixing with "non-whites." Scientists did not articulate the threat to white racial purity in terms of blood droplets, yet their evident concern about degeneracy in effect endorsed the one-drop rule. White racial purity (of the Anglo-Saxon sort) had to be preserved on all fronts: immigration restrictions halted contamination by inferior whites; Jim Crow legislation and de facto segregation kept whites and nonwhites apart. Concern about intrawhite contamination, however, quickly receded. Although (social) scientists and politicians perceived racial differences among whites to be real and consequential, they did not long hold to those views. By the late 1920s, (social) scientists wrote increasingly of the "white" or "Caucasian" race, which included, without invidious distinctions, many of the groups formerly disparaged.[127] In any case, the census had always counted European immigrants as "white," although enumerators' instructions never defined *white*. Such was not the case, however, for "non-white" groups, and with the 1930 census, detailed definitions were provided for certain of them.

As in law, social customs, and science, the census upheld and reinforced the ideas of white purity and the one-drop rule, although not consistently. The 1930 census enumerators' instructions were as follows:

1. Negroes.—A person of mixed white and Negro blood should be returned as a Negro, no matter how small the percentage of Negro blood. Both black and mulatto persons are to be returned as Negroes, without distinction. A person of mixed Indian and Negro blood should be returned a Negro, unless the Indian blood predominates and the status of an Indian is generally accepted in the community.

2. Indians.—A person of mixed white and Indian blood should be returned as Indian, except where the percentage of Indian blood is very small, or where he is regarded as a white person by those in the community where he lives.

3. Mexicans.—Practically all Mexican laborers are of a racial mixture difficult to classify, though usually well recognized in the localities where they are found. In order to obtain separate figures for this racial group, it has been decided that all persons born in Mexico, or having parents born in Mexico, who are definitely not white, Negro, Indian, Chinese, or Japanese, should be returned as Mexican ("Mex").

4. Other mixed races.—Any mixture of white and nonwhite should be reported according to the nonwhite parent. Mixtures of colored races should be reported according to the race of the father, except Negro-Indian [see the definition of *Negro* above].[128]

Although "Chinese," "Japanese," "Filipino," "Hindu," and "Korean" were also included on the 1930 and 1940 censuses, enumerators were not given specific definitions or instructions about them. The 1930 instructions (except for Mexicans) also guided the 1940 and 1950 censuses. The definition of *Negro* on the 1960 census removed the explicit reference to the one-drop rule by employing no blood terminology at all. However, it still defined as Negro anyone with at least one Negro parent.

The introduction and then removal of the "Mexican" category shows how census methods in one case both upheld the "white" and "non-white" rule of classification and relaxed it. The minutes of the advisory committee's 1928 meeting neither mention the Mexican category nor provide an explanation for its introduction. However, an August 1931 press release explained that the category was added in response to massive Mexican immigration in the 1920s.[129] During and after the Mexican Revolution, large numbers of Mexicans entered the southwestern United States. Both the U.S. Immigration Service and the Mexican Department of Foreign Relations estimated that nearly 500,000 Mexicans legally entered between 1889 and 1928.[130] The 1930 census returns reported 1,422,533 Mexicans living in the United States. In earlier censuses, Mexicans had been classified as white, and the category "Mexican" was added in response to their larger numerical presence. In smaller numbers, Mexicans had been presumed to be of Spanish descent, and thus white,[131] but with the intent of counting them separately, larger numbers of them were necessarily defined as "racially mixed," in keeping with the white/nonwhite, pure/impure dichotomy.

Although the Census Bureau included "Mexican" only in the 1930 census, the category might well have been retained in subsequent censuses but for what the advisory committee minutes call "an accidental circumstance."[132] The committee's draft memorandum, written by Leon Truesdell, chief statistician for population, is slightly more informative, saying it was "because of political complications resulting from what might be termed an accidental circumstance,"[133] but it does not specify what the "political complications" were.

With the Mexican government's assistance, Mexican Americans lobbied against the continuance of the "Mexican" category.[134] They protested because they perceived a connection between its introduction and the forced repatriation of nearly 400,000 Mexicans and Mexican-Americans from the Southwest in the 1930s. The category itself suggested discriminatory intent, regardless of how far removed it was in actuality from the policy and mechanisms of forced repatriation.[135] Mexicans were subsequently counted as "white," until the introduction of the "Hispanic Origins" question in the 1980 census.[136]

The state of racial discourse was more unstable than the 1930–60 census instructions would lead us to believe. By the 1940s, its scientific foundations had shifted noticeably. Scholars have identified internal and external destabilizing forces. Internally, cultural anthropologists, under the guidance of Franz Boas, compellingly challenged the basic tenets of race science. Boas, his students, and like-minded anthropologists and biologists argued that race had no biological basis and thus had no bearing on the customs, intelligence, temperament, or character of individuals or groups.[137] Such similarities and differences were best understood in terms of culture. They argued that "physical characteristics were completely unreliable indicators of race."[138] Externally, Nazism forced (social) scientists worldwide to reexamine their thinking on race. In 1950, UNESCO (the United Nations Educational Scientific and Cultural Organization) issued the first of a series of official statements on race. The anthropologist Ashley Montagu noted: "[I]n the decade just passed more than six million human beings lost their lives because it was alleged that they belonged to an inferior race. The horrible corollary to this barbarism is that it rested on a scientifically untenable premise."[139]

Shifting (social) scientific ideas about race alone do not account for changes in racial discourse. The demise of the South's cotton economy, the massive migration of southern blacks to northern and midwestern cities, increased political participation and agitation, more successful legal challenges to segregation, and the onset of the Cold War decisively transformed the political landscape. The explanation here is admittedly schematic; it identifies neither precise causal factors nor a sequence of events that triggered the shift in thinking. The point is that prevailing racial discourse now existed on a far less nourishing terrain. The acceptance of race, even in scientifically biased ways, did not mean that American social, political, and economic life would or should continue to be organized around it in the ways it had been. Ideas of race and the attendant (and proper) public policies had long been inseparable, but they were so no longer. The issue of race was detached from questions of how it mattered politically, socially, and economically, and whether it should or should not do so. If race had no biological basis, it was easier to loosen the connection.

At the same time, it became increasingly difficult to discuss what race was in a coherent way, other than to say that it did not biologically exist. Civil rights discourse focused exclusively on racism, discrimination, and equality, leaving aside the question of race itself. Census-taking in the era after the Civil Rights Movement has reflected this tension: census data are used to remedy racial discrimination, while census categories are themselves supported by a decentered, conflicting, and in certain ways, anachronistic racial discourse. The controversies over racial categorization in the 2000 census reveal the extent to which these two views—civil rights discourse and racial discourse—are on a collision course.

Civil Rights, Race, and the Census

The Civil Rights Movement and resulting civil rights legislation of the 1960s dramatically changed the political context and purposes of racial categorization. Federal civil rights legislation, most notably the Civil Rights Acts of 1964 and 1968 and the Voting Rights Act of 1965, dismantled the most egregious discriminatory mechanisms, namely, black disenfranchisement in the South, rigid residential segregation, and wholesale exclusion of blacks from certain occupations and American institutions. Civil rights discourse promoted and sustained these political changes. It held that racial discrimination was morally wrong, politically and socially corrosive, and legally suspect. Legal segregation and southern black disenfranchisement flagrantly disregarded the Constitution's Fourteenth and Fifteenth Amendments. Racial discrimination in employment, housing, and education vitiated the notion of equal opportunity and treatment. Although federal laws and programs required racial and ethnic census data for monitoring legislative compliance and for delivering federal services and funds to groups, neither civil rights strategies nor rhetoric addressed race or racial classifications directly.[140] In large part, the categories were taken as they were. They had been the basis of discrimination, and it was presumed that they would be the basis of remedy. It did not seem to matter whether they were real or not in a scientific sense. Race categories remained politically, socially, and economically salient. Civil rights advocates had clear political goals but faced real political constraints: they had to secure enduring victories within a slightly opened, but still resistant, political environment. Southern segregation had to be broken; southern black enfranchisement enforced and protected. The federal government had to be compelled to protect black political rights and made to stop deferring to southern states' rights. The federal government also had to be made to direct federal attention and funds to deep-rooted poverty and disadvantage. With this agenda, there was neither much evident need nor much room for thinking about race as an idea, or about racial classifications, either in society or in censuses. This oversight has not, however, been cost-free for subsequent civil rights advocacy.

The Census Bureau and, later, the Office of Management and Budget have had to think about racial classification. This rethinking process has occurred in stages over the past thirty years and reached its most systematic phase in the 1990s. Most simply, the Census Bureau and OMB have had to examine, if not fully explain, what is meant by the term *race* and by the use of racial data. If race is not a scientifically valid concept, why does the census continue to count by it?

Present-day Census Bureau and OMB officials labor under intellectual and political conditions significantly different from and more complex than those of their predecessors. In the past, officials had little serious doubt about either the biological reality of race or the propriety of using census data to support and justify segregatory public policies. Nor did they hesitate to use the census to shape and advance race theory itself. Yet, however intertwined the aims of past scientists, census officials, and politicians, their work assumed and projected a veneer of (social) scientific objectivity. Scientists considered race fundamental to human existence, census officials counted by race, and politicians used these data to formulate public policies. Today, the veneer of objectivity, for race and for the purposes of counting, is gone. Counting by race is justified precisely because of the subjectivity of race and its political salience in American life, not because of any objective reality. Today the census cannot classify and count at a political distance, any more than it has done so historically. The principal difference for census-taking is that past racial discourse was firmly anchored in contemporary science; today it is not.

In one significant way, however, the role of the census in the late twentieth century is similar. Past censuses contributed directly to shoring up the scientific underpinnings of racial discourse. Today, a wide range of actors also attempts to use the census to form and support racial discourses, albeit new ones. On what conceptual basis and by what reasoning should the census count by race? The answer(s) matter(s) enormously to the coherence of racial thought, public policy, and political strategy. Should it count because it considers racial categories benign demographic descriptors, based on some notion of geography or culture? In that case, the census would support the idea that race is now best understood as an imperfect marker of "groupness." To satisfy statutory requirements? The census would here seem to be endorsing the view that race is chiefly a political category, made meaningful by its legislative uses. Should the census not count by race at all? Perhaps the best racial discourse is no racial discourse? Eliminating the question would seem to be one step in that direction.

These ideas are not inconsequential abstractions. Behind them stand vocal constituencies. Organizations representing multiracial and multiethnic Americans, Arab Americans, Irish Americans, and German Americans have lobbied for the addition of new categories, such as "multiracial" and "middle-eastern," or for the disaggregation of the "white" category itself.[141] These groups argue that census categories should capture demographic diversity accurately and reflect personal self-identification, two tasks they equate. In contrast, civil rights organizations have lobbied against any significant change in race categories, stressing their legislative purposes: race categories are now most meaningful in terms of civil rights. The task of counting must be judged by the extent to which it reinforces or weakens the enforcement of civil rights legislation. Finally, academics and political pundits have called for the elimination of the term *race* (liberals) or of the question itself (conservatives).[142] Liberals charge that the term *race* is outdated and scientifically indefensible, proposing that it should be replaced by *ethnicity*. Conservatives demand removal of the question, with the express aim of undercutting race consciousness and eliminating the racial data on which many public policies at present rely.

Federal officials are far from powerless, as we shall see, but they work under political constraints unknown to their predecessors. The Civil Rights Movement resulted in both significant federal legislation and powerful new political constituencies, with which the Census Bureau and OMB have had to contend. In the past, Census Bureau officials made decisions about "non-whites" with few interventions from the groups themselves, and decided on racial categories without public input, review, or accountability. More recently, the bureau and OMB have opened themselves up to public view, in keeping with a desire to make their deliberative processes and technical methods more transparent. They are now more accountable to the public in terms of racial classification than ever before. In 1960, self-identification replaced enumerator identification by instructions, signaling the bureau's attempts to be at once more accurate and more responsive to public sentiment. Finally, there is today no presumed objective science of race to which officials can refer. Yet these constraints have not ruled out the rol of the census in creating racial discourse. How the Census Bureau and OMB approach race in some important way affects how we think about race and how race organizes American political and social life.

STATISTICAL DIRECTIVE NO. 15

In 1977, expressly to enable better compliance with civil rights legislation, OMB issued its Statistical Directive No. 15, which mandates the five official racial/ethnic categories used in all statistical reporting by federal agencies, including the Census Bureau.[143] The directive's categories were not drawn directly from the census, and since its promulgation, the Census Bureau has had to comply with its standards. It permits federal agencies to use other "sub" categories, but they must be able to aggregate them into the original five. The Census Bureau has been one of the few agencies to exercise this option, which it has done in response to direct lobbying and congressional influence.

In 1964, an executive order created the Federal Interagency Committee on Education (FICE), and in January 1974, Executive Order 11761 updated FICE's mandate.[144] More than 30 federal agencies were either members of FICE or participants in its responsibilities, which included coordinating federal educational policies and advising the secretary of health, education, and welfare (HEW). In 1973, the FICE subcommittee on minority education submitted a report entitled *Higher Education for Chicanos, Puerto Ricans, and American Indians* to then HEW Secretary Caspar Weinberger. Weinberger took particular interest in the report's recommendation that uniform, compatible, and nonduplicative racial/ethnic categories be developed for use across federal agencies. In June 1974, FICE created an ad hoc committee on racial and ethnic definitions, chaired by Charles E. Johnson, Jr., assistant chief of the Census Bureau's Population Division. All federal agencies using racial and ethnic data heavily were summoned to join the committee; these agencies included OMB, the General Accounting Office (GAO), the Department of Justice, the Department of Housing and

Urban Development, and the Equal Employment Opportunity Commission (EEOC).

Representatives met together and through "considerable discussion, disagreement, give-and-take, and compromise" devised the categories.[145] They were guided by two principal aims: to devise categories that would satisfy the multiple federal needs for such data and to develop categories that made sense in some general way. In this regard, the representatives reasoned that all race categories needed to refer to a geographic location from which the race originated. This idea, and the use of race as a geographical marker, caused the committee some difficulty in certain cases. For example, the committee debated whether persons from India should be categorized under the "Asian or Pacific Islander" category or under the "White/Caucasian" category, since they were purportedly Caucasians, "though frequently of darker skin than other Caucasians."[146] In the trial directive they were classified as Caucasian, but they were reclassified as Asian in the final version (most likely in response to Asian Indian lobbying efforts to ensure racial minority status).[147] Committee members relied on their own personal understanding of race, not on expert testimony or opinion. Judging from the committee's deliberations and the directive itself, members viewed races as natural human groupings, each with its own original geographic home.

In May 1977, OMB adopted Directive No. 15 for use by all federal agencies. The directive's preamble states simply: "[T]hese classifications should not be interpreted as being scientific or anthropological in nature. . . . They have been developed in response to needs expressed by both the executive branch and the Congress."
The categories were:

  1. American Indian or Alaskan Native—A person having origins in any of the original peoples of North America, and who maintains cultural identification through tribal affiliations or community recognition.

  2. Asian or Pacific Islander—A person having origins in any of the original peoples of the Far East, Southeast Asia, the Indian subconti-

nent, or the Pacific Islands. This area includes, for example, China, India, Japan, Korea, the Philippine Islands, and Samoa.

3. Black—A person having origins in any of the black racial groups of Africa.

4. Hispanic—A person of Mexican, Puerto Rican, Cuban, Central or South American or other Spanish culture or origin, regardless of race.

5. White—A person having origins in any of the original peoples of Europe, North Africa, or the Middle East.

Directive No. 15 defines "Hispanic" as an ethnic category, meaning that there are, for example, "white" Hispanics and "black" Hispanics. It instructs that persons of "mixed racial or ethnic origins" be classified according to "the category which most closely reflects the individual's recognition in his community."

After the directive was issued, the Census Bureau added several Asian and Pacific Islander subcategories and a new "Hispanic Origins" question, in response to the direct lobbying of minority advisory committees and congressional pressure. In these cases, specific categories and questions are in contention, not the ideas of race or ethnicity as such. Groups organized to secure an official statistical existence and to participate in federal programs intended for racial minorities. In the mid 1970s, Asian Pacific, Black, Hispanic, and American Indian and Alaska Native advisory committees were established to advise the bureau. These committees exert considerable influence on all matters related to racial and ethnic enumeration, including the new Asian-Pacific Islander (API) subcategories and the "Hispanic Origins" question. The 1980 census contained nine API subcategories, up from five on the 1970 census, as a result of lobbying.[148] The 1990 census contained the same nine plus an additional "other API," where respondents could fill in their desired term. Coalitions of Asian-American groups have lobbied for the addition of two more subcategories in the 2000 census. Likewise, the Census Bureau added the "Hispanic Origins" question to the 1980 census under pressure from the Hispanic Advisory Committee and in the absence of a satisfactory alternative method.[149] Previously, the bureau had not assigned persons of "Spanish heritage" and/or with "Spanish surnames" to a separate group. They were generally categorized as "white," except when they were, in the words of census manuals, "definitely Negro or Indian."

Prompted by growing public criticism that Directive No. 15 was incapable of accurately measuring the number of new immigrants or offspring of interracial marriages, OMB set out in 1993 to assess the adequacy of current categories, devise principles to govern revisions of the directive, and solicit specific recommendations for changes in categorization. This review was significantly more open to public input and expert evaluation than the 1977 meetings had been. In March 1994, OMB established an interagency committee for the review of racial and ethnic standards, which included representatives from thirty federal agencies, including the Census Bureau, the Department of Justice, and the Department of Education. In addition, OMB actively sought public comment through congressional subcommittee hearings in 1993 and 1997 and by notices posted in the *Federal Register*. At OMB's request, in 1994, the National Research Council's committee on national statistics conducted a workshop that included federal officials, academics, public policy analysts, corporate representatives, and secondary school educators.[150] Finally, OMB sponsored research on and testing of the possible effects of a new multiracial category and of the reformatting and resequencing of the Hispanic Origins question.[151]

The demand for the addition of "multiracial" to Directive No. 15 proved the most contentious issue, because it challenged the premise of mutual exclusivity on which U.S. racial categorization has been based. The "mulatto" category of past censuses is not a proper analogue to the "multiracial" category. There the "mulatto" category was a qualifier of the "negro" category, not a wholly independent category. At the same time, the term *multiracial* itself presumes the existence of discrete, if not pure, races. In its July 1997 report, the interagency committee recommended that OMB allow respondents to choose more than one race on their census schedules for the first time in history, while also recommending against the adoption of a multiracial category. It further recommended the addition of "Native Hawaiian or Other Pacific Islander," making it the fifth racial classification. It also called for slight alterations in the wording of existing categories, suggesting that "Alaska" Native replace "Alaskan" Native in the title of the "American Indian or Alaska Native" category, that "Latino" be added to that of "Hispanic," making it "Hispanic or Latino," and that "African-American" be added to that of "Black," making it "Black or African American."[152] OMB, which was empowered to accept, modify, or reject the committee's recommendations, accepted them in toto. The strong institutional, political, and methodological bias against major changes in categorization ensured that such changes would be highly improbable. The interagency committee, composed of representatives from thirty federal agencies, worked to satisfy the legislative requirements and institutional demands for racial data, just as FICE had been impaneled to do. Minority organizations in support of civil rights enforcement lobbied against major changes, and statisticians and demographers most concerned with data comparability (or at least the appearance of such) over time, warned of the dangers of extensive changes.

That OMB and the Census Bureau considered the multiracial category at all demonstrates the influence of the organized multiracial movement and OMB's receptivity to group demands. It also signaled a growing acceptance of the idea, within OMB at least, that the future will somehow be more multiracial than the past. However, the interagency committee chose its words carefully on this issue, saying: "[T]he multiracial population is growing, and the task of measuring this phenomenon will have to be confronted sooner or later."[153] It described growth of the multiracial population as a "phenomenon" but did not indicate what it meant to be "multiracial." Is this phenomenon social, natural, or some combination of the two? Are Americans becoming "multiracial" now because they choose to and are allowed to assert themselves as such? Or is becoming "multiracial" a new natural process? The interagency committee avoided these basic questions, as has OMB. In so doing, they ensured that neither the multiracial idea nor multiracial population will grow, at least with federal support or in official numbers. Multiracial activists unsuccessfully attempted to enlist the census in their larger political project of creating a self-consciously multiracial community. For the moment, Americans who assume and assert multiracial identities can only reveal them by checking separate categories on census forms. Yet, it is important to emphasize that these activists were not alone in their pursuits. As the history of racial categorization in the United States amply shows, the census today, as in the past, remains the arena where ideas about race are worked through, categories constructed and then applied to public policy.

CHAPTER 3

With "time . . . , they will be white"

Brazilian Censuses and National Identity

Writing in the late 1930s, Vera Kelsey, an American observer, sought to capture Brazil's essence in her book *Seven Keys to Brazil*.[1] Borrowing liberally from the Brazilian anthropologist Gilberto Freyre, Kelsey concluded that Brazil's people of color did not object to white domination because "one day, on the turn of wheels of time and evolution, they will be white themselves." Until the 1950s, Brazilian census texts assured both Brazilian and foreign readers, but Americans especially, that Brazil's population was "whitening." Today, census texts refer to Brazil's population as racially mixed, with a large nonwhite plurality. Brazilians and outsiders, mostly Americans, increasingly describe Brazil as a "black" nation, with the largest black population outside of Nigeria. They too refer to census data. How is it then that Brazil could be a "white" country at the beginning of the century and a "black" one at its end? And why does it matter? The answers lie more in census methods and in competing interpretations of census data than in demographic shifts. They also lie in racial discourse, in its ways of determining racial membership and assigning value to it. For Brazilian elites, at least, Brazil's identity as a white and racially harmonious nation has mattered enormously. The Brazilian Statistical Institute has not only reflected these images but upheld and protected them.[2] In the same way, however, census methods of racial categorization, the availability of color data, and the analysis of such data now assist in Brazil's transformation into a nonwhite and racially stratified nation.

This chapter analyzes the history of color categorization in Brazilian censuses from the first modern census in 1872 to the 2000 census. It argues that in Brazil, as in the United States, censuses have served to maintain and advance racial discourse. In Brazil, this means that the census has shaped and transmitted the ideas of "whitening" and "racial democracy." It also means that the census will necessarily be involved in the rejection of these ideas. As in the United States, the Brazilian Statistical Institute is in the thick of racial politics, not detached from it. The census is not an adjudicator but a political participant. Whereas past U.S. censuses contributed to a racial discourse that justified racial discrimination, however, in Brazil, the census has contributed to a racial discourse that denied that racial discrimination existed, thus justifying state inaction.

Counting by Color

Brazilian censuses have contained a question about color for the same basic reason that American censuses have contained a question about race. Brazilian elites presumed that race was a fundamental and natural component of human identity, and, like Americans, they viewed race as an independent factor in human affairs. However, Brazilian censuses have not counted by race as such. The Portuguese word *côr* ("color") refers to physical appearance, not racial origins. Of course, racial origins are not unconnected to color, because color is derived from the "mixture" (or not) of Europeans, Africans, and Indians, Brazil's three "original" races. Brazilian censuses registered color as it was and is understood. American censuses also used the term *color*, but usually as a synonym for *race*. In United States, there was no meaningful conceptual distinction between race and color. When "racial" identification seemed incongruous with "color" (e.g., a "light-skinned black"), the census employed "blood quantas" as the arbiter. Blood marked racial status when color proved unreliable. In Brazil, color and race are related but have been conceptually distinguished: color refers to appearance, race to origins.[3] In the United States, race trumps color: in Brazil color trumps race. Although hardly unambiguous, this distinction is the key to Brazilian racial discourse and the support the census provides for it.

The thinking has gone as follows: Brazilians are of different colors and thus racially mixed, and such racial mixture has made counting by race impossible. Two of Brazil's most influential twentieth-century thinkers, Oliviera Vianna (1883–1951) and Gilberto Freyre (1900–1987), argued respectively that this mixing would lead to whiter Brazilians and to a "new" Brazilian race. Census inquiries themselves have organized the fluid boundaries of racial mixture that were presumed to exist. Brazil's intelligentsia, political elite, and census officials have emphasized racial "mixture" with the same vigilance that their U.S. counterparts have emphasized racial "purity." American (social) scientists have struggled to prove the existence of discrete and unequal races, even as they presumed them to exist. Brazilian social scientists have largely accepted the reality of races and their inequality, although not with the same intensity as Americans and Europeans. American elites obsessed over racial mixture and labeled "racially mixed" persons "nonwhites" in general and "blacks" in particular. Brazilian elites also obsessed over racial mixture but concluded, first, that Brazilians were becoming "whiter," and then that they were becoming an entirely new race.

Unlike their U.S. counterparts, nineteenth-century Brazilian censuses were neither involved in slavery debates nor directly advanced racial thought. These principal differences are clear in the century's two modern censuses: that of 1872 and that of 1890. Although the 1872 census was conducted a year after the passage of major abolitionist legislation, neither census questions nor census data were marshaled for a debate over slavery. Likewise, although

Brazilian intellectual and political elites were preoccupied with the perceived calamity of racial mixture, they did not employ the census to examine the problem. But this changed dramatically in the twentieth century. The census ceased to be a bystander and became an active participant in promoting the dominant racial discourses of "whitening" and "racial democracy."

The First Censuses: 1872 and 1890

The first meaningful victory for Brazilian abolitionist legislators, although weakly enforced and later judged a failure, was the Rio Branco Law of 1871, which freed government slaves, emancipated slave children upon their adulthood, mandated that all privately owned slaves be registered with the state, and, to ensure slaveowner compliance, stipulated that all unregistered slaves be regarded as free.[4] Even in the face of the penalty of losing slaves, slaveowners did not, however, rush to comply with a law that sought to undermine the institution of slavery. Abolitionism was not a significant political issue among party politicians until the mid 1860s, 300 years after slavery was established in Brazil and twenty years before its final abolition in 1888.[5] Abolitionist rhetoric focused little on race as such, mostly because the supporters of slavery did not defend it in terms of the racial inferiority of blacks or their suitability as slaves.[6] They argued, when required to argue at all, that slave labor was the basis of the country's economy. Brazilian slaveowners believed in white superiority and black inferiority,[7] but these views were not prominent in their defense of slavery. They defended slavery as a system of labor. On the other hand, abolitionists argued that Brazil, even during slavery, was less racially prejudicial than the United States.[8] These same abolitionists were also committed to the idea of Brazil's eventual "whitening" after abolition.

The first modern census in 1872 was conducted in a political and intellectual environment strikingly different from that of the United States. Political debates about slavery did not turn on the idea of race, but political debates about free labor did. Both abolitionists and slaveowners welcomed the prospect of free European laborers for racial reasons. Brazilian (social) scientists were deeply attuned to scientific developments in the United States and Europe, and Brazilian institutions were consuming and creatively applying such knowledge, especially knowledge about race.[9] But the census was not used to further scientific racial thought, as it had been in the United States.

In addition, census-taking was not tied by constitutional mandate to representational apportionment, and the absence of such a direct procedural imperative, coupled with the Brazilian state's slow centralization, accounts for its unstable beginnings. The 1872 census included one color question with the terms white (*branco*), black (*preto*), *pardo*, and *cabaclo*,[10] but color data were not politically significant at the time.

Brazilian theorists in the late nineteenth century—well aware of prevailing European ideas on race and racial mixture—focused on documenting, discerning, and arresting the presumed negative consequences of racial mixture.[11] European thinkers had not taken polygenism as seriously as had their American counterparts. They were interested in racial mixture as such, not in using it as proof of the existence of distinct species. Like American polygenists, however, they viewed racial mixture, especially between Europeans and non-Europeans, negatively.[12] In their writings, Brazil exemplified the dangers of mulatto degeneracy and tropical decay.[13] The perception by both Brazilian and foreign thinkers that Brazil was a *mestiço* nation went much further than mere description:[14] it seemed self-evidently to pronounce Brazil's national limitations. National progress rested on its people, and a nation of racially mixed and hence degenerate people could not progress. As the Brazilian historian Lilia Moritz Schwarcz has richly documented, museums, historical societies, law schools, medical schools, and scientists all fixed on racial mixture as the key to understanding Brazil and its national possibilities.[15] Nevertheless, perhaps because of the limited institutional capacity and inadequate statistical methods of the Brazilian census agency, the Directoria Geral de Estatística, Brazil's 1890 census was neither preoccupied with racial mixture nor used to decry the national calamity that racial mixture was certain to engender.

Immigration policies and a new spin on European racial theory provided the answers to Brazil's national problem. Elites sought to create a surplus supply of low-cost labor, while at the same time achieving "racial uplift." Indeed, the planter class largely controlled the gradual transition from slave labor to free labor.[16] In order to ensure a steady supply of cheap labor and maintain production levels, Brazilian planters recruited large numbers of European workers to cultivate Brazil's coffee plantations, and in 1884, wealthy São Paulo planters established the Society for the Promotion of Immigration. Although private, the society was heavily subsidized by the provincial government of São Paulo.[17] Between 1882 and 1934, approximately 2.3 million immigrants arrived in São Paulo state,[18] and from 1888 to 1900, 73 percent of the incoming emigrant population was Italian.[19] European immigrants were preferred for racial, as well as economic reasons.[20] First, planters were convinced that black and *mestiço* laborers would return to their natural indolence without the firm control by whites that slavery provided.[21] Thus, even though ex-slaves and free people of color were available as workers, planters neither assumed nor aggressively sought to enforce labor availability through legislation like the U.S. Black Codes.[22] Ex-slaves were largely left to their own devices. Many briefly left their plantations but soon returned to work as fieldhands. Many others worked independently as artisans, and still others sought work in urban factories and shops or as domestics.[23] Second, Brazilian elites perceived European immigrants especially as "civilizing" agents. They initially resisted Japanese immigration on racial grounds, but overcame their reluctance when supplies of European workers decreased.[24] Voluntary African immigration, however, was consistently discouraged and legally barred from 1890 to 1907.

"Whitening" would also be achieved in another way. Brazilian thinkers posited that the disastrous consequences of racial mixture would be averted through racial mixture itself. In a sharp reversal of earlier ideas, Brazilian intellectuals began to view miscegenation not as degenerate but as fortifying for whites and cleansing for nonwhites. The prominent literary critic Sílvio Romero (1851–

1914) argued that racial mixture enabled whites to thrive in the tropics. In the process of intermixing Brazil's three founding races, the white race would "predominate through natural selection until it emerges pure and beautiful as in the Old World."[25] Brazilians would become "whiter" over time. In the hands of Brazilian eugenicists and others, the "whitening" idea took several contradictory forms: first, Brazil's large mixed-race population was degenerative, but this degeneracy could be reversed through better public health and mixing with whites; second, blacks and mulattos were dying at a higher rate than whites, thus ensuring Brazil's white future. Variations on the central theme of "whitening" dominated official census texts until the mid twentieth century. Whether census officials stressed the redemptive power of racial mixture or high mortality depended upon their reactions to European racial ideas and their own assessment of the Brazilian people. In all instances, census methods and census data were crucial to their interpretations. Census texts themselves, moreover, were highly influential vehicles for the articulation and dissemination of these ideas in narrative form.

It is hardly possible to overemphasize the centrality of census data to twentieth-century claims of a racially mixed Brazilian society and the political, social, and economic arguments that have flowed from such claims. In the first half of the century, census texts happily reported that Brazilians were becoming whiter. Political, social, and economic progress were guaranteed by and through whitening. In the latter half of the century, census texts have reported color statistics in a matter-of-fact way, and referring to these color data, political and intellectual elites have proclaimed Brazil a "racial democracy," meaning that Brazilian citizenship is neither enhanced, diminished, nor stratified by race. Presumed racial differences have not been a way of distinguishing between Brazilians, because they are racially mixed. Beginning in the 1970s, however, census officials, academics, politicians, and activists have openly questioned categorization methods and the ability of the census to accurately capture Brazil's diversity. Two opposing sets of claims have emerged. Certain academics, politicians, and activists charge that census terminology has deliberately obscured Brazil's racial reality: Brazil is neither a racial democracy nor a "white" country. On the other hand, some academics and census officials have argued that adequate methods have yet to be developed. Clearly, the official truth about Brazil's racial or color composition is derived as much from census terms and methods—and the racial ideas that undergird them—as from individual human bodies.

Brazilian racial discourse thus tells a shifting story about who Brazilians are racially and the nature of Brazilian social relations, both of which are at the core of national identity. Twentieth-century census-taking has contributed to this shifting discourse and sustained it in fundamental ways. For most of the century, political elites have successfully used one aspect of this discourse—the notion of racial mixture as racial democracy—to disguise and ignore the profound disadvantages accorded to color.

Twentieth-Century Censuses: A "Whiter" and "Blacker" Brazil

THE 1920 CENSUS: THE CERTAINTY OF WHITENING

Brazil's Old Republic began with the dethronement of Emperor Pedro II by the military in 1889 and ended with the military coup d'état in 1930 that installed Getúlio Vargas as president. The 1891 Constitution established a decentralized federal structure that served and protected the interests of state political and economic elites. Brazil's economic engine ran on coffee cultivation and export. During this period, political elites of the south-center states of São Paulo, Minas Gerais, and to a lesser extent Rio Grande do Sul controlled national politics. Indeed, nearly all the civilian presidents (1894–1930) came from one of these three states. Moreover, the franchise was limited, voting and social mobility were low, and clientelism, political patronage, and illiteracy were high.[26] The transition from the monarchy to a constitutional republic continued oligarchical rule, merely transferring power from the emperor to the landed aristocracy of the southeast and to the military.

Within this decentralized political context, the development of federal bureaucracies was slow and haphazard. This was certainly true of the national statistical agency, the Directoria Geral de Estatística (DGE), which was reestablished under the Republic in 1890.[27] Historians consider each of the censuses conducted under the DGE unreliable.[28] The 1890 census schedules were incompletely distributed and returned. At the same time, the number and complexity of inquiries significantly impeded the tabulation and publication of census results.[29] The 1900 census was even less reliable than that of 1890, and no census was taken in 1910. The 1920 census was also poorly executed, and there was no 1930 census owing to the military coup d'état. The failure of these early censuses can be explained by a lack of centralization, lack of resources, weak command of statistical methods, and poor administrative coordination between federal and state offices. However unreliable the data, the DGE could not have existed without the effort of a small group of dedicated officials.[30]

The "whitening" of Brazil was one of the Old Republic's dominant ideas. It found full expression in a section of the 1920 census entitled "Evolution of the Race," which recorded each racial group's contribution to the country's fused racial heritage and charted its inexorable march toward whiteness; this section was later published unaltered as a separate volume entitled *Evolução do povo brasileiro* (Evolution of the Brazilian People).[31] Given the pervasiveness of the elite belief in whitening, it is not surprising that this belief was communicated in the census text. (The text of the 1860 U.S. census had predicted the eventual disappearance of Negroes, reflecting the beliefs and wishes of American elites.) The 1920 Brazilian census schedule did not even ask a color question, however, so that its predictions were not based upon contemporary data, however unreliable and ambiguous such data would have been.

Why then did the 1920 census tell the story of whitening? One reason may be that the author of *Evolução do povo brasileiro,* the prominent social theorist Francisco José Oliveira Vianna, insisted that Brazil's future was white, and that recruitment of European workers could be terminated.[32] Over the previous decade, it had become clear that the honeymoon with immigrant workers, Italians and Spaniards especially, was over. Their militancy alarmed industrialists and politicians. European immigrants dominated Brazil's first labor unions, which were anarcho-syndicalist in their ideological orientation.[33] During the Old Republic, labor organizing increased, and by 1917, the number of unionized workers had grown to unprecedented levels, as did strike movements from 1917 to 1920. Labor activity diminished with government and industrial repression, however, and the unions had been significantly weakened by 1921. São Paulo's elites finally discontinued the immigrant recruitment program in 1927. Their decision was slow in coming, because they had invested "considerable financial and ideological capital" in the idea of immigrant labor's superiority.[34] The 1920 census text was perhaps intended to reassure them that their ideological investment had paid off: Brazil was becoming whiter and would continue to do so without further European immigrants.

The whitening idea did not derive only from the anticipated results of European immigration. Whitening was also a response to, and an appropriation of, the science of eugenics, disseminated from Europe and the United States. According to European and American eugenic theories, racial improvement was possible through reproduction of a race's fittest individuals. Not every race, however, was suitable for eugenic remedy. European and American eugenicists theorized that Europeans, but only certain Europeans, were both worthy of and capable of improvement. They judged racial betterment in Latin America an impossibility, however, given its large indigenous and African populations. Latin American and specifically Brazilian eugenicists saw it differently.[35] While agreeing on the racial inferiority of Africans and the country's indigenes, they argued that the Brazilian race could be improved through better breeding, better living conditions, and the power of "white blood." Their eugenics was a mix of social reform and neo-Lamarckian theories of heredity. Brazilians would improve racially as their genes improved physiologically, first through sanitation, hygiene, and exercise and then through reproduction with other "fit" (meaning white) persons.[36]

The 1920 census text is one of the clearest explications of the whitening ideal and makes explicit references to eugenics.[37] Although there is no evidence that Vianna was an active participant in Brazil's eugenics movement, he was a prominent racial theorist,[38] and he premised almost all his writing on race.[39] He justified authoritarian-oligarchical rule in racial terms: only whites were capable of competent governance. Unlike other intellectuals, most notably the politician Rui Barbosa (his intellectual nemesis, who defined governance and institutional development in terms of legislation), Vianna concentrated on Brazil's lived political realities.[40] In his eyes, Brazilian realities exposed large numbers (although never the majority) of degraded, backward Africans, Indians, and mixed bloods to an even larger number of civilized whites. "Whiteness," especially the intellectual and cultural guidance provided by white elites, was both a prerequisite for and guarantor of progress.

In relation to other Brazilian thinkers of the day, Vianna's ideas were most clearly associated with contemporary Western science's tenets on race. He did not, for example, celebrate the virtues of "mulatto-ness" or "mixture" in and of itself. Rather, he understood it as an intermediary step to "whiteness." At times, however, his writings betray an uncertainty about the possibilities of either rescuing Africans and Indians from barbarism or transforming mulattoes into whites. His assurances in the 1920 census of the inevitability of whitening appear, in this sense, uncharacteristically optimistic.[41] In his most celebrated work, *Populações meridionais do Brasil* (Southern Populations of Brazil) (1920), Vianna wrote that his study of the racially mixed inhabitants of rural southern states would "reveal faults, accentuate defects, demonstrate lines of inferiority and destroy, with a certain frankness, numberless illusions of ours regarding ourselves and our capacities as a people."[42] In later works, such as *Raça e assimilação* (Race and Assimilation) (1932), Vianna lamented what he perceived as the declining interest in the study of racial difference among Brazilians, to their peril.[43]

How, then, are we to assess Vianna's *Evolução do povo brasileiro*? It would be easy to dismiss it by declaring it to be little more than a political tract and not a social scientific document. After all, the census did not ask about color, making its discussion of whitening even more incredible, and the overall validity of the census itself all the more suspect. But Vianna's book was most certainly a political document, and therein lies its significance. Brazilian elites purposefully used the census to promote their views of Brazil's population, with little regard for how those views corresponded (or not) to the country's complicated racial reality. To a varying extent, this pattern of elite domination has characterized twentieth-century Brazilian census-taking.

In the end, whether Brazilians were becoming "whiter" was not measured by the census as much as the idea of "whitening" was created and promoted by it. Did the census text have an impact outside elite circles? Yes and no. Increased political advocacy and social organizing among black Brazilians and rejection by certain Brazilian intellectuals critical of Eurocentric thought suggest that whitening was not universally embraced.[44] Over time, however, the idea has permeated Brazilian culture in obvious and subtle ways. It has infused standards of intelligence, beauty, health, and wealth.[45] It is learned from schools and textbooks and is promulgated widely in print, especially in visual media.[46] The belief in whitening extends far beyond the census, but the important point here is that the census has been the creator and promoter of the idea, not a detached register of its existence.

THE 1930 REVOLUTION AND
RACIAL DEMOCRACY

Brazilian politics and society were dramatically transformed by the 1930 military coup d'état and presidency of Getúlio Vargas of the state of Rio Grande do Sul, which resulted primarily from a political impasse among the political elites of the three southern states that had historically brokered national political power. Its less immediate causes were the political exclusion of Brazil's majority and the discontent of a small but growing urban middle class with the disproportionate political power of the landowning elite. The military coup signaled fundamental changes in political, economic, and social arrangements. Although Vargas did not abandon the politically weakened rural oligarchy, he aggressively courted the growing urban middle and working classes. He implemented economic policies aimed at expanding Brazil's industrial base and centralized and expanded the Brazilian state. Of particular interest here is that the Instituto Brasileiro de Geográfia e Estatística (IBGE), the successor to the Directoria Geral de Estatística, was established as a permanent state agency in 1938.[47]

Vargas's populism incorporated a new notion of Brazilian peoplehood. According to this view, racial mixture meant neither individual degeneration nor national decline. Brazilians were an ever-evolving, ever-mixing, and ever-whiter people. Moreover, racial mixture itself was positive and accounted for the uniqueness of the Brazilian people and for the "racially democratic" nature of Brazilian social relations and political institutions. Unlike the United States, there was neither de jure racial segregation nor apparent racial animus among citizens. The anthropologist Gilberto Freyre was the most influential thinker and proponent of this view. Freyre's corpus of work, from the 1930s through the 1970s, was dedicated to the celebration of the new Brazilian race and to Brazil's unique contribution to world civilization: racial democracy.[48]

In his most important work, *Casa-grande & senzala* (1933; later published in English as *The Masters and the Slaves*), Freyre directly challenged the dismal forecasts of racial theories by positively re-evaluating African and Indian cultures and embracing racial mixture. The "backwardness" of Africans and Indians was a result of social and historical circumstance—namely, slavery and colonization—and not exclusively, or even primarily, nature. With this conceptual move, Freyre rescued Africans and Indians from permanent denigration while affirming the superiority of Europeans. Each group had made its own contribution to Brazilian culture, but, predictably, the European contribution was both the most evident and most important. Biological explanations did not disappear from Freyre's claims, since he embraced the central idea of racial mixture itself and the creation of a new race. But where Vianna spoke of "aryanization," Freyre spoke of "Brazilianness." In an obvious way, Freyre's new identity was a recasting of the old, but it was also a departure. Freyre offered a way of viewing Brazil and its national possibilities on its own, not Europe's, terms. He provided an interpretation that favorably assessed Brazil's past and optimistically predicted its future: the process of mixing, begun during slavery, would result in the eventual creation of a new Brazilian race. According to Freyre, racial mixture, itself the purported result of racial harmony, was the foundation of Brazil's racial democracy.[49]

Freyre's ideas about Brazilianness converged powerfully with the populist discourse and nation-building ambitions of the Vargas regime, outlasting Vargas and subsequent political regimes and confounding attempts to test whether racial democracy has existed in economically, politically, and socially meaningful ways. Indeed, even as Freyre formulated his idea of racial democracy, Brazil's most visible black political organization, the Frente Negra Brasileira (Black Brazilian Front), was at the height of its strength,[50] vigorously disputing claims of racial democracy and nondiscrimination.[51] Until recently, Freyre's ideas have enjoyed a transhistorical and metaphysical status; for this reason, among others, racial democracy is referred to as a myth. Yet myths are socially and politically consequential precisely because they are given life in the world. In Brazil, as in the United States, census methods and texts are creators and conduits of racial myths and boundaries.

THE 1940 CENSUS: NAZISM AND WHITENING

German and Italian racism bore directly on the deliberations of the Brazilian National Census Commission about whether to include the color question in the 1940 census, and if so, what terminology to use. The rise of fascism in Europe in general was of particular concern to Brazilian political and intellectual elites, given Brazil's large Italian and sizable German immigrant populations. Brazilian leaders worried that these immigrants would harbor political sympathies with the fascist regimes, and organize themselves accordingly.[52] European fascism, particularly its strident anti-

Semitism, resonated deeply with Brazil's own anti-Semitism and na-
tivism.[53] The Ação Integralista Brasileira (AIB), Brazil's own viru-
lently anti-Semitic fascist party, held its first public meeting in
January 1933. Its members were drawn from "the middle classes,
the armed forces, many of Italian and German descent in southern
Brazil and a few very wealthy Industrialists."[54] AIB quickly became
Brazil's fastest-growing political party.[55] In response, a small group
of Brazilian intellectuals, including Gilberto Freyre, issued a "Manifesto Against Racial Prejudice" in October 1935.[56] In it, they cautioned that the "transplanting of racist ideas and especially their social and political correlates," posed a particular danger for Brazil,
given that its "ethnic formation is extremely heterogeneous."[57] In
December 1937, consolidating his power in the authoritarian
Estado Nôvo (new state), President Vargas outlawed AIB, along
with all other political parties, including the Black Brazilian Front.[58]

This concern about the dangers of racist ideas, especially those of
European fascism, emerged in IBGE's decision not to include *pardo*
(connoting "mixture") among the census choices. As the text
stated: "The preparation of the 1940 census developed within a period in which racist aberrations appeared headed toward world
domination."[59] IBGE's explanation focused on Brazil's supposed
traditional belief in "the equality of races." The intention, the
document explained, was to quell fears that census results might be
used for discriminatory purposes or for anything other than purely
scientific objectives. Thus, hoping to avoid asking Brazilians to respond to terms "sometimes used with disdain," IBGE decided to
limit the choices to white, black, and yellow, with a horizontal line
for "mixed." After the census was taken, however, all horizontal
lines were tabulated and published under the category *pardo*. It is
important to note that the meaning of *pardo* was—and remains—
ambiguous. In Portuguese-language dictionaries, it is defined as
both "gray" and "brown," and its connotations are equally ambiguous, because Brazilians infrequently use it in common parlance.
Its most significant use is as a census term. Although controversy
did not then surround *preto* (black), it has also been a peculiar term
for IBGE to use. Brazilians usually use it in the third person, not the

first person, as the census requires. Even more illuminating, it is commonly used to describe objects, not human beings. Black activists raised the issue of terminology most forcefully as IBGE prepared for the 1991 and 2000 censuses.

According to IBGE, the decision to exclude *pardo* may have had "little technical basis" but it preserved "human dignity," in the end, the best solution to a "difficult problem." IBGE also presented two key considerations that informed its decision on the color categories: first, it wanted to distinguish Brazilians who retained the color characteristics of Brazil's "three fundamental ethnic groups"— "whites, for those of European origin; black, for those of African origin; and yellow, those of Asiatic-Oriental"—from those of mixed origin. In addition, it wanted to avoid appearing like the United States, with its rigid color line, which might have resulted had it tried to distinguish among the many "mixed" Brazilians. IBGE explained that those persons who would be classified as "black" in the United States because they had "one-eighth or one-sixteenth black blood" would in contrast be considered "white" in Brazil. Moreover, inasmuch as "whites" were held to constitute the majority of the economic and intellectual elite, well-educated and well-mannered people of mixed race were also considered white, even if "clearly brown" in appearance.[60] Similarly, in marriages in which one spouse was white and the other brown, the family usually assumed the color of the white spouse, at least as far as censuses were concerned.

Not only did IBGE officials debate the exclusion of a "mixed" category, they also debated the exclusion of the color question itself.[61] In fact, their decision hinged on the advice of IBGE's technical division. Although other members of the Census Commission thought it should be excluded, because the results would inevitably be inaccurate, upon consultation with the technical division, as advised by IBGE's president, the balance tipped back toward inclusion. Giorgio Mortara, the chief consultant, held that the question was more political than technical.[62] Lourival Fontes, the Estado Nôvo's minister of propaganda, concurred with Mortara, adding that it was necessary to include the color question for foreign

propaganda.[63] Unfortunately, Fontes's point was not further elabo-
rated, so it is not exactly clear what he meant by "fundamental to
foreign propaganda." One might speculate, however, that the data
it generated were expected to bolster Brazil's image as a nonracist
nation.

IBGE reported that the census results met official expectations.
The data showed that whites were the majority of the population,
63 percent, while *pardos* made up 21 percent, and blacks 15 percent.[64] These numbers were considered reliable, but IBGE cautioned
that given the plasticity of Brazilian color boundaries, they were not
completely accurate. Had it been possible to use an "objective" criterion, meaning one based on scientific definitions of racial group
membership, the numbers of whites and blacks would have been
perceptibly lower and the number of browns higher, since many
browns were "incorrectly" classified as blacks and, more frequently, whites. With these qualifications, IBGE confirmed the census results.

The text that accompanied the 1940 census, however, revealed
nothing of the concerns about racist ideology, the stated commitment to the equality of races, or the suspicion that the number of
pardos was higher than the official numbers indicated. Instead, it
provided a narrative unwavering in its optimistic belief in Brazil's
whitening. Paradoxically—but not surprisingly—this text shared
with Nazism a preoccupation with races and their natural order
that IBGE had supposedly desired to repudiate. Repudiation was
not possible, however, because whitening presumed the existence of
unequal races, just as Nazism did. Whereas Nazism called for
physical extermination, whitening called for absorption. There is
obviously a profound difference between mass murder and absorption; the point here is simply that Nazism and Brazilian whitening
were both based on prevalent racial ideas.

The text of the 1940 census immediately became the standard interpretation of Brazilian culture.[65] The work of the esteemed educa-
tor Fernando de Azevedo, it once again recounted the myth of the
founding of Brazil and the evolution of its unique people. Race remained at the core of the discussion, which emphasized the distinc-

tive physical, cultural, and intellectual characteristics of each race and its contributions to Brazilian civilization. An English translation of the 1940 census text was published in the United States in 1950 under the title *Brazilian Culture*.[66]

In a chapter entitled "Land and Race" (race, like land, was assigned a natural and fundamental status), Azevedo carefully described the three constitutive elements of the new Brazilian race. As Vianna had done in *Evolução do povo brasileiro*, Azevedo too pointed out the diversity within the groups of European colonizers, African slaves, and indigenous inhabitants. The Portuguese were not a "pure race," but rather a product of "the mixture of the primitive inhabitants of the peninsula—the early Iberians—and races and peoples which mingled in constant migrations across that peninsula, such as the Celts, the Greeks, the Phoenicians, the Romans, the Visigoths, and the Arabs, not to mention the Jews, of whom at a single time it received fifty thousand families, moved thither by order of Hadrian."[67] Similarly, enslaved Africans were not a homogeneous group, but were people taken from different nations and cultures at varying historical junctures. "The Africans of Brazil," according to Azevedo, included "authentic Negroes like the Hottentots and the Bushmen, and the Fulahs, who are sometimes called 'white Negroes'" and "mixtures like the slaves drawn from Senegambia or Portuguese Guinea, who are considered by some to be superior to the rest from an anthropological point of view."[68] Evaluation and hierarchical ordering pervaded Azevedo's interpretation. He identified and organized the "primitive" and "civilized" European sources of the "impure" Portuguese race and then of Africans and Indians. Thus not only were Europeans in general above Africans and Indians, but among the "primitives" themselves, the "racially mixed" ones were considered superior to the "authentic."

Whatever the biological, and hence cultural, contributions of the Tupi and other indigenous inhabitants and enslaved Africans to Brazilian civilization, the European contribution had been most fundamental and most obvious. It was "white blood" into which "black" and "red" were mixed and "diluted," creating a mixed but whiter people. Although it was impossible to discern with certainty all of the dimensions of race mixture in Brazil, Azevedo assured readers that it would lead to a white Brazil. He concluded the chapter with the following comforting prediction:

> If we admit that Negroes and Indians are continuing to disappear, both in the successive dilutions of white blood and in the constant process of biological and social selection, and that immigration, especially that of Mediterranean origin, is not at a standstill, the white man will not only have in Brazil his major field of life and culture in the tropics, but be able to take from Old Europe—citadel of the white race—before it passes to other hands, the torch of Western Civilization to which Brazilians will give a new and intense light—that of the atmosphere of their own civilization.[69]

That the census was the main outlet for expounding the whitening idea is clear. In publishing it, state officials had two audiences in mind: Brazilians themselves and English-speakers, principally Americans. How did these audiences respond? It is difficult to know with any certainty how Brazilians viewed individual or collective identity. However, the ideas of whitening and of racial democracy did not exist in a vacuum. Larger political and economic developments supported the racial democracy ideal or at least made it very difficult to disprove.

In 1945, after a military coup overthrew Vargas's fascist regime, competitive party politics were established in Brazil for the first time in the country's history. In contrast to the Democratic party in the United States, for example, Brazil's numerous political parties did not, however, treat racial (or color) politics as a major plank. Whereas the first stage of Brazil's industrialization at the turn of the century had almost exclusively employed immigrant laborers, import-substitution industrialization and the creation of large state-owned enterprises in the post-1945 period generated jobs for native Brazilians. Brazilian unions, although firmly under state control, provided new avenues of political participation and incorporation. Political elites argued that nature, not politics, offered the best solution to the race problem: racial mixture was a guarantor of racial harmony and unity. Color was not a serious barrier to social and

TABLE 3

Brazilian Census Color Questions and Categories, 1872–1991

Year	Color Question	Color Terms Used
1872	Yes	*Bránco* (white), *Preto* (black), *Pardo* (mixed white and black), *Caboclo* (*Mestizo* Indian).
1880 no census		
1890	Yes	*Branco* (white), *Preto* (black), *Mestiço* (mixed white and black), *Caboclo* (*Mestizo* Indian).
1900	No	
1910 no census		
1920	No color question, but extended discussion in census text about the "whitening" of Brazil.	
1930 no census		
1940	Yes	*Branco* (white), *Preto* (black), *Amarelo* (yellow). If respondent did not fit into one of these three categories, enumerator was instructed to place a horizontal line on census schedule. These horizontal lines were later tabulated under *Pardo* (used by IBGE to connote "mixture"; literally means brown or gray).
1950	Yes	*Branco* (white), *Preto* (black), *Pardo* (mixed or brown), *Amarelo* (yellow). Self-classification according to designated categories is introduced.
1960	Yes	*Branco* (white), *Preto* (black), *Amarelo* (yellow), *Pardo* (mixed or brown), *Índio* (Indian).
1970	No. National Census Commission appointed. Experts recommend inclusion of question, Commission decides exclusion.	
1980	Yes	*Branco* (white), *Preto* (black), *Pardo* (mixed or brown), *Amarelo* (yellow).
1991	Yes. Question asks race or color. Race corresponds to the new indigenous category.	*Branco* (white), *Preto* (black), *Pardo* (mixed or brown), *Amarelo* (yellow), *Indígena* (indigenous).

SOURCE: Instituto Brasileiro de Geografia e Estatística (IBGE).

TABLE 4

Color Composition of Brazilian Population, 1940–1991

(in thousands)

Color	1940	1950	1960	1980	1991
White	26,172 (63.5%)	31,028 (61.7%)	42,838 (61.0%)	64,540 (54.2%)	75,704 (52.0%)
Brown	8,744 (21.2%)	13,786 (26.5%)	20,706 (29.5%)	46,233 (38.8%)	62,316 (42.0%)
Black	6,036 (14.6%)	5,692 (11.0%)	6,117 (8.7%)	7,047 (5.9%)	7,335 (5.0%)
Yellow	242 (0.6%)	329 (0.6%)	483 (0.7%)	673 (0.7%)	630 (0.4%)
Indigenous	—	—	—	—	294 (0.3%)
Missing	42 (0.1%)	108 (0.2%)	47 (0.1%)	517 (0.4%)	534 (0.3%)
TOTAL	41,236 (100%)	51,944 (100%)	70,191 (100%)	119,011 (100%)	146, 813 (100%)

SOURCE: Instituto Brasileiro de Geografia e Estatística (IBGE).

economic mobility, and it would eventually cease to be a significant issue as Brazilians became whiter. There was no need for positive state intervention because racial (or color) discrimination was not a social or political problem. Black organizations repeatedly challenged these claims, although their efforts were also directed at taking advantage of the opportunities that industrialization and greater political openness afforded.[70]

Among Americans, especially white academics, Brazil enjoyed a reputation as a racially harmonious society, one that was not hard to maintain given contemporary de jure and de facto racial segregation and discrimination in the United States. Presenting an image of a white Brazil was more challenging, and Brazilian elites lamented and strategized about it. In 1935, Ambassador Oswaldo Aranha wrote from Washington, D.C., to a friend: "We need a Brazil of white men . . . nothing of other races."[71] Ambassador Aranha repeatedly lauded the United States as a "Nordic society" and privately advised President Vargas that members of the diplomatic corps should be chosen with a view to the racial impression they would make.[72]

THE 1950–1960 CENSUSES: THE TRIUMPH OF RACIAL DEMOCRACY

The profound shifts in scientific thinking about race after World War II reverberated in Brazil as they did in the United States. Brazilian censuses also supported and advanced a new racial discourse. IBGE texts spoke less often and less aggressively of "whitening" and of the regenerative and redemptive powers of mixture. Instead, race mixture was reported matter-of-factly. However, the idea of distinct races remained and scientific knowledge retained its authority in IBGE efforts to fend off critiques of its methods, interpretations, and decisions; until recently, IBGE argued that its color terms were based, however imprecisely, on scientific knowledge. The ways in which educational and economic standing and regional customs affect how Brazilians understand and use color terms complicate, but do not invalidate, IBGE's presuppositions about race and color.

An official 1956 report analyzing the 1950 census is clear evidence of IBGE's evolving conceptual moves.[73] The report spoke briefly and dispassionately of the various ethnic groups that came together to form the Brazilian people. Widespread racial mixture was, of course, cited as the principal reason for ambiguities in color classification, and hence for difficulties in conforming to scientifically legitimated color categories. The nonexistence of U.S.-style racial prejudice meant that the "white" category had been applied with "a liberty inconceivable in Washington."[74] Even with the caveat that the numbers of "white" people might have been inflated, the 1956 text offered assurance that whitening was progressing. However, unlike earlier explanations, IBGE did not discuss shrinking numbers of blacks and browns in terms of the superiority of an all-white group. Rather, it attributed the decrease to higher mortality rates among browns and, especially, blacks. The report also identified the influx of European immigrants at the turn of the century as a factor in the higher numbers of whites, an interpretation that relied on social and historical factors and not primarily on the premise that white blood was superior. As for the 1950 census itself, *pardo* was added to the white, black, and yellow categories, and auto-classification was introduced. Auto-classification meant that enumerators were bound to record the respondents' actual answer. As with past censuses, controversy about the unreliability of color data persisted, and again there were suggestions that the question be excluded. But IBGE decided to retain it, despite the unease its inclusion engendered, because it provided the best—albeit flawed—way of charting the progress of Brazil's "melting pot."[75] The overall accuracy of the 1950 census was not questioned, since it was associated with the Committee on the 1950 Census of the Americas (COTA).[76] The 1960 census included the color question, but results were not publicly available until 1978, and even then the data, including color, were never fully released.

The evident Brazilian sensitivity to developments in Western scientific thought is not surprising. Closely attuned to scientific racial thought in Western Europe and, later, the United States, the Brazilian intellectual and political elite tried to discern the meanings and implications of these theories for Brazilian national identity. Thus, when the idea of inherent racial superiority and inferiority was rejected, Brazil's elite responded by promoting the racial democracy idea even more aggressively. In the past, given their adherence to scientific authority, the Brazilian elite had had two choices: they either had to resign themselves to the supposed horror of racial mixture or minimize its perceived ill effects by promoting the notion of "whitening." They chose the latter, although not without contorting the very racial ideas upon which whitening was based. With the apparent revolution in scientific thinking, these efforts were less necessary and less disjointed. Race mixture was not, on its face, a national liability; rather, it was a national asset.

Emboldened by this profound shift in thinking about race, from the 1950s on, the state deliberately advanced the idea of Brazilian racial democracy. Within Brazil, it was encouraged by state *inac-*

tion in response to the claims of black Brazilians that racial/color discrimination was common and consequential. Although in 1951 the Brazilian Congress passed the *Lei Arinos* (Arinos Law), the first law to outlaw overt racial discrimination in hiring and public accommodations, it was largely ineffective. Moreover, congressional debates prior to its passage focused on one particular incident and on the supposed foreignness of racial discrimination to Brazilian society. In 1950, Katherine Dunham, a black American dancer and anthropologist, had been denied entry at a luxury São Paulo hotel. She protested loudly and publicly, and the incident proved an embarrassment. Senator Afonso Arinos de Melo Franco of the conservative Democratic National Union party secured passage of the law that bore his name despite considerable resistance from fellow legislators. Franco claimed to be motivated, not by the Dunham incident, but by his black chauffeur's experiences with immigrants in Rio de Janeiro.[77] Franco argued that racial discrimination was more widespread than was openly admitted, and that the Constitution did not adequately address the problem. (In 1945, a national convention of Brazilian blacks had decided to lobby the Constituent Assembly for constitutional protections against racial discrimination and federally funded educational scholarships for blacks, but the Second Republic's Constitution made provision for neither.)[78] Franco read from letters he had received from all over Brazil recounting racist incidents. Senator Plinio Barreto, a member of Franco's party, concurred with him, pointing out that certain civil service jobs, such as posts in the diplomatic corps, and commissions in the navy and air force were effectively closed to blacks.[79]

Yet underneath this apparent recognition and admission that racial democracy was a myth lay an unmistakable commitment to it. Franco attributed most racially discriminatory actions to gringos, not to immigrants more generally or to Brazilians themselves: "[T]he agents of [racial] injustice are almost always *gringos* who are ignorant of our traditions and insensitive to our old customs of racial fraternity."[80] His fellow senator Gilberto Freyre reluctantly supported the bill, thinking it unnecessary in Brazil. Not surprisingly, he too thought that racially discriminatory behavior was a

foreign, specifically a U.S. import, and thus antithetical to true Brazilianness. In his words to the Congress: "It is not surprising that
this [the Dunham incident] occurred in São Paulo, because com-
mercialism, mercantilism, business, the dollar ["dollarism"], imme-
diacy, all the 'isms' inseparable from the vigorous and triumphant
civilization in industrial America operate in São Paulo and with a
vengeance."[81]

From its passage in 1951 until 1988, when it was replaced by the
Lei Caó (Caó Law), the Arinos Law was a spectacular failure, despite mounting evidence that it was necessary. In thirty-eight years,
only three cases had come before the courts, and of these, only two
brought convictions with penalties.[82]

Along with census texts, diplomatic tracts and international reports served as outlets for Brazilian racial discourse. The Brazilian
elite viewed foreigners (especially Americans) both as outsiders to
Brazil's racial fraternity and as consumers of Brazil's celebratory
self-proclamations of racial democracy. In the foreword to a 1951
Ministry of Foreign Relations booklet entitled *An Essay on Race
Amalgamation*, Freyre commented glowingly on the observations
made by its author, Eugene Gordon, a North American. Referring
smugly to dismal assessments of racially mixed Brazilians by American thinkers in the past, Freyre commented, "the fact that in countries like the United States, young researchers are turning with sym-
pathy to the once alarming 'Brazilian solution' is a matter of particular interest."[83] The "Brazilian solution" to racial antagonism,
according to Freyre, "becomes of greater importance day by day as
an experiment and perhaps as an example to be followed."[84] Brazil's 1979 report to the United Nations outlining the steps it had
taken to comply with the International Convention on the Elimination of All Forms of Racial Discrimination (ICERD) read as follows: "[Brazil's] harmonious racial and ethnic heritage formed a
unity and attested to the wholeness of the Brazilian nationality. The
Indian, African, European, and Asian elements had combined to
form a single *ethnos*, which could be found in the personality of
every Brazilian."[85]

In an ironic way, Brazil's foreign relations efforts were perhaps *too* effective. In the early 1950s, UNESCO commissioned a team of foreign and Brazilian scholars to study Brazil's apparent success at achieving racial harmony in light of the Holocaust. Contrary to their expectations, these scholars documented extensive and consequential racially discriminatory practices throughout the country, but especially in the southeast (São Paulo).[86] Studies of the northeast stressed overall regional underdevelopment, in addition to color discrimination, in explaining the low standing of nonwhites.[87] The studies all revealed a close correspondence between color and socioeconomic standing, and suggested that discrimination was a significant factor in the disparities between whites and nonwhites. These reports punctured the racial democracy bubble, especially in academic circles. In political and popular circles, however, the idea and the language of racial democracy remained resilient. Moreover, IBGE upheld and protected the idea by continuing to use the terminology of color on censuses, although not by producing relevant socioeconomic data. In fact, IBGE did not peg color to socioeconomic indicators such as income and education until the 1976 Household Survey (PNAD).[88]

THE 1970 CENSUS: REMOVAL OF THE QUESTION

In 1964, the military overthrew the democratically elected president, João Goulart, ushering in twenty-one years of military rule. The military's principal objective was rapid modernization of the economy. It entrusted key economic policy decisions to an elite cadre of foreign-educated economists and planners (the technocrats). From 1964 to 1973, the technocrats' planning largely paid off: Brazil's capital market was modernized, thereby attracting foreign investment, the government's budget deficit decreased, and public funds were invested in infrastructural projects.[89] In the six years before the oil shock of 1973, Brazil's GDP grew at an average annual rate of 11.5 percent, and the industrial sector at a rate of 13.2 percent.[90] The upper and middle classes enjoyed a disproportionate share of the benefits of economic growth.[91] The military governed through a series of Institutional and Complementary Acts that did not replace the Constitution but superseded it. During the 1960s, the acts became successively more authoritarian and repressive, granting the military executive expanding powers to suspend political and civil rights, purge the civil service, restrict congressional powers, and alter administrative procedures.[92] Military leaders also changed the rules of political party organization, reducing the number of parties that had existed prior to the military coup from thirteen to two: the National Renovating Alliance (ARENA), the government party, and the Brazilian Democratic Movement (MDB), the official opposition.

Not surprisingly, military leaders displayed low tolerance for discussions of any sort about race. They characterized criticism of racial democracy as "acts of subversion" carried out by "leftists seeking to create new sources of tension and dissatisfaction with the regime and its duly constituted authorities."[93] Brazilian scholars—such as Florestan Fernandes, Fernando Henrique Cardoso, and Octávio Ianni—who had participated in the UNESCO studies of the 1950s, continued their work at the University of São Paulo. Their thinking developed into what is known as the São Paulo School of Race Relations.[94] As they saw it, Brazil's racial problems derived from the particularities of Brazilian capitalist development, that is, the deliberate exclusion of blacks from the industrial labor market in the early twentieth century. Once blacks were more fully integrated into the labor force, racial inequalities would lessen. The more fundamental class inequalities, however, would remain. In 1969, the military forced these scholars out of their university positions because of their leftist views in general, not only their critiques of racial democracy. In the same year, the National Census Commission (CCN) held a public forum to consider the possible removal of the color question from the 1970 census. Although submitted written testimonies recommended that the question be included, CCN decided that it should be removed.[95] There has been much speculation on the reason or reasons for this decision, and the publicly available IBGE documents do not provide an answer. In an obvious way, its exclusion was in keeping with the regime's general stance on race. CCN recommended, however, that the 1976 national survey include a color question, which suggests that long-standing concerns about IBGE methods and the accuracy of census color data were also involved in the commission's decision. Equally important, concerns about methodology, not allegiance to racial democracy, informed the testimonies of the two experts called before the commission.

In his written opinion, Dr. Manuel Diegues Junior acknowledged the difficulty of fixing a definitive concept of color for Brazilians. Predictably, he identified the three founding races, "the Caucasian Portuguese, the Mongoloid Indian, and the Negroid African," and argued that Brazil's already extensive process of miscegenation was still continuing. A specific ethnic type had not yet developed, although the color *moreno* most closely approached a distinctively Brazilian ethnic characteristic.[96] Further confounding these difficulties, he noted, was the extent to which "ethnic expression" took on social or cultural meanings. In other words, "ethnic" identity was a signifier of cultural and/or social status. Diegues argued that color was not the decisive element in determining the ethnic classification of a population; physical anthropologists used other methods in determining a group's ethnicity, such as classifying facial features (i.e., eyes, nose, lips) and skull sizes. However, these techniques could not be used in a national census. Brazilians were then left, according to Diegues, with color. He recommended that the color question be retained until scientifically valid color categories able to capture Brazil's ethnic reality were devised. He argued, in short, that the question be kept for two reasons: (1) it provided an idea of how the Brazilian population defined itself, and (2) color data allowed for comparison with past censuses.

Dr. José Arthur Rios was the other specialist, and like Diegues, he supported the inclusion of the color question. He argued, however, that an arbitrary and superficial characteristic such as color neither captured other potentially significant characteristics of race membership nor identified distinct cultural traditions. Challenging the optimism of Oliveira Vianna's 1920 census introduction regarding whitening—although Rios never explicitly called it such—he argued that it was impossible to interpret Brazil's racial future based upon superficial classifications of color. The ambiguity, superficiality, and inconsistency of the term and its use had led to consistently imprecise and deficient results. Skin color was distinct from any physical anthropological type, so it provided no reliable measurement of the "true" anthropological or racial types and mixtures among the Brazilian population, and even the social use of color categories varied regionally and contextually. Rios maintained that the inclusiveness of the *pardo* category disqualified it as a precise marker of Brazil's racial composition. However, like Diegues, he concluded that the question should be included on the census. He thought, as did Diegues, that, although useless scientifically and anthropologically, the question could provide a useful picture of the "mentality of the Brazilian in relation to the *problem* of color" (emphasis added).[97]

Neither Diegues nor Rios predicted or celebrated "whitening." Instead, they emphasized the difficulties that extensive racial mixture presented for classification and the conceptual difficulties of race and color themselves. However, their recognition of science's tentativeness about race did not lead them to abandon their belief in the potential for a scientifically sanctioned method of categorizing according to race. Until such a method was devised, however, Brazilian color (not racial) enumeration had only social, and not scientific, significance.

Although the commission did not follow Diegues's and Rios's recommendations, their arguments about the social value of the color question and color terms were taken into account. Thus, the commission also recommended that the 1976 National Household Survey (PNAD) include a Supplement on Social Mobility and Color with two color questions, one consisting of four pre-coded options and the other open-ended. The expressed purpose of PNAD's special color question was to advance the development of a color question and of color categories that were (social) scientifically sound and would generate more accurate data.

In the survey's aftermath, the search for satisfactory methods and terminology persisted. In the three southern states of Paraná, Santa Cantarina, and Rio Grande do Sul, Brazilians responded to the open-ended sample question asked with 136 different colors. The responses (literally translated) included "dark white," "dirty white," "brown well arrived," "half brown," "half black," and "very dark."[98] These results generated competing interpretations. The responses proved that a color question produced hopelessly imprecise and subjective data, some politicians and intellectuals argued. Conversely, demographers and activists contended that the 136 responses provided striking evidence of color's social significance. Finally, certain statisticians interpreted the data to show that official census terms were not necessarily at odds with the 136 responses. Statisticians condensed the 136 responses, which fell within existing census categories in the following percentages: white, 41.9 percent; black, 7.6 percent; yellow, .97 percent; and *pardo,* 7.6 percent. The three other terms most frequently offered did not correspond to IBGE options; they were: "light," 2.5 percent; "light brown," 2.8 percent; and "brown" (*moreno*), 34.4 percent.[99]

The assumptions behind the 1976 PNAD supplement had been spelled out in a 1974 article by Tereza Cristina N. Araújo Costa, a statistician in IBGE's Social Indicators Group, which argued that color should be included in the Brazilian census.[100] Like Diegues and Rios, Costa contended that the color question was important not only to IBGE but to Brazilian society. She addressed not only scientific objections to inclusion of the color question in censuses but also the objections arising from the concept of racial democracy, proponents of which relied on census data in arguing their case but nonetheless deemed census questions about color unnecessary.

Referring to U.N. and U.S. Census Bureau documents, Costa noted the difficulties scholars have faced in defining race: demographers must live with the impossibility of conforming to scientific standards of racial categorization and content themselves instead with the methods of physical anthropology; accurate racial measurement is impossible because of the irreversible and unchartable trend toward global race mixture. And it was on these claims that Costa based her argument. For Costa, the color question and color terms (both social and census) are important in Brazil precisely because they do not conform to scientific standards, but this lack of conformity does not deprive them of either social meaning or social scientific utility.

Costa contended that racial mixture in Brazil, as elsewhere, is a natural fact, and that it could not be adduced by IBGE to avoid enumeration by color. Like her IBGE predecessors, Costa believed that "race mixture" in a biological sense exists, and she recognized the conceptual ambiguities of racial demography. However, in a break with past IBGE thinking, she recommended that IBGE retain the color question in censuses, arguing that although color is a "fragile approximation to racial classification," it is the only feasible measure.[101] It is fragile because, in Brazil, color imperfectly corresponds to "racial" origins, and more than that, because color encompasses social and class status. Finally, color is the only feasible vehicle because methods more closely aligned with physical anthropology (i.e., classifying by facial and other physical characteristics) are financially and technically impossible. Having demonstrated the necessity of color categories on censuses, she proposed a sample survey using both open-ended and multiple-choice color questions, the method of the 1976 PNAD.

Costa repeated her point about the importance of the census color question more sharply in a 1987 article.[102] In both articles, Costa appeared as an important, if isolated, voice within IBGE. Responding to the repeated claim that Brazilians are racially mixed, she did not conclude, as had technicians and ideologues alike, that such ambiguity rendered color enumeration pointless and made race a nonissue in Brazil. She argued the contrary. If the categories are merely (if not only) of social and not scientific significance, the question remains, what is their social significance? This is a question that IBGE and many Brazilians have been loathe to answer fully.

THE 1980 CENSUS: THE BATTLE OVER
THE QUESTION'S RETURN

Brazil's transition to democratic governance was protracted and tightly controlled, beginning in the late 1970s with political liberalization, the *abertura* (opening). Military President General Ernesto Geisel ended press censorship and eased censorship of television and radio. Although still subordinate to military leadership, the Congress was allowed to pass several liberalizing measures; these included "the abolition of the Institutional Acts; the restoration of habeas corpus; the return of political liberties, after ten years, to those prosecuted under the provisions of the Institutional Acts; limitations on the president's powers to close Congress; and the creation of new political parties."[103] In October 1978, however, the military government submitted a new bill to Congress that essentially reframed the Institutional Acts. This bill became law in 1979, thus making it clear that the military would control the pace and content of liberalization. However, societal pressure was not inconsequential. In the mid 1970s, university students had begun to organize against the dictatorship, women's organizations and neighborhood associations formed. The Catholic Church remained a staunch advocate of human rights and a facilitator of organization and communication across groups. In 1978, São Paulo's metalworkers organized a massive strike, a sign of resurgent unionism.[104] In the same year, progressive members of São Paulo's business community issued a manifesto calling for redemocratization.[105] Also, in the same year, the Movimento Negro Unificado Contra a Discriminacão Racial (MNUCDR) was formed in São Paulo, joining a number of black cultural organizations established earlier in the decade.[106] Democratization was not an entirely top-down process.

Within this political climate, scholars and black activists demanded the restoration of the color question to the 1980 census and the subsequent publication and availability of its color data. Simmering issues, including those of enduring economic disparities along color lines, reemerged.[107] IBGE at first designed the 1980 census without the question but changed its decision in response to lobbying. This time around, neither opponents nor supporters of inclusion referred to the scientific or conceptual soundness of the idea of color itself. Proponents emphasized the necessity of current data for social scientific analysis, while opponents stressed fiscal constraints and the question's purported unconstitutionality. On

October 24, 1979, Congressman Marcello Cerqueira introduced a bill demanding that IBGE include a color question on the 1980 and subsequent censuses.[108] He rejected IBGE's explanation that time and fiscal constraints render this unfeasible, arguing that such false explanations had been offered for the 1970 census. In that instance, according to Cerqueira, military leaders were eager to import U.S. capital, not U.S. social activism as demonstrated by the North American Civil Rights Movement. The military were fearful, Cerqueira asserted, that inclusion would enable such a movement in Brazil. He argued that the color data generated by the 1980 question would equip legislators to "reach a racial democracy, which exists presently only on paper." On November 8, 1979, IBGE President Montello met officially with representatives of academic and black movement organizations.[109] Academics stressed that without new data derived from such a question, researchers and government officials had no alternative to data from the 1950 census, the last for which color data were available. Black organization representatives emphasized that including a color question would ensure that the contemporary color composition of Brazil would be registered and provide current data for further statistical computation and analysis. After the meeting, Montello announced that IBGE would restore the question, although he himself had labeled it unconstitutional.[110]

Gilberto Freyre's opposition to reintroducing a color question was exceptional precisely because he addressed science and the ideological underpinnings of color. In a São Paulo newspaper article entitled "Brasileiro—sua côr?" ("Brazilian—Your Color?") which appeared a month after IBGE's decision, Freyre lamented the return of the question and thus of an issue that, he thought, had long ago been successfully resolved.[111] According to Freyre, the question was unnecessary, because Brazilians were simply Brazilians. Each had transcended his or her consciousness of racial origin and become a member of a Brazilian "meta-race." It was impossible to capture with four choices the multiplicity of a "miscegenated and nationally Brazilian" people. Moreover, he argued, IBGE's use of the question threatened to undermine its very respectability, since at the very moment of IBGE's decision to restore the question, scientists and anthropologists were questioning the notion of race itself and its connection to skin color. For Freyre, the correct response, or, in his words, "the Brazilian response," was *moreno* (brown). *Morenidade* (brownness) corresponded most closely to Brazil's meta-racial reality and thus stood above the ideological positions of "whiteness, blackness or yellowness." Freyre quoted a Colombian observer who had praised Brazil as "the triumph of the mixed person," calling it a nation in the "vanguard" in terms of its "assimilation of people of color."

In addition to displaying his skill in redirecting the terms of the debate, as he had done so effectively in the past, Freyre's article revealed precisely what was at stake. Although he acknowledged that race is ambiguous, at least in scientific terms, he nonetheless touted a racialized national identity—one resulting from and yet transcending racial mixture. At issue, then, was the discursive construction of Brazilian identity both collective and individual. Who would tell the story of Brazilian identity and what would that story be? Until the 1980 census, following Freyre's reasoning, the story had been one of racial mixture and racial democracy, and IBGE had appeared to be a capable transmitter. But given the uncertain scientific and anthropological status of race, IBGE's decision to restore the color question was not only bad social science but also bad, almost treasonable, national policy. To underscore this latter point, Freyre advocated the use of the term *moreno*, one not used by IBGE. As Freyre presented the matter, IBGE was so out of touch with true Brazilianness that it had not only restored the question but had also offered inappropriate color terms. As we shall see, since the 1990 census, the use of *moreno* has had an increasing number of Brazilian and American advocates. It was not by accident that Freyre concluded the article with the remarks of a foreign observer. The narrative of a unified Brazilian identity and racial democracy has derived its value, in significant measure, from its influence abroad.

The 1980 color question allowed for a type of socioeconomic analysis that academics and activists desired and proponents of racial democracy did not. Scholars have since produced important research using census color data and other national surveys.[112] *O lugar do negro na força de trabalho* (The Black's Place in the Labor Force), published in 1985, was the first public IBGE publication that specifically included color as an independent variable in analyzing employment, income, and education data.[113] It was completed in 1983 but was not made publicly available for two years because an IBGE director considered its findings politically embarrassing.[114] Overall, this book and other, similar research have shown clearly that color is a significant variable in determining levels of educational attainment, employment prospects, and income.

From Color to Race?

In restoring the color question, IBGE still had to address the issue of terminology and, by extension, the ideas that animate color terms. This time the issue was taken up, not because of the prompting of a national census commission, but because a small group of statisticians and analysts within IBGE's Department of Social Studies and Indicators (DIESO) were preparing the aforementioned book on black labor force participation.[115] The analysts' reasoning again demonstrates that racial democracy existed as much in words as in social reality. Different terms generate different data, which engender different interpretations. Freyre, for example, had argued that the question was unnecessary: color was no longer a significant marker of difference, nor was it a source of division among Brazilians. Moreover, IBGE's terminology was wrong; if the question needed to be asked, *moreno* was the proper term. The task for DIESO analysts was to separate, or, more accurately, to attempt to separate, the terms from the meanings and political claims attached to them. Not surprisingly, the analysts were unsuccessful: by using one set of terms instead of another, they unavoidably advanced a view of Brazil's population and societal relations that was antithetical to racial democracy.

In writing their book, the DIESO analysts had to decide whether *race* or *color* would be the term of reference and which words— *black, white, nonwhite,* and *brown*—would be used for the categories.[116] They drew an analytical distinction between race and color. Past analysts had often used the terms interchangeably, or, more frequently, had privileged *color*, having concluded that racial mixture made racial distinctions insignificant. The DIESO analysts' decision to distinguish between *color* and *race* was important, because it laid bare the suppositions beneath these terms: if *race* (i.e., white race, black race) rather than *color* was used, it exploded the notion of a Brazilian meta-race with many colors. Moreover, if color categories were used in a bipolar way (i.e., black and white or white and nonwhite), the image of a racially egalitarian society was replaced by one of a society divided along a major color faultline.

The DIESO analysts decided to unite *pardos* and *pretos* (blacks) under the term *negro* (black) because both groups shared a similar socioeconomic profile, and further justified *negro* because of its use by Brazilian social scientists and black organizations.[117] The term *race*, they concluded, captured this unity of "browns" and "blacks" in a way that *color* did not. The problem with using *color*, they explained, was that in its emphasis on phenotypes, it ignored "the cultural and historical aspects of the constitution of these social groups."[118] Conversely, the term *race* signified "a common origin of groups and their historical trajectory."[119] Yet they did not mean *race* in a biological sense. Rather, their use of the term was in keeping with that of some social scientists and black organizations. DEISO's efforts within IBGE mirrored grassroots efforts in Brazil to change the terms of discussion and analysis from color to race.

The 1991 Census and the Campaign

IBGE began preparing for the 1990 census early, three months before the inauguration of Fernando Collor de Mello, Brazil's first popularly elected president in thirty years. Immediately after taking office, Collor announced the "Collor Plan," an economic shock plan designed to reduce Brazil's runaway inflation.[120] Because Collor did not have a working majority in Congress, until congressional elections in October 1990, he ruled by decree. His economic plan was socially, politically, and institutionally disruptive, as were some of his administrative and budgetary reforms. Thus, although the census was at first scheduled to begin on September 1, IBGE postponed it until 1991 because of lack of funds and government mishandling.[121] Outside the new government, civil society remain enlivened, although not with the same intensity that characterized the redemocratization efforts of the late 1970s and 1980s. Brazil's black organizations and activists continued their rhetorical and political strategies of denouncing racism and promoting a distinct black cultural identity.

By this time, certain black activists had come to view the census as a potential vehicle for creating a "blacker" Brazil. As we have seen, IBGE officials and intellectual elites paid great attention to devising and justifying methods of census-taking and then rendering their intended interpretations. In their 1991 census campaign, black activists focused on the preferences of Brazilians themselves, as well as on IBGE methods. Their campaign, "Don't Let Your Color Pass in White: Respond with Good Sense," is discussed in greater detail in Chapter 4. The point to be made here is that it publicly raised two fundamental issues: first, it challenged IBGE methods and terms by asking why color was being used and not race, and if color, why *preto* and not *negro*; second, it sought to address the preference of most Brazilians to choose "lighter" colors, and especially not to choose black (*preto*), when identifying themselves on census schedules.

The color question in the 1991 census was like previous questions, but with one important exception: the terms *raça* (race) and *indígena* (indigenous) were added. The question was rephrased to ask, "What is your race or color?" and *indigenous* was added to the listing of *black, white, brown,* and *yellow.* The two new terms were linked—*race* applied only to the new indigenous option—but this qualification was not spelled out explicitly either in the census enumerator manual or on the census schedule itself. In the past, IBGE had classified Indians as *pardos,* and it reportedly decided to include the "indigenous" option after consulting with anthropologists and representatives of FUNAI, the federal government's Indian Affairs Bureau.[122] Persons connected to the "Don't Let Your

Color . . ." campaign speculated, however, that the category had been included at the request of the World Bank, which needed such demographic information for upcoming initiatives on the protection of indigenous territories. The addition of the category did not, however, portend greater cooperation from indigenous people. Several indigenous tribes disallowed census enumerators on their land, charging that the Brazilian government intended to use the data to reduce indigenous territories.[123]

Because of its one-year delay and other difficulties, the reliability and accuracy of the 1991 census were initially questioned by demographers, statisticians, and other consumers of census data.[124] Color data were released belatedly in 1995. In an important way, however, the data themselves remained quite beside the point. They were once again overshadowed by the ongoing issue of terminology and the resulting interpretations of Brazilian society and politics. Since 1991, growing public and scholarly discussion about IBGE's methods and terms have forced IBGE, more often than not, to explain, if not defend, its past and current methods. The sources of this pressure are varied, and include demographers, self-identified black activists, and politicians. With the unraveling of the racial democracy idea, the question of who Brazilians *really* are has emerged in powerful ways. There is good reason for this connection: as we have seen, the image of a racially democratic and non-discriminatory society has hinged on the idea of racial mixture. In fact, the causal link was often presented tautologically: Brazilians are racially mixed, and therefore there can be no racial discrimination, or there can be no racial discrimination because Brazilians are racially mixed. But the acknowledgment of the existence of discrimination, as substantiated by census data, has unavoidably led to a rethinking of IBGE terms that have defined who Brazilians are. It may well be that the divisions between Brazilians extend far deeper than color, as that term has been understood in Brazil, and are rooted in notions of distinct racial origins. The public review of IBGE terms, both unsettled and unpredictable, is currently under way.

The 2000 Census: From Racial Democracy
to "Cordial Racism"?

Fernando Henrique Cardoso, a sociologist, was elected president in 1994 and reelected in 1998. In outlining his government's aims, Cardoso observed: "Brazil is no longer an underdeveloped country. It is an unjust country."[125] Elected with a popular mandate, Cardoso entered office with ambitious plans to control inflation, reduce the public sector, attract foreign investment, and address deep social problems. On the last point, Cardoso issued a "National Program on Human Rights" in 1996 that outlined his administration's short-, medium-, and long-term goals. While the program reads like a wish-list rather than a feasible plan of action, it offered two goals of particular interest: (1) it recommended that color be included in all population statistics and registries; and (2) it directed IBGE to aggregate *mulattos* and *pardos* together with *pretos* as *negros* (blacks). The report does not give the specific reasons for these recommendations, but democratization itself provides a general explanation. By masking the deep inequities among Brazilians, the notion of racial democracy has hindered the deepening of political democracy. Of course, the racial democracy ideal alone is not responsible for the absence or impoverishment of political democracy, but there exists a converse relationship between the two: as substantive democracy has become more real (however slowly), the unreality of the idea of racial democracy has become more perceptible. Moreover, it is clear that the new vision of Brazil as a multiracial society composed of distinct racial groups will hinge as much on census categories as has the idea of a single Brazilian race. Cardoso's human rights program appears to be a promotion of this new image.

Without doubt, the racial democracy idea in Brazil is dying, however slowly. The signs of its impending death are everywhere. Brazilian political discourse is now peppered with references to Brazil's "racial diversity," not its racial unity. On Independence Day 1995, President Cardoso remarked in his presidential speech:

"[W]e wish to affirm, and truly with considerable pride, our condition as a multi-racial society and that we have great satisfaction in being able to enjoy the privilege of having distinct races [*raças distintas*] and distinct cultural traditions also. In these days, such diversity makes for the wealth of a country."[126] Affirmative action policies, although a long way from legislation and implementation, are now openly discussed and advocated.[127] Brazil's black movement, although tiny in relation to its claimed constituency of approximately 73 million people (half of Brazil's population), has been extraordinarily successful in undermining the image of a nondiscriminatory society.[128] It has been far less successful in growing its ranks. The census campaign was driven, in part, to do just that. Although it currently appears unlikely that many Brazilians will join black political organizations, many more seem willing to embrace the idea of a distinct black Brazilian culture and experience. Several popular magazines geared to Brazil's black population have been launched: *Black People* (its title is in English, the rest is in Portuguese) appeared in 1993, and *Raça: A Revista dos Negros Brasileiros* (Race: The Magazine of Black Brazilians) in late October 1996.[129]

In June 1995, the influential newspaper *Folha de São Paulo* ran a special Sunday supplement entitled "Racismo cordial: A mais completa analise sobre preconceito de côr no Brasil" ("Cordial Racism: A Comprehensive Analysis of Color Prejudice in Brazil"), later published as a book.[130] It was extraordinary in its comprehensiveness and in its brazenly accusatory tone: the book's introduction proclaimed that "Brazil is a racist country against black people."[131] This bold conclusion was based on data from a survey that polled 5,000 Brazilians on a series of questions ranging from the color terms that Brazilians prefer to their views on the prevalence of racism in the country to sexual stereotypes about the various groups. However, for all its certainty about Brazilian society's racist nature, certain of the survey data were apparently contradictory. For example, while 89 percent of Brazilians polled agreed that racism against blacks exists, only 10 percent stated that they themselves behaved in prejudicial ways. Even more interesting and puzzling,

64 percent of blacks and 84 percent of browns stated that they themselves had never felt discriminated against. According to this survey, Brazil is a racially prejudicial society without either conscious perpetrators or conscious victims.

More germane, however, are the survey data on self-identification according to color, and *Datafolha* researchers' interpretations of such data.[132] Intent on exposing the impropriety of IBGE's color terms, researchers devised a method that they claimed gave them a more reliable approach to Brazilians' real preferences in self-identification. The interviewers noted the color of the interviewees in three ways: first, according to their own observation of the respondent; then the respondent's self-description; and finally, the interviewee's choice from the list of IBGE color terms. With this method, the researchers found that the vast majority of respondents rejected IBGE's term *pardo*; that is, only 6 percent freely self-identified as *pardo*. It is interesting to note, however, that the number of persons who freely identified as *preto* or *negro* was only slightly higher, at 8 percent. A plurality, 43 percent, freely identified themselves as *moreno*, and 39 percent as white.[133]

In response to these results, *Datafolha* researchers openly advocated the replacement of *pardo* with *moreno* on census schedules, and they accused IBGE of falsely presenting Brazil as a white country, a portrait greatly at odds with Brazilians' own views of themselves and their country. In their words, "[F]or IBGE, Brazil is a country with a white majority and a plurality of *pardos*." In contrast, "[F]or Brazilians, a white majority does not exist in the country." Based on *Datafolha*'s data, the sum of persons who described themselves as *moreno*, *negro*, or *preto* was 51 percent. If those who described themselves as *pardo* (6 percent), *mulato* (1 percent), and *escuro* (dark) (1 percent) are added, the final percentage is 59 percent. The use of *moreno* also received qualified support from demographers, who suggested that IBGE conduct further research on the subject. (Of course, IBGE had conducted such a test, the 1976 Household Survey, which elicited 135 responses to the open-ended color question. IBGE consultants then concluded that *pardo*, while not a synonym for *moreno*, was a more reliable and precise term, its low social salience notwithstanding, and *pardo* was retained on the subsequent 1980 and 1991 censuses.)

IBGE is clearly at fault according to the *Datafolha* researchers. Yet IBGE officials have expressed no intention of adopting the term *moreno*, even though they admit that *pardo* is, in significant ways, unacceptable. An IBGE official, Valéria Motta Leite, for example, described *pardo* as the "trash can" term of the census, in that all responses that have not fitted into white, black, and yellow have been classified as *pardo*.[134] Here, mixture, the centerpiece of Brazilian racial ideology so touted in IBGE texts, is curiously divested of all positive meaning. *Pardo* is now viewed as so expansive a term as to be meaningless. This characterization of *pardo* by certain IBGE officials makes its resistance to *moreno* difficult to understand, its stated explanations notwithstanding. *Moreno* is clearly the more socially salient term; it is widely, if variously, used. Should it be adopted, it is likely that the number of persons self-identifying as "black" and "white" would decrease.[135] Brazil would indeed have a nonwhite majority, but it would not necessarily be a black majority.

Moreno and Not Black?

Growing support for a *moreno* category seems to signal the death of the "whitening" ideal and the triumph of Gilberto Freyre's notion of *morenidade* and Brazilianness. At the same time, racial mixture has been detached from the concept of racial democracy, and in this sense, there has been a significant rupture. "Mixture" or "brownness" is embraced, but the idea of a nondiscriminatory Brazil is not. IBGE is not alone in its resistance to adopting the term *moreno*. Many black activists also resist it, but for different reasons. Although black activists have directed their efforts toward the dismantling of racial democracy, talk of *moreno* and *morenidade* receives a lukewarm reception. They recognize that the vast majority of those who self-identify as *moreno* (and *pardo*, for that matter) most likely do not see themselves as part of a black group or even as partners in a common cause. Indeed, the census campaign was an attempt to flatten the distinctions between the "black" and "mixed" terms by urging Brazilians to see common African ancestry as the primary tie that binds. *Moreno* on the census would directly undercut these efforts.

For the government's part, recent efforts directed at the "black population" presume that blacks and *mulattos*, *pardos*, and so on are constituent members of the same group. With this aggregation, the "black population" becomes a large plurality within, if not the majority of, Brazil's population. Yet neither Cardoso's human rights program nor public discussions about affirmative action and other social policies view this calculated majority as a real majority. Discussion does not then proceed to consider how political, economic, and social benefits might be redistributed to this new black majority. At the same time, Brazilians who are "nonwhite" (*mulattos*, *pardos*, etc.) do not view themselves or others like them as black. This apparently includes the president. In a 1997 interview with Cardoso, a reporter described the majority of Brazil's Congress as "not exactly white." Cardoso replied, "No, they are not white, but they don't know they are not. And who wants to know? This is why I always call attention to the color of my skin. I say: 'Look at my skin.' "[136] Cardoso does not say that he is black, however, although he would be returned as such on census forms based on his human rights program's recommendation. For the moment, Brazil's black majority is a paper creation. The full social, economic, and political implications of deeming Brazil a country with a black majority are quite another, distant, matter.

As the twentieth century began, Brazil was moving toward whiteness; as the century ends, the country is heading toward nonwhiteness, if not blackness. This, at least, is the story told by the Brazilian censuses. It is also a story that is virtually impossible to prove or disprove, because ideas about race and color, and the corresponding terminology, do not hover above the contexts in which they operate. As we now know, whether Brazil's population is white, *mestiço*, or black depends largely on how such terms are understood and defined. It also depends on who is providing the definitions and interpreting the data. Human bodies, in a paradoxical but real way, do not much matter. As in the United States, however, the census approach to color/racial categorization in Brazil is not simply a conceptual or terminological problem. The rationales for race- or color-conscious public policies, either negative or positive, hang in the balance. For most of this century, the Brazilian state not only ignored deep inequities compounded by color discrimination, it obscured the existence of such discrimination by deliberately promoting racial democracy. IBGE's reluctance to produce official socioeconomic data along color lines, coupled with the insistence that the plasticity of color terms made such data unreliable, ensured and sustained the idea of racial democracy. At the same time, it was the idea of racial democracy itself that shaped IBGE methods. Today, official data show the depth and the persistence of inequality in general and of color inequality in particular. Such inequality suggests that color terms may be flexible, but they are not materially inconsequential.[137] As Brazil's elites and activists contemplate positive state action, they look to the census for assistance in proper categorization. Politics, not nature or (social) scientific thought, will determine the outcome.

CHAPTER 4

Identities in Search of Bodies

Popular Campaigns Around Censuses

In 1996, the American multiracial movement organized its first March on Washington in the spirit of the famous 1963 civil rights march. Although not well attended, the event borrowed freely from and laid claims to being the rightful heir of the Civil Rights Movement. Participants marched to demand the addition of "multiracial" to OMB's Statistical Directive No. 15 and to the 2000 census schedule. Earlier, in 1990–91, Brazil's Black Movement had mounted a campaign to urge Brazilians to check off a darker color on their census schedules. For both movements, census categorization is an essential way to establish an official statistical presence and to bolster political claims. Their goal is to change the racial discourse upon which such categorization draws and advances itself. Their movements depend for their existence as much on their rhetorical as on their organizational strategies. The size of the American multiracial population and the number of black people in Brazil rest on the success of these movements in attaching identities to bodies.

This chapter aims to tell the story of racial discourse and census politics from the bottom up. It argues that both movements responded to new political opportunities and to shifts in racial discourse by promoting their own countervailing discourses and by organizing politically. Changes in census methods (or the potential thereof) have in turn strengthened the movements' rhetorical claims and may potentially increase their numbers. However, this kind of organizing presents a paradox. Movement leaders use the census to create identities as much as to energize preexisting identities, yet securing a new census category and galvanizing a self-conscious group of people with new political and social allegiances are two different tasks. The second does not necessarily follow the first. The political success of social movements rests on their organizational strength and their popular appeal. Organizations need actual bodies, not simply abstract numbers. Even if the American multiracial and Brazilian black movements soon achieve the desired categories and numbers, the bodies are another matter.

The Multiracial Movement in the United States

When multiracial organizations were formed in the late 1980s and early 1990s, America's culture wars were well under way. According to conservative critics, "multiculturalism," affirmative action policies, and a liberal ideological orthodoxy were undermining American politics and society. Liberals were attempting to hold on to the political and legal gains of civil rights advocacy by protecting and defending multiculturalism and affirmative action policies, if not political correctness. Although scholars, politicians, and policymakers alternately bemoaned or celebrated the latest manifestation of identity politics in American public life, the origins of racial or ethnic identities themselves went unexplored. The dominant racial discourse presumed the social, if not the biological, certainty of racial categories. They no longer required deep explanation. Public discussion and political contention now turn on the political, economic, and social meanings and consequences of racial group membership.

Within this discursive and political context, there was little mention of multiracialism, but avenues were available for activists to force recognition. Although variously defined, "multiculturalism" has at least meant the visibility of separate minority cultures within the larger public sphere in general and within public school curriculums in particular.[1] These cultures are presumed to be discrete wholes, ever separate from a white majority. "Multi" here connotes many, but not necessarily the melding of the many. Census categorization has rested on the mutual exclusivity of racial categories. "Mulatto" was treated as a subset of Negro, even as (social) scientists tried to prove mulattoes to be a distinct type of persons. As multiracial activists saw it, their first job was to fight for visibility and recognition on their own terms. They wanted persons they defined as "multiracial" to have a publicly recognized and validated group identity, one more group among the many in a multicultural America. Securing an official census category has been one of their main political goals. It has also been their principal vehicle for creating and disseminating the discourse of multiraciality. Given the history of the census in forming and furthering racial discourse, their choice is a logical one.

The multiracial movement is a national one comprising several organizations and publications, most of which were established in the late 1980s and early 1990s, and not all of which still exist today. The two major organizations are the Association of Multiethnic Americans (AMEA) and Project RACE, an acronym for "Reclassify All Children Equally." AMEA, a national confederation of local interracial organizations based in San Francisco, was founded in November 1988.[2] Its stated mission is to "promote a positive awareness of interracial and multiethnic identity."[3] Project RACE was founded in the fall of 1991 by Susan Graham, its current executive director, and Chris Ashe. Based in Roswell, Georgia, with eight regional branches around the country, its mission (with its emphasis on children, more narrowly defined than AMEA's) is to advocate for a "multiracial classification on all school, employment, state, federal, local census and medical forms requiring racial data." "A Place for Us" is a Chicago-based organization, founded and led by Ruth and Steve White, which its leadership describes as "the nation's largest multiracial establishment promoting racial harmony." There are also multiracial student organizations on many college and university campuses across the country.

Founder and editor Charles Byrd designed the Internet news journal *Interracial Voice* (*IV*) to provide the movement with its worldview. Transmitted from New York City, *IV* began as an e-mail journal in the early 1990s and then became a full-fledged web page in September 1995.[4] In the words of its masthead, *Interracial Voice* is "the voice of the Global Mixed-Race, Interracial Movement." Whereas securing an official multiracial category was a driving motivation of AMEA and a stated raison d'être of Project RACE, it was an initiative deserving support for *Interracial Voice,* whose stated mission is to advocate for the "universal recognition of mixed-race individuals as constituting a separate 'racial' entity." *IV* does not exist alone in cyberspace, however; Project RACE and AMEA also maintain web pages. All three web pages provide links to other web pages with multiracial themes and to the Census Bureau and OMB web pages. Several print magazines also emerged in the early 1990s, most of which are no longer published, although *Interrace* magazine, which first appeared in 1989, is still available. Finally, several scholarly books and law journal articles have provided theoretical underpinnings for multiraciality and openly advocated in favor of a census category.[5] Most notable among these are *Racially Mixed People in America* (1992) and *The Multiracial Experience: Racial Borders as the New Frontier* (1995), both edited by Maria P. P. Root; and *Race and Mixed Race* (1993) by Naomi Zack, and *American Mixed Race* (1995) edited by Zack.

MULTIRACIAL DISCOURSE: MULTIRACIAL IDENTITY AS RIGHT AND VIRTUE

Multiracial discourse is built on the premise that persons who have multiple racial heritages should be able to claim and assert all of them and not be forced to choose or assume only one. Multiracial identity is a discrete and integral racial identity that stands alone; it is not a subset of another racial identity. As Maria Root writes, persons who assert multiracial identities "assert access to membership and privileges of their multiple heritages."[6] Race itself is ambiguously defined. On the one hand, advocates present multiracial identity as a natural phenomenon: races mix. On the other, advocates also argue that race is a social construct, and that many

so-called pure whites, Asians, blacks, Native Americans, and Hispanics are really multiracial. Through its explicit rejection of the
"one drop of nonwhite blood" rule, multiracial discourse directly
challenges traditional racial categorization, both in the census and
in society. At the same time, it is a response to and product of the
rigidity and mutual exclusivity of traditional categorization: multiracial identity presupposes monoracial identities.

Although American multiracial discourse is itself most fully intelligible in the political and social context of the United States, the
claims made on its behalf are now universal. Multiracial activists
claim that multiracial identity bestows rights, political authority,
and inherent moral virtue. The UN Universal Declaration of Human Rights, other international legal conventions, and political
theories of multiculturalism all presume the right to possess and
preserve particular cultural, ethnic, and/or racial identities.[7] Multiracial activists have not, however, appealed to international law;
their objectives, audiences, and opponents are domestic. According
to advocates, multiracial persons have a right to their identities and
to authority over their identities. In the words of the "Bill of Rights
for Racially Mixed People," "I have the right not to keep the races
separate within me."[8] Multiracial persons, not members of other
racial groups, exert political and moral authority over their own
identities. Multiracial activists have directed this claim most
sharply at black leaders. Charles Byrd, the editor of *Interracial
Voice*, has argued that neither the black intelligentsia nor civil
rights organizations have the political or moral authority to constrain black/white multiracials from asserting multiracial identities.
In his view, black leaders, in their apparent acceptance and enforcement of the one-drop rule, have "lustfully embraced one of the
most vicious aspects of American racism."[9] According to Byrd, the
lack of such authority has led black leaders to employ strong-arm
tactics in order to keep multiracials in the black fold and artificially
inflate the number of blacks.

Moral virtue inheres in multiracial identity, according to activists. It is the very embodiment of racial harmony. Multiracial persons are themselves natural enemies of racial antagonism and sepa-

ratism. "We are the living, breathing antithesis of separatist and racial dogma! We cannot be separated!" Byrd declared at the multiracial solidarity march.[10] Multiracials are thus at once the natural heirs to the Civil Rights Movement and uniquely suited to lead America into its multiracial and "raceless" future. "We," declared another march speaker, "the multiracial community, are the ones poised to move this country forward toward racial liberation. We are the next wave of the Civil Rights Movement."[11] This claim of racial harmony is similar to Brazil's racial democracy narrative. Yet American activists have never invoked Brazil, at least not in a positive way. At congressional subcommittee meetings, multiracial activists have deliberately distanced their ideas from a Brazilian context by condemning racial democracy as a myth.[12] They have also argued that multiracial activists are not trying to create a "colored buffer group" between black and white.[13] Rather, American multiracialism seeks to create an ever-broader racial identity that "dismantle[s] the dominant 'either/or' mode of racial thinking."[14]

Although it would seem clear who the presumed and desired members of the multiracial community are, it is not. Activists have had to create and communicate the boundaries of membership. Through language, they have sought to erect boundaries that are neither too inclusive nor too restrictive. If, as multiracial arguments propose, a large number of Americans are racially mixed, they would be the target audience. But activists have not made mass appeals. Such appeals would have vitiated the claims of multiracial distinctiveness and "newness." If activists focus too much on the "one drop of black blood" rule, they run the risk of alienating black leadership and black people in general. They also reach only a very select group, since it is far from clear how many black/white biracial persons would want to join the multiracial community. A confrontation with black organizations was unavoidable, however, given the history of racial categorization and current civil rights laws and policies. In the end, multiracial organizers have had to develop a Janus-faced rhetorical strategy: multiracial people are both America's "new people" and America's historically neglected minority.

AMEA and Project RACE present "multiethnic" and "multi-racial" as the identities of the future and point to rising rates of immigration and intermarriage. Project RACE emphasizes the necessity of an accurate racial identification for multiracial children. It casts "multiraciality" as a new social phenomenon and characterizes the lack of a multiracial category as an issue of accuracy and fairness. The Project RACE web page states it this way:

> Biracial and multiracial people do not have a box to check on forms. Being forced to choose only one race forces us to deny one of our parents. It also requires us to do something illegal, since we are defining ourselves as something we are not. Multiracial people should have the option of recognizing *all* [italics in original] of their heritage. "Multi-racial" is important so that children have an identity, a correct terminology for who they are. "Other" means different, a label that no person should bear. Also, without proper racial and ethnic classifications, multiracial people are "invisible" in the health care system.[15]

Members of other racial groups, children especially, have their own categories. Multiracial children deserve their own. Moreover, Project RACE maintains that it is unfair to make a child choose between her or his parents when filling out the race inquiry on an official form. It is also unfair that government procedures and bureaucrats are empowered to make the final decision. The public statements of the AMEA and Project RACE leadership minimize, if not ignore, past legal definitions of racial membership and anti-miscegenation laws. Multiracial identity begins today, with parents who impart it to their children and with adults who choose it for themselves. *Interracial Voice*, which identified "black/white" multi-racials as its principal constituency, was directed at multiracial adults exclusively, while Project RACE and the AMEA identified all multiracial/multiethnic people. *Interracial Voice* directly faced America's past by openly acknowledging and rejecting the "hypo-descent rule" and its most closely observed "one drop of black blood" corollary. The "hypodescent rule," according to the anthropologist Marvin Harris, "means affiliation with the subordinate rather than the superordinate group."[16] As the editor, Charles Byrd, explained, "The history of hypodescent is such that, at this time, the vast majority of black/white multiracials will go to their graves identifying as black—as is their right. For those of us who have freed ourselves mentally from this cradle-to-grave indoctrination, we deserve to be able to say so on U.S. Census forms or wherever else we please!"[17] Multiracial adults who have lived by force of law and custom and now by volition as blacks can elect to claim a multiracial identity. Should they make that choice, multiracial blacks purportedly free themselves from the ignoble and confining standards of the hypodescent rule.

In addition to verbal descriptions, multiracial leadership has used visual images to convey the boundaries, however porous and ambiguously defined, of the budding multiracial community. Facial photographs figure prominently in movement publications and public presentations. In his May 1997 testimony before a congressional subcommittee, for example, Nathan Douglas of the Interracial Family Circle brought along a very large picture of his eight-year-old son. In Maria Root's books, facial photographs and descriptions of all of the contributors' ancestries are listed in the back. Thus, the reader sees Ms. Root's face and learns not only of her prior publications but of her "Filipino, Spanish, German, Portuguese, Chinese, and Irish" ancestry as well.[18] Photographs are also featured on the book jackets.

For activists, proprietorship and authority over multiracial identity and its virtues are rendered impotent without official recognition. Asserting and living a multiracial life out in the world is not only inadequate, but diminished without an official multiracial category. As an AMEA spokesperson, Carlos Fernandez, testified before Congress: "[T]his society must first recognize and acknowledge our existence. In concrete terms, this means accommodating our identity on official forms if not in common parlance."[19] Theirs is a politics of recognition. As the philosopher Charles Taylor describes it:

[I]dentity is partly shaped by recognition or its absence, often by the misrecognition of others, and so a person or group of people can suffer real damage, real distortion, if the people or society around them mirror back to them a confining or demeaning or contemptible picture of themselves. Nonrecognition or misrecognition can inflict harm, can be a form of oppression, imprisoning someone in a false, distorted, and reduced mode of being.[20]

The type of recognition that multiracial activists demand of the census bureau is decidedly different from past efforts. For the 1910 census, black activists lobbied for more hiring of black enumerators to ensure a more accurate count. They also demanded that black enumerators be allowed to interview whites, just as whites were allowed to interview blacks.[21] Black activists viewed participation in the census as a validation of black citizenship and of membership in the public sphere. Allowing blacks to enumerate whites was thought to be a blow struck against Jim Crow. Recognition rested not in proper racial categorization but in the right to participate fully in a civic duty. Racial categories were then unambiguous, at least as far as the distribution of rights and privileges were concerned.

Today, the push for a multiracial census category has led the politics of recognition into direct confrontation with contemporary civil rights politics. Multiracial activists have argued that if the government asks a race question, it is obliged to use categories that approximate self-identifications. Census categories are not mere technical or administrative devices; they are, or should be, mirrors of personal identities. Multiracial activists have expressed little reverence or deference for the uses of racial categories in civil rights legislation and little concern about the potentially detrimental effect that siphoning off blacks, Asians, Native Americans, and Hispanics might have on civil rights advocacy and politics.

Civil rights organizations (i.e., African American, Hispanic American, Asian American, and Native American) have largely viewed the multiracial movement as a direct threat to their political and legal interests, fearing a slow, but perceptible flight from monoracial to multiracial identification. With smaller numbers and smaller percentages of the nation's population, they would be weakened in their advocacy. Further, they have viewed multiracial discourse itself as the latest effort to dismiss the continuing social, political, and economic ramifications of race by declaring it to be at once too fluid for simple classification and a matter of individual choice. As one legal scholar argues, the multiracial movement "can be viewed as a metonym for the more general color-blind approach to race evident in recent Supreme Court cases."[22] In an obvious and ironic way, the multiracial movement is itself an outcome of the Civil Rights Movement's victories. Racial membership and segregation laws were dismantled. The U.S. Supreme Court declared anti-miscegenation laws unconstitutional in the 1967 *Loving vs. Virginia* decision. Civil rights enforcement and public policies require that positive attention be paid to racial difference. Statistical descriptions of racial disadvantage, along with the statistical monitoring of racial progress, have enhanced the uses and heightened the visibility of census categories and data.[23] Finally, racial discourse itself has become decentered. There is no dominant language for discussing and describing what race is.

THE STRUGGLE OVER A MULTIRACIAL CATEGORY

The multiracial movement followed a differentiated strategy of congressional and bureaucratic lobbying and of arousing multiracial identification. Project RACE and AMEA acted as interest groups in their pursuit of a fairly narrow and well-defined goal—adding "multiracial" to Statistical Directive No. 15—within established institutional channels. Both organizations presented their objective to OMB, the Census Bureau, and members of Congress as nonnegotiable. When OMB finally decided that Americans would be allowed to check more than one racial category, however, each organization reacted differently. AMEA supported the decision, but Project RACE did not. The Internet journal *Interracial Voice*, on the other hand, more akin to a social if not a mass movement in its aspirations, rhetoric, and actions, sought to usher in a multiracial consciousness that would manifest itself politically, socially, and culturally. An official category was only a part, albeit an important one, of this larger design. And lobbying proved the more effective strategy, especially since designating a new official category was largely an administrative decision, albeit driven by and freighted with politics. OMB's review of Statistical Directive No. 15 was the main catalyst for multiracial organizing, because it offered a real opportunity to change census policy. OMB solicited recommendations, and multiracial organizations offered theirs. Even before the federal review, however, Project RACE had focused on changing state legislation, using what its director, Susan Graham, described as a "bubble up" strategy: getting state legislatures to adopt a multiracial category in order to push the federal government forward on the issue. Project RACE had pursued this tactic, as well as lobbying and providing public testimony before congressional committees. By July 1997, as OMB concluded its review of Statistical Directive No. 15, Georgia, Illinois, Indiana, Michigan, and Ohio had already enacted multiracial legislation. Of these five, Georgia, Indiana, and Michigan defined multiracial as "a person having parents of different races."[24] California's pending legislation goes back several generations further than the laws in other states. It defines *multiracial* as meaning "an individual whose biological parents, grandparents, or great-grandparents are of more than one race."[25] These state laws also require that all state documents and records include a multiracial category, and that, for federal reporting, such persons be reclassified according to the rates at which OMB's five officially categorized groups exist within the general population.

This state-level tactic worked successfully in getting federal officials to take notice of the issue of multiple racial origins, if not to establish multiracial as a separate category. As the federal interagency committee that advised the OMB commented, "Legislative activity at the State level generates further impetus for considering a modification to the Federal Standard to provide reporting of more than one race."[26] But this tactic was also significant for another reason. Legal definitions of race have had enduring effects in U.S. law and politics. Two of the five OMB categories—black and American Indian—have had long and complex legal lives. The authority of the multiracial category is confirmed by state legislation endorsing the concept of multiracialism, which creates an equivalence of sorts between it and the other official race categories.

Between the initiation of the OMB review in 1993 and its completion in July 1997, two rounds of congressional hearings were held, in 1993 and 1997, and then a final hearings in late July 1997. In 1993, Representative Thomas Sawyer (D–Ohio), of the House Subcommittee on Census, Statistics, and Postal Personnel, organized the first round of public hearings on Statistical Directive No. 15. Project RACE's Susan Graham and AMEA's Carlos Fernandez testified before the committee, both arguing that the government's stated commitment to accuracy, fairness, and nondiscrimination demanded that the addition of the multiracial category, and that the absence of such a category undermined the accuracy of other racial data. In the interest of fairness, multiracial individuals deserved a multiracial category; its omission constituted discrimination. Graham and Fernandez also introduced their proposal for reworking Directive No. 15: "multiracial" would become a sixth category, with the five existing categories serving as subidentifiers. The same format would apply to censuses; a person would check "multiracial" and then "all that apply" from the official five.

All the major civil rights groups—the National Coalition for an Accurate Count of Asians and Pacific Islanders, the National Council of La Raza, the Mexican American Legal Defense Fund, the Urban League, and the National Council of American Indians— also testified at this first round of hearings and advised OMB to proceed cautiously in adopting the multiracial category. Behind their caution, however, lay opposition. Every speaker questioned how the multiracial category would affect monitoring of compliance with civil rights legislation. Federal civil rights laws and programs are premised on exclusive racial membership, as was the discriminatory treatment that prompted such laws. The term *multiracial*, they argued, was too broad to be statutorily useful. Henry Der of the National Coalition for an Accurate Count of Asians and Pacific Islanders asked, "What generalizations can be made about multiracial persons of white, American Indian, and Pacific Islander backgrounds with multiracial persons of African-American, Japanese, and Hispanic backgrounds?"[27] Social scientists, OMB and Census Bureau officials, and representatives from several federal agencies who testified at the hearings also expressed caution about adopting the multiracial category. They stressed that statistical categories need to be discrete, broadly understood, few in number, capable of eliciting consistent responses, and comparable with past categories. They were heavily biased against any major changes in Directive No. 15.

In tallying the positions of those who testified at the first congressional hearings, advocates of the multiracial category were clearly outnumbered by opponents. Among congressional representatives, however, multiracialism had supporters and champions. Republicans tended to support the idea. House Speaker Newt Gingrich spoke favorably of the category and testified at the July 25, 1997, hearings. In February 1997, Congressman Thomas Petri (R–Wisc.) introduced H.R. Bill 830, which mandated that federal agencies, including the Bureau of the Census, adopt a multiracial category. This bill became known as the "Tiger Woods Bill," in reference to the young golf celebrity's self-description as "multiracial," and more specifically as "Cablinasian."[28] The bill had two co-sponsors, Martin Frost (D–Tex.) and Merrill Cook (R–Utah). Democrats tended to oppose adoption. Representatives Carolyn B. Maloney (D–N.Y.), Danny K. Davis (D–Ill.), Eleanor Holmes Norton (D–D.C.), and Carrie P. Meek (D–Fla.) all announced their opposition at subcommittee hearings. The reasons for this partisan divide are not hard to figure out. Garnering Republican support was relatively easy. The constituencies of the civil rights organizations do not vote Republican, at least not in large enough numbers to matter. In addition, Republicans were attracted to the idea that "multiracial" further complicated the country's already complex and highly charged racial politics. Democrats, in contrast, dared not risk alienating their key constituencies, and they remained committed, on some level, to monitoring civil rights violations and enforcing of civil rights legislation, both of which use census data.

The second round of hearings, in May 1997, was organized by Congressman Stephen Horn (R–Ca.), chair of the Subcommittee on

Government Management, Information, and Technology.[29] At these hearings, all sides held to their earlier arguments, notwithstanding Census Bureau research conducted in the interim. The 1996 National Content Survey (aka U.S. Census 2000 Test) found that of the 94,500 households surveyed nationwide, approximately 1 percent reported as multiracial in versions of the race question that included a multiracial or biracial response category.[30] The 1996 Race and Ethnic Targeted Test (RAETT) found that neither the multiracial category nor the multiple response options had any statistically significant effect on the percentage of persons reporting as white, black, American Indian, or Alaska Native. However, the percentages of persons who reported as Asian and Pacific Islander was affected.[31] Although the NAACP acknowledged that a very small number of those self-identified as black chose the multiracial category, they remained opposed to it on the grounds that the Census Bureau test was not the census itself. The danger lay in the future. Over time, its constituency would grow, just as the self-identifying Hispanic population had. Paradoxically, the La Raza representative expressed the same concerns, arguing that "multiracial" would over time "dilute other race categories" and undermine the coherence of legislation and programs aimed at historically disadvantaged groups.

Multiracial spokespersons were undaunted by the small percentage of those who chose "multiracial" in the Census Bureau tests and did not view the test results as a referendum of sorts on their cause. Their rhetoric, after all, has hinged on "newness" and representing "new" people. According to Susan Graham and Ramona Douglass, the small numbers showed that the category would not negatively affect other racial groups, and that there hence remained no good reason for excluding it. Moreover, in their attempts to justify the multiracial category in terms of civil rights and historical discrimination, they stressed their long-standing commitment to and involvement in the civil rights struggle. Graham and Douglass also referred to their ongoing research, which they claimed proved that multiracial persons had been historically discriminated against as such, and not as members of other racial groups.[32] It is interesting that, while multiracial activists spoke vaguely of past legal discrimination, they rarely invoked the history of the mulatto category on the U.S. census, mostly because it offered ambiguous benefits and clashed with the very meaning of "multiracial." Past census-taking was profoundly and negatively preoccupied with "mulattoness," which would seem to buttress claims that "mulattoes" have endured a distinct brand of discrimination. Yet census methods grouped "mulattoes" with the larger Negro population, thereby undercutting their distinctiveness. Activists view multiraciality as the wave of the future, not an anachronistic throwback to the past. "Multiracial" is a new and independent category, neither synonymous with mulatto nor a subcategory of some other nonwhite category.

The movement also pressed forward with measures to generate wider support and exposure. Spokespersons appeared on numerous television shows and radio programs, usually in debate formats with opponents.[33] Since 1993, the movement has also been written about widely in the *New York Times*, *Washington Post*, and *Los Angeles Times*.[34] The effect of this wider exposure on actual membership in organizations is unclear. In July 1996, Charles Byrd of *Interracial Voice* organized the "Multiracial Solidarity March" on Washington, intended, as are all marches, to be a show of strength. However, it was poorly attended.[35] The low turnout, approximately 200 people, did not immediately appear to undermine the legitimacy of the movement. In its wake, the multiracial category and its advocates continued to command public, and especially political, attention.

In early July 1997, the federal interagency committee recommended to OMB that the census allow for multiple responses to the race question. But it also recommended against the addition of "multiracial" as a sixth official category. Project RACE, A Place for Us, and *Interracial Voice* all expressed dissatisfaction with the recommendations and continued to press the issue. Project RACE had lobbied for a multiracial category with subidentifiers, while *IV* had advocated simply for multiracial, without subidentifiers. Both Project RACE and *IV* viewed the multiple origins proposal as at best a partial victory and at worst a perpetuation of the perception of "multiracial" as a sub- and/or incoherent identity. On the other side, AMEA accepted the committee's recommendation, stating that the outcome satisfied its basic concern that the government recognize multiracial persons by allowing them to check more than one box. AMEA also viewed the recommendation as "the best compromise at this time."[36] The committee's report notwithstanding, advocates still hoped for the passage of federal legislation. Yet at the third round of congressional hearings in late July 1997, Congressman Petri testified that the multiple-origins recommendation satisfied the goals of the "Tiger Woods Bill," although as law, it could have compelled OMB to add "multiracial" to Directive No. 15. Advocates reacted angrily, charging Petri with sacrificing their cause to an "unspoken political agenda."[37] They would not concede defeat, vowing to find a sponsor for an amended version of the "Tiger Woods Bill," and to show public support at a second multiracial solidarity march, in Hollywood, California, but the battle was over. In October 1997, OMB announced its final decisions. The movement was defeated.

ASSESSING THE MULTIRACIAL MOVEMENT:
A CATEGORY IS NOT ENOUGH

The defeat of the multiracial category has not resulted in the demise of the multiracial movement, although it revealed an underlying schism between the organizations: AMEA on one side and Project RACE and *Interracial Voice* on the other. AMEA accepted the multiple check-off option, while the other two did not. Their rejection of the decision has left them with no alternative but to return to grassroots organizing for the 2010 federal census and to lobbying state legislatures. It is unlikely, however, that state-level lobbying will be effective, because state statistical reporting will now conform to the new classification standards. Project RACE's "bubble up" strategy worked precisely because the federal government had not yet decided how multiracial identifications would be handled. The *Interracial Voice* web page now openly urges multiracial people to check "American Indian" as a way of expressing dissatisfaction with the absence of a single multiracial category *and* as a way of expressing solidarity with a similarly disrespected group. It remains to be seen how Native American political organizations will respond to this apparently benevolent overture. AMEA's acceptance of the decision has led to its even greater participation in the 2000 census process, although not always producing the desired results. AMEA President Ramona Douglass now sits on the 2000 Census Advisory Committee, and she continues to press for greater influence and visibility for multiracial issues. The Census Bureau plans to launch a huge advertising campaign celebrating America's diversity and urging Americans to take the census seriously. According to AMEA, however, no ads or even segments of ads refer specifically to multiracial identity and the option to choose more than one racial category.[38]

Multiracial organizations continue to form throughout the country and on college campuses, ensuring the issue a future. Although Susan Graham of Project RACE minimized the multiple-check off option as a "bittersweet victory" and Carlos Fernandez of AMEA described it as "the best compromise," it is in fact a substantial and far-reaching change, one produced largely by their efforts. Without the multiracial movement, it is unlikely that there would have been either serious consideration of a multiracial category or the final decision to allow multiple racial choices. Indeed, although OMB's decision fundamentally alters tabulation methods, Statistical Directive No. 15 itself was not significantly changed. Considerable institutional, political, bureaucratic, and technical bias weighed in against major changes in categorization. At the same time, the multiracial movement has been forced to become more than a one-issue movement. It can no longer base its fate on a census category alone. It will have to find bodies through deliberation, argument, persuasion, and organizing, not through statistical methods alone.

Brazil's Black Movement and the
1991 Census Campaign

The Brazilian *movimento negro*, or black movement, is much older than the U.S. multiracial movement, although the exact dates of its beginnings depend upon how broadly or narrowly it is defined and who is doing the defining. Activists tend to describe the movement in terms of resistance, beginning with slavery, and thus locate its origins in a seventeenth-century maroon society of runaway slaves known as Palmares.[39] Other activists, mostly academics, define the movement more narrowly, focusing on black political, social, and cultural associations formed since the abolition of slavery. They tend to locate its beginnings in the Old Republic with the Frente Negra Brasileira (Black Brazilian Front), and trace its evolution through more prominent incarnations, such as the Teatro Experimental do Negro (TEN) (Black Experimental Theater) of the 1940s and 1950s, "Black Soul" in the 1970s, and the Movimento Negro Unificado (United Black Movement) of the 1980s and 1990s.[40] The umbrella label *movimento negro* subsumes a variety of activities and organizations that are held together only by the term *negro*, which glosses over the regional, class, political, and ideological divisions between and among them. More important, the use of "black movement" conceals the absence of a broadly shared understanding of "black" and to whom "black" should be applied.

Brazil's black movement has been fragile and small precisely because of the fluidity of color categories and the negative connotations associated with black and being called black. That Brazilians now question the notion of racial democracy is partly a result of black leadership's long-pursued strategy of denouncing it as a myth. But black leaders have been far less successful in creating a politically committed and self-consciously black constituency among Brazilians. Black activists argue that Brazil is a "blacker," not a "whiter," country, thus contradicting the whitening and racial democracy ideas. Census data are as important to them as they have been to Brazil's elite. Such data buttress their claims of black political underrepresentation, disproportionate impoverishment, and overall social marginalization. If Brazil's majority is black in the ways in which activists define that term, Brazil may be compared with apartheid South Africa: it is a country of white minority rule and privilege. This comparison is sometimes advanced by activists, especially in international circles. Brazilian activists have, for example, delivered lectures to Transafrica, the premier African American lobby and think tank on U.S. foreign policy toward Africa and the Caribbean, in hopes of getting Brazil onto its action agenda.[41] Transafrica was a central player in the anti-apartheid and divestiture campaign. In Brazil, the black movement has faced two major challenges: first, to contest census data and interpretations of such data that point to an ever-smaller percentage of blacks; and second, to create a consciousness about "blackness" that can contend with the dominant consciousness of "whiteness" and "whitening." Large numbers of Brazilians may become "black" if they come to think of themselves as such. Black activists seek to show the way by organizing around the census but at the same time challenging census methods.

THE 1991 CENSUS CAMPAIGN

The black activist Father David Raimundo dos Santos described the 1991 census campaign "Não Deixe Sua Cor Passar em Branco: Responda com Bom C/Senso" ("Don't Let Your Color Pass in White: Respond with Good Sense") as "a test of fire for the black movement."[42] It would prove whether its consciousness-raising rhetoric, enlivened by the 1988 centennial commemoration of the abolition of slavery, had worked or not.[43] When Brazil completed its transition to democratic rule in the 1980s, the *movimento negro* was active, as were other social movements. Women's organizations, neighborhood associations, church-based communities, and unions all reoriented their activities and objectives from opposition to authoritarian rule to participation in democratic governance and society. These groups negotiated democratic consolidation by attempting to secure real policy and material gains through established party and bureaucratic channels, while resisting cooptation and marginalization.[44] During the transition, union leaders and leftist activists formed the Workers' Party (PT), which has since become one of Brazil's most ideologically consistent and cohesive parties. Black activists also faced opportunities and challenges. With the return of competitive congressional elections in 1982, numerous political parties actively courted the black movement in hopes of garnering votes. In São Paulo state, for example, numerous political parties nominated a total of 54 black candidates for municipal, state, and national offices,[45] and the Rio de Janeiro gubernatorial candidate Leonel Brizola, of the Democratic Labor Party, ran on a platform of *socialismo moreno* ("brown socialism") in a deliberate attempt to link color and class.[46]

Of the 54 candidates fielded in São Paulo, however, only 2 were elected: one to the state legislature and the other to the São Paulo city council. Brizola was elected governor of Rio de Janeiro state, and he appointed blacks to three cabinet positions, as secretaries of labor and housing, military police, and social affairs. Although black candidates fared poorly in São Paulo, the elected Brazilian Democratic Movement party (PMDB) established a special state agency to address the concerns of São Paulo's black community.[47] Many black activists welcomed this agency and Brizola's cabinet appointments as real inroads into the state apparatus and resources. Others criticized them as token gestures and replications of Brazilian clientelism. Since 1983, an "estimated 29 blacks" have served in the national Congress and 17 have served for two or more terms.[48] (The word *estimated* is used because this number includes persons who do not self-identify as black.)[49] The self-identified black federal deputies and senators have faced enormous difficulties in developing race-conscious legislative agendas and gaining wider support from fellow legislators. And although the Workers' Party has successfully run more self-identified black candidates than any other party, the discussion of race and color remains a difficult one; party leaders see racial/color issues as derived from and reducible to the more fundamental issue of class inequalities.

The black movement faced additional difficulties, however, beyond those posed by democratic consolidation and party politics.

These difficulties are basic and long-standing, deeply rooted in the nature of twentieth-century Brazilian racial discourse and racial identification. Neither the women's movement nor neighborhood-based associations faced the fundamental problem of identifying a constituency and then having that identification questioned by the persons themselves or by others. A women's movement activist is not likely to be asked, Who is a woman? Am I a woman? whereas a black activist is likely to be asked, Who is black? What do you mean by that term? Am I black? Black activists themselves often recount stories of self-discovery. As Father dos Santos tells it, he discovered that he was black in the late 1970s, when he was discriminated against.[50] "Before," he stated, "even with my black features, I thought I was white."[51] The black movement has been as consumed with creating a constituency as it has with pressing demands on that constituency's behalf or getting candidates elected to political offices. The census campaign was one of the first direct efforts to address Brazil's masses, the movement's audience.

The campaign was supported by nine nongovernmental organizations; seven were part of the black movement and two were affiliated with academic institutions. Although they came to the campaign with different and at some level conflicting understandings of its purpose and objectives, all agreed that Brazilian color statistics were flawed, because Brazilians tended to self-select as "white," rather than as "brown" or, especially, "black," meaning that the number of "whites" was artificially inflated, while the numbers of "browns" and "blacks" were deflated. The campaign was not solely a black movement effort, but it was of critical importance to the movement. At stake was the size of the black population, which is either a very small percentage of the Brazilian population or the majority, depending on whether the black category includes the number of blacks or whether it also includes the number of browns and those other Brazilians who falsely check "white." The seven black movement entities included well-established organizations and newly formed ones: the Research Institute of Black Cultures (IPCN), the newspaper *Maioria Falante*, the Palmares Institute for Human Rights (IPDH), the Center of the Articulation of Marginal Populations (CEAP), the Center of Ne-gromestiça Reference (CERNE), Black Pastoral Agents (APN), and the Institute of Religious Studies—Brazilian Negritude Program (ISER).[52] Although none of these entities has a large membership, a few of them have been quite effective at calling public and political attention to the existence of discrimination in Brazil. Since its establishment in 1975, IPCN has pursued a dual strategy of advocating for civil rights and working for the development of black social and cultural institutions. For this reason, other black organizations have considered it in both admiring and critical ways as "American" in its approach.[53] CEAP, founded in 1989, is not a black organization, although it pursues issues that affect nonwhite persons (for example, the murder of street children by policemen). The two academic-affiliated groups were the Center of Afro-Asiatic Studies (CEAA) of Candido Mendes University and the Laboratory of Social Research at the Federal University of Rio de Janeiro.

Unlike those in the American multiracial movement, Brazilian black activists did not launch the campaign in response to a direct institutional precipitant. IBGE had not announced a review of its classificatory standards. The census campaign was in part a continuation of efforts begun in the late 1970s to have the color question restored to the 1980 census. It was also the brainchild of its originator, Wania Sant'Anna. While working at the Brazilian Institute for Social and Economic Analyses (IBASE), Brazil's premier leftist nongovernmental organization, Sant'Anna was often hampered by a lack of sufficient data about the socioeconomic conditions of Brazil's black population.[54] The absence of data in turn undermined her ability to advocate within IBASE for greater sensitivity to the racial dimensions of Brazilian class inequality. She thought that the census campaign would be a way of involving IBASE in the "racial question" and of putting the issue of racial identity "into the mouth and head of the black community."[55] Establishing what was meant by the "black population" and who would (and could) be deemed a member was the campaign's raison d'être.

The Ford Foundation's contribution to the campaign was modest, but until the postponement of the census (and hence the campaign), it was its sole source of financial backing. In 1991, Terra Nuovo, an Italian foundation, provided limited support for campaign activities in Salvador, Bahia, where it was based. But even with this addition, the Ford Foundation remained the campaign's chief source of revenue. It is significant that all financial support came from foreign sources. Foreign funding has often presented problems of political legitimacy for the recipients in the *movimento negro*. Reliance on foundation funding has fueled the charge, often leveled by white political and intellectual elites, that the movement itself is both materially and ideologically un-Brazilian. (This rationale was used to justify the military government's decision to ban the Inter-American Foundation from Brazil in 1978, based in part on the foundation's support of "subversive" black cultural and community organizations. The foundation was allowed to return in 1983.)[56] Black activists who are denied funding or choose not to accept it consider those who do to be politically compromised and at some level unauthentic.

Most campaign organizers were dissatisfied with the precodified census terms. In their view, "color" was an imperfect and obfuscating measure. "Race" was their preferred measure, and the corresponding census category would have been simply black (*negro*), meaning "black race." This alternative would replace not only the existing census term for black (*preto*), one commonly used to describe objects, but the census term for mixed or brown (*pardo*) as well. As one organizer explained, "*preto*" connotes only color, but *negro* connotes both culture and history. For all the apparent agreement among organizers, however, there was no firm consensus on terms. For example, Januario Garcia, the president of the Institute for the Study of Black Cultures, preferred simply "white" and "nonwhite."[57] Regina Domingues, Sant'Anna's successor as the campaign coordinator, thought that there should be a better way of accommodating the notion of "mixture" than the term *pardo*, which she maintained meant little.[58] Father David Raimundo dos Santos suggested that there be two questions, one that asked about race and the other about color; that way a person could assume both his or her race and "brownness."[59]

The campaign's slogan in Portuguese conveyed two types of messages: one addressed the color preferences of Brazilians and the other their general participation in the census. "Não Deixe Sua Cor Passar em Branco" ("Don't Let Your Color Pass in White") meant that Brazilians should not choose "white" as their color; it also meant that they should be counted. (Deliberate abstention from voting in an election as a form of protest is referred to as letting one's vote "pass in white.") The slogan urged the opposite: willing participation. The second half, "Responda com Bom S/Censo" ("Respond with Good Sense"), reinforced these messages. To respond with "good sense" (*senso*) meant to choose a "darker," more sensible color for self-identification; to respond with "good census" (*censo*) meant to participate in the census. The propaganda centerpiece of the campaign was its poster and accompanying pamphlet. The poster was intentionally provocative: below the campaign slogan was a photograph of three nude bodies, each of a different skin tone, with only their backs revealed. At the center of this photograph was a small rectangle in which the precodified census terms were listed, each followed by a question mark. The text of the pamphlet spelled out clearly the stakes, the reasons for, and the objectives of the campaign. It identified its audience immediately: those Brazilians with African origins who were embarrassed to claim them. The assertion of black identity was clearly linked to claims of deepening democratic citizenship. Being black ought not to preclude full participation in the political and especially the economic life of Brazil. The pamphlet identified whiteness as the ticket of admission into full Brazilian citizenship:

> Here in Brazil, many people are embarrassed to be *pretos* [blacks] and because of this they say that they are *mulatas*, *morenas*, etc. Many white people also feel ashamed to have black friends and generally say that these friends are a little dark [*escurinhos*] or are blacks of white souls [*pretos de alma branca*]. Have you frequently perceived such occurrences? Blacks and whites, therefore try to disguise that here in Bra-

zil exists a population descended from Africans who have contributed to the construction of our country's wealth.

The text attributed the embarrassment of so many Brazilians to the "ideology of whitening," "the desire to be white and all that white represents. And what does white represent? It represents a better house, a better education, a better salary, good food, a new car, a bank account, good social relations, a fashionable wardrobe, vacations, a good marriage, better medical attention, a beautiful face on T.V., etc." Significantly, nearly all these associations with "whiteness" are materially based, clearly revealing the intimate connection of color with class standing. The campaign message also included a claim of fairness and just due: persons of African descent have contributed to the country's wealth; they have the right to share and enjoy its benefits. The benefits and privileges of "whiteness," the pamphlet reminded readers, are really "the right of anyone of our society, independent of his or her color. And in order to obtain this right, it is not necessary to abandon being *preto, mulato, pardo, moreno*, etc." In other words, it is not (nor should it be) necessary to check "white" on a census form or otherwise hide from or deny one's blackness. The three main objectives of the campaign were to encourage *negros* and *mestiços* to declare their color; to foster more positive self-images; and to generate more accurate color data. The brochure also provided general information about the census, in which the census was presented as a potentially empowering and unobtrusive state action. IBGE officials were most comfortable with this last aspect of the campaign—its potential to generate public interest in the census.

Campaign organizers were unable to gain access to census enumerators in order to sensitize them to the complex "social etiquette" surrounding asking questions about color.[60] In fact, IBGE could not fulfill the organizers' requests for reasons beyond its general resistance to and apparent indifference toward the campaign. First, the entire census undertaking was disorganized. The census was postponed for one year, but during the period leading up to the

1991 census and during the census-taking itself, labor disputes, budget problems, and lack of census materials tainted the whole process. IBGE hired temporary workers to serve as enumerators quite late in the preparatory process, and there was barely enough time to train them in their basic responsibilities, never mind sensitize them to the social dynamics of color and the corresponding interviewing techniques.

Campaign organizers had good reasons to meet with census enumerators. The "accuracy" of the data depended on the accuracy of their collection. Subsequent interviews by researchers who accompanied census enumerators disclose the deeply contingent and relational nature of counting by color. The interviews also reveal larger ideas about color terms and the values attached to them. As one white enumerator explained his approach, for example, it was clearly at odds with the official instructions.[61] Enumerators were instructed to ask the respondent to select his/her color from among the categories *branca* (white), *parda* (brown or mixed), *preta* (black), *amarela* (yellow), and *indígena* (indigenous) and to mark the response given. The enumerator explained that if the respondent looked white to him, he checked "white." If the social setting required that he not ask the respondent's color, in observance of color etiquette, he chose the color he thought most appropriate. When he was tired and bored, he also decided the color of respondents. He deviated from these practices, it is interesting to note, only when he encountered persons he considered black. Then he asked their color, because he expected that they would attempt to whiten themselves. Some unspecified number of them did declare themselves white. Of those who declared themselves black, nearly all used the social and political term *negro* (black), and not the census term *preto* (black).

As yet, researchers have not conducted any systematic or comprehensive postcensus interviews with enumerators, so knowledge about the actual methods of 1991 census data collection remain sketchy. However, other studies have shown that interviewers often "whiten" respondents, meaning that they will assign a lighter color to the interviewee than the interviewee would self-select.[62] In addition, using indirect methods (similar to those applied in estimating rural to urban migration), demographers have found that those who earlier in their lives have categorized themselves in censuses as black later reclassify themselves as brown, in keeping with their upward mobility.[63] Taken together, these sources confirm what past research has shown and what common sense knows: Brazilians will alter how they identify themselves and others depending upon shifting perceptions of themselves, their perceptions of those asking (including social status), and their relationships with these persons.[64] At the same time, even though to whom it is attributed depends on the social situation, the values attached to color remain relatively consistent: "white" and "lighter" indicate higher status than "black" and "darker."

In 1990, when the census was postponed, the campaign had yet to mount a full-scale effort. The starting date for the 1991 campaign was May 12, not 13. May 12 was chosen as a way of challenging official state commemorations of the abolition of slavery scheduled for May 13. Organizers decided that the campaign would not participate in the "farce" of celebrating abolition when, in their view, living conditions that resembled slavery still existed. Quinta da Boa Vista Park was chosen as the site for the Rio launching because many poor black and brown residents of Rio's Zona Norte and Baixada Fluminese gathered there. Besides grassroots activities, the Rio operation used local and national media channels to disseminate the campaign's message. Globo TV, for example, Brazil's most powerful media conglomerate, aired a commercial promoting the campaign. But while the commercial stressed the importance of answering the color question, it advocated self-selection of brown (*pardo*), to the campaign organizers' consternation. The organizers did not, however, demand either that the commercial be stopped or the message changed. They calculated that having this commercial was better than having none at all. Throughout the month of September, the campaign's message was run across an electronic bulletin board during soccer matches and read to radio listeners, with the support of the Bureau of Sports for the State of Rio de Janeiro (SUDERRJ). Campaign materials were also distributed as soccer fans entered Brazil's famous Maracana Stadium.

Yet of all these events and outreach efforts, the visit of Nelson and Winnie Mandela, in August 1–6, 1991, most energized the campaign. Their visit received extensive media coverage, and they attracted large crowds to all of their public appearances, at which campaign workers distributed pamphlets and buttons.[65] As important, the visit set the stage for a public debate about Brazilian racial politics. That the Mandela visit enlivened public discussion about race is not, in and of itself, surprising. Historically, external forces, such as the Katherine Dunham incident in 1950 and the 1950s UNESCO studies, have been an impetus for such discussion and for opening up the issue of racial democracy. What was surprising about the Mandela visit, then, were the terms of public discussion and who set them. Given Brazilian politicians' and intellectuals' pervasive use of apartheid South Africa as an external referent for all that Brazil was not, one might have expected those same politicians and intellectuals to tout Brazil as an example of what South Africa could become. They did not.

Upon arriving in the city of Rio de Janeiro, Mandela, in his first speech, thanked the Brazilian government and people for their support of the anti-apartheid struggle. He then went on to say that Brazilian society, like that of South Africa, was comprised of a "mixture of people," and that Brazil as a successful multiracial society would serve as a "guide" for South Africans.[66] Further, he said that "black Brazilians had already reached the stage where they could use their own resources, leaders, and schools for their betterment," while South African blacks were still fighting for the right to vote.[67] In contrast, several prominent Brazilian politicians and newspaper editors used the visit to point up Brazil's failings, not its achievements. The governor of Rio de Janeiro, Leonel Brizola, and São Paulo's governor, Luiz Antonio Fleury, were reported to have initiated a discussion about racism in Brazil and the struggle against it in their private meetings with Mandela.[68] The newspaper *Folha de São Paulo* ran an editorial that questioned the suitability of Brazil as a symbol for a multiracial and yet nondiscriminatory society and urged Brazilians neither to abandon, in face of the Mandela visit, recent efforts to unmask racism in Brazil nor to return to the false security provided by the myth of racial democracy.[69] Yet, even with this open repudiation of the myth, the image and fable of the three races proved irresistible.

Among the numerous articles on the Mandela visit run by the national *Jornal do Brasil*, one included a photograph of Mandela, Governor Brizola, and Juruna, a leader of Brazil's indigenes, walking down a corridor, with the comment that "in that instant, representatives of the three races which comprise the Brazilian population were together."[70]

In the wake of Mandela's remarks, black activists found themselves weakened. Not only had party politicians stolen their thunder about racism, but they were in the awkward position of contradicting and being contradicted by Nelson Mandela. Brazilian black activists had frequently used South Africa as a point of comparison, viewing South African apartheid more, not less, favorably than Brazil's purported racial democracy. According to their characterizations, Brazil, like South Africa, was ruled by a white minority, but at least in South Africa, whites openly acknowledged their racism, and blacks, as blacks, actively fought against it. Moreover, they also perceived the socioeconomic status of Brazilian blacks as at least as bad as, if not worse than, that of South African blacks. Thus black activists did not openly refute Mandela but charged instead that they had been purposely prevented from meeting with him. Januario Garcia, president of the Institute of Black Culture (IPCN), accused both the federal and the Rio de Janeiro state government of racial discrimination in its organizing of Mandela's visit to Rio.[71] Benedita da Silva, then federal deputy of Rio de Janeiro (PT), charged that Mandela's visit had been hijacked by party politicians and that "neighborhood associations, labor unions, Indian groups, etc.," in addition to black movement organizations, had been excluded.[72] The importance of symbolically embracing the Mandelas while scoring political points was not lost on Brazilian party politicians or black movement activists. For Benedita da Silva, Winnie Mandela's appearance before the Brazilian Congress provided an occasion to compare Brazilian and South African racism.[73] President Fernando Collor de Mello, in contrast, used his meeting with Mandela to confirm Brazil's connection with Africa, remarking in English, "Between Brazil and Africa there is no distance because we have the same roots."[74]

Despite their displeasure at Mandela's initial comments, black movement activists abandoned neither their comparisons of Brazil and South Africa nor their attempts to have Mandela speak about the "true" conditions of black Brazilians. In response to attempts to eliminate a Rio state-level secretariat agency dedicated to "the defense of the black community," for example, Secretary Abdias do Nascimento retorted that "the apartheid of Brazil is much worse than that of South Africa."[75] Meanwhile, in later speeches, Mandela spoke less glowingly about the multiracial character of Brazilian society or of blacks' place within it. In a speech delivered in Salvador, Bahia, on August 3, Mandela said that black Brazilians had not been totally integrated into the nation's economic and social life. Even with these efforts, Mandela was quoted as having felt "bitterness" among the blacks he met.[76] In one of his last interviews in Brazil before returning to South Africa, Mandela was asked to clarify what he meant when he said that he felt "at home" in Brazil. Was that, the interviewer wanted to know, an endorsement or a critique of the assertion that there were similarities between Brazil and South Africa? He responded: "When I said upon my arrival that I felt at home, I was referring to the warm reception of Brazilians. However, in my discussions with governors and mayors, they spontaneously raised the question of racism in Brazil. We are confident that the Brazilian people will courageously confront the problem of racism in Brazil, as the American people were able to do in the 1960s."[77]

In these final words, Brazil was cast, not as a country that had already solved its racial problem, but as one that had yet to confront it. It was precisely this stripping away of the official narrative of racial harmony that the campaign had sought to encourage. At the same time, the Mandela visit also highlighted the instability of Brazil's political and discursive terrain. In the early 1990s, few politicians were willing to acknowledge the existence of racism, yet none would go on public record as adherents of the idea of racial democracy. At the same time, however, there existed (and still exists) only one ineffectual law prohibiting racial discrimination. Racial or color issues were not featured significantly on political party agendas, and compensatory or redistributive legislation (i.e., affirmative action) seemed a distant possibility. Meanwhile, even as it became increasingly inappropriate, black activists continued to invoke South African apartheid as a symbol of racial tyranny and Nelson Mandela as a resistance leader. By August 1991 South Africa was on its way to majority rule, and Mandela was acting more like a future president than a resistance leader. Given Mandela's remarks, it was clear that he and Brazilian black activists were not reading from the same script. The campaign's targeted constituency had openly expressed feelings of black racial pride and solidarity during the visit, yet it was far from clear how such apparent pride and identification would translate on census schedules.

By the official start of the census on September 1, 1991, the campaign was over. In mid September 1991, IBASE sponsored a day-long seminar to continue discussion about preferred methods for the then distant 2000 census.[78] Seminar participants, drawn from the ranks of nonprofit organizations, universities, and IBGE, were as divided over and perplexed about the issues of color categorization as campaign organizers were and IBGE had been. Yet, for all of the contention and confusion, certain political realities were now clear. IBGE could no longer decide on methods of color enumeration without taking organized public concerns seriously. The black movement, which had identified IBGE as a central contributor to its aim of creating Brazil's black majority, could no longer issue broadside denunciations of the Brazilian state.

ASSESSING THE CAMPAIGN: THE LIMITS
OF COUNTERINTUITIVE APPEALS

How then to assess the campaign? Judging from the full census results, belatedly released in 1996, the campaign had a negligible impact on preferences, at least as far as the black option was concerned. The percentage of Brazilians who chose black (*preto*) in fact *decreased* slightly, from 5.9 percent in the 1980 census to 5 percent in 1991. The percentage of those identifying as "brown" (*pardo*) increased from 38.8 percent in 1980 to 42 percent in 1991. This increase is consistent with past censuses, however, in which *pardo* percentages have increased. Although both white and black percentages have decreased over time, "black" is now only a small percentage of the population count, while "white" remains more than half of it (52 percent). Perhaps the campaign influenced those who checked "brown" but would have checked "white" without it. Yet, if the *pardo* percentages have increased steadily over this century, attributing the latest increase to the campaign would likely be an overstatement.

The campaign was a limited effort. Its small staff worked with paltry financial resources. Despite its national aspirations, most of its activities were centered in the city of Rio de Janeiro, although there were noteworthy efforts in the five cities/states of Salvador, Bahia; Belém, Pará; São Luis, Maranhão; Recife, Pernambuco; and Belo Horizonte, Minas Gerais. As formidable as these obstacles were, however, they were overshadowed by the campaign's inherent tension. Why would anyone say he or she was black if allowed not to? As we know, the colors white, brown, and black are valued differently. Via mass media and school curricula, Brazilians receive a steady diet of images and declarations in which "whiter" and richer Brazilians are more valued and more representative than "darker" and poorer ones. As important, the positive meanings attached to "whiteness" and "lightness," and the negatives ones attached to "blackness" and "darkness" bear real social and economic consequences, from birth until death. Infant mortality rates for blacks and browns are now 40 percent higher than they are for whites.[79] Analyses of 1980 census data show that while overall school attendance has increased for all Brazilians, it is still racially differentiated. Black and brown children tend "to start school later, leave school earlier, and at all ages display a lower probability of being in school."[80] As wage earners, black and brown men and women are concentrated in less skilled and lower-paying jobs, and even when controlling for education and job experience among blacks, browns, and whites, wage differentials persist.[81] Poor black and brown people, as both children and adults, are routinely subjected to excessive police harassment, often resulting in murder.[82] Important political and cultural changes are now afoot. In the early 1990s, however, campaign organizers had little to offer beyond symbolic incentives (i.e., an assertion of black pride). The material benefits of self-selecting as black loomed on an uncertain political horizon, contingent on how many other Brazilians so identified and on how successful black leaders would (and could) be in advancing claims on the group's behalf. It remains forever unknown how the masses of Brazilians would have responded to the campaign's slogan as individuals, had they been exposed to it. Nonetheless, given the negative meanings and consequences of blackness in Brazil, it is clear that self-selecting as black was neither an obvious nor an easy choice. In fact, it may well be that the census form provides a way of escaping stigmatization that living in Brazil does not.

The final census numbers neither diminished the legitimacy of the black movement nor made the campaign a failure. Rather, the movement was strengthened and more strongly positioned to influence the 2000 census process. Wania Sant'Anna, the campaign's originator, now serves as an unofficial advisor to IBGE on color enumeration, joining experienced academics and demographers. Indeed, the current open discussion about census methods within IBGE and in the media is directly, if not wholly, attributable to the census campaign. Yet, while the black movement may be advancing in the battle of census methods, it still has a much larger war to win. Activists must still persuade a vast number of Brazilians to identify themselves differently and to act politically in new ways. Claiming to represent a black majority (or a large black plurality) based on census numbers and actually organizing Brazilians as blacks and being recognized as legitimate leadership are entirely separate tasks. Like the American multiracial movement's leaders, Brazil's leaders have been more concerned about numbers than bodies. They have not mistaken or confused the tasks, but they have deliberately chosen to challenge the census because it was the easier of the two. The hard work of organizing bodies still lies before them. Nonetheless, both movements were right in identifying the census as the place where ideas about race are partly made and can be remade. Census categories are not free-floating; ideas undergird them. By demanding new categories and calling older ones into question, these activists force recognition and discussion of the role of the census in upholding certain ideas about race and displacing others.

CHAPTER 5

Counting by Race

More than Numbers

Whether censuses should count by race and/or color may be the obvious question to ask, but it is neither the first nor sole question. There are really two related first questions: why have censuses counted by race, and what is race? There are neither simple nor independent answers to the whys, whethers, and hows of racial categorization. Nor are there now simple or obviously right or obviously wrong answers to whether American or Brazilian censuses should continue to count by race or color. Censuses count by race for reasons that are complex, shifting, and always political. Official understandings of race have been equally fluid and complicated. In the case of the United States especially, these two questions have themselves been interrelated: the census has been used to construct scientific ideas of race. Yet the methods of census-taking and the status of census bureaus as detached registers have obscured this basic reality, sustained by the impossible demand and expectation that the census stay out of politics.

Political contestation over racial categorization in censuses persists, not in spite of larger racial politics, but precisely because of them. The recent decisions of the U.S. Office of Management and Budget (OMB) and the Instituto Brasileiro de Geográfia e Estatística (IBGE) are the latest developments in fundamental political contests in which census bureaus are players and not mere adjudicators. This chapter analyzes these decisions and their larger political implications and reassesses comparative scholarship on race and Brazilian and American politics in light of the arguments presented in this book. It concludes with a discussion that places these ideas in the context of other social categories and national experiences.

U.S. Censuses: From What to Count to How to Count

OMB's public review of its Statistical Directive No. 15 and public reaction to it brought the issue of official categorization out of the shadows. It is no longer possible either to ignore the political and social origins of racial categories or to treat racial categorization and data as functions of demography. Moreover, the process of counting has not—indeed, cannot—escape the pull of politics any more than categorization. How a person's race is counted is as important as the race that person self-selects. As the contention over tabulation shows, there is no guaranteed correspondence between the category (or categories) an individual self-selects and the category under which that individual is officially counted.

In its announcement of the revisions of Statistical Directive No. 15, OMB did not discuss how the data would be tabulated. However, it did hint at the concerns and commitments that would guide its thinking on tabulation: "[I]n general, OMB believes that, consistent with criteria for confidentiality and data quality, the tabulation procedures used by the agencies should result in the production of as much detailed information on race and ethnicity as possible."[1] OMB has finally decided on a set of preliminary tabulation plans that allow for maximum flexibility and accuracy in accordance with the intended uses of the data.[2] For example, Public Law 94–171 requires that the Census Bureau provide state legislators with population data for apportionment and redistricting down to the block level. The Census Bureau will supply minimal racial data using the six single-race response categories "White," "Black or African American," "American Indian and Alaska native," "Asian," "Native Hawaiian and other Pacific islander," "Some other race," and the multiple-race response category "Two or more races."[3] The Census Bureau will also produce a far more detailed file (100-Percent Summary File) that will include data on both single-race and multiple-race responses. It will provide certain racial population totals down to the block level and more detailed racial information down to the census tract level only.[4] In arriving at these preliminary plans, OMB had a choice of five methods of tabulation, each with the potential to produce its own political implications and each having its own supporters and detractors.[5]

The first method was the "full racial distribution" approach, meaning that all responses would be tabulated. Those choosing a single race would be tabulated as such, and those choosing two or more races would also be tabulated as such. Adding the "Some other race" category to OMB's 5 official categories means that there are 57 possible multiple-race combinations. Thus, there would be a total of 63 racial categories in the final tabulations: 57 multiple-race categories plus the 5 official single-race categories and "Some other race."

The second method was the "all-inclusive" approach, meaning that people would be included in all of the racial categories that they marked. Thus, a person might conceivably be counted one or six times, depending upon her or his responses, and the total number of people would consequently be greater than 100 percent.

The third method was the "collapsing" approach, which only tabulates categories that pass a predetermined size threshold. Not all possible multiple-race responses would be tabulated separately, only the most numerous. All other multiple-race responses would be aggregated and tabulated together, presumably under "multiracial" or some such term.

The fourth method was the "historical" or "combining or priority reassignment" approach, according to which those who checked multiple races would be reassigned to one category according to rules that have governed past census-taking and/or the political imperatives of current census-taking. A person who checked "Japanese" and "White," for example, would be classified as "Japanese."

The fifth and final approach was a series of possible algorithmic reassignments. The first was called an "equal fractional" variant, meaning that multiple-race responses would be equally divided among the categories chosen. For example, a person who chose "White" and "Chinese" would be half tabulated in "White" and half in "Asian." (Final tabulations use OMB's official categories, according to which "Chinese" is aggregated under "Asian.") The second or "unequal variant" option, would divide responses unequally. Using the same example, a response of "Chinese" might count for two-thirds and "White" for one-third.[6] The third or "random reassignment," variant would randomly reassign, with equal probabilities, multiple-race responses. The fourth, or "whole reassignment or imputation" would require reassigning a multiple-race response to one of the five official categories based on a formula, "which may or may not take into account the races actually reported."[7] For example, such a formula would mean assigning of a multiple-race respondee to the same racial category as that chosen by his or her neighbor. The last, or "proportional distribution" technique would reassign multiple-race responses in accordance with the proportions of the official racial categories within society.

OMB's decision shifted the battle from one of categorization to one of tabulation, with easily identifiable battle lines. For advocates of a multiracial category, the "full racial distribution" and "collapsing" approaches were the most desirable. Each in its own way would have given the categories of "multiple race" equal standing with the official racial categories in tabulation, which they were denied by Directive No. 15 and in the census itself. The "full distribution" approach treats every possible combination of multiple-race responses as equivalent to each other and to a single-race response. The "collapsing" approach, while not as comprehensive, also treats multiple-race responses as equivalents to single-race responses, if not to each other. At the same time, however, the precise and comprehensive tabulation of every multiple-race response directly undercuts the unifying idea of "multiraciality" so forcefully advocated by *Interracial Voice* and Project RACE.

People could well check multiple races on their census schedules without in any way embracing multiraciality or viewing their responses as parts of a grander multiracial identity. However, from the viewpoint of multiracial advocates, full distribution and collapsing, even with their shortcomings, were unmistakably preferable to the other approaches. Each of the other approaches makes hollow the act of choosing multiple races by reassigning such responses to one of the five official categories, and for certain techniques, by completely disregarding the responses themselves (e.g., imputation and proportional distribution algorithms). Each of the other approaches also ensures that the notion of "multiple-race" identity will not take root at the tabulation stage, just as it is disallowed from taking root by Directive No. 15 and the census schedule. In short, advocates of a multiracial category viewed the adoption of any approach other than full racial distribution or collapsing as equivalent to defeat of the multiracial category itself.

In contrast, because legislative and administrative remedies for discrimination are premised upon the continued salience and stability of historical constructions of racial identities, civil rights organizations supported the methods that adhered most closely to past methods of tabulation. This "historical," or "combining and priority reassignment," approach disallows the tabulation of multiple-race responses by reassigning persons according to the logic that governed past census-taking and tabulation. Although that logic now bears a different name, "priority reassignment," engenders profoundly different political consequences, and bears different meanings, it operates as it always has. If a person checks both "White" and a "nonwhite" category such as "Black" or "Chinese," the person is categorized as "Black" or "Asian," respectively. However, if another person checks multiple nonwhite races such as "Chinese" and "Black," then that response is placed within a residual category. How such multiple nonwhite race responses are finally tabulated depends on the uses of the data.

In the end, OMB and Census Bureau officials have opted to use various formulations of the "collapsing" approach, because they offer a safe middle ground between competing groups and a way of satisfying the statutory and administrative requirements for racial/ethnic data. It allows for a select number of multiple-race responses to be tabulated along with the five official racial categories but is also based upon the mutual exclusivity of categories, thus leading to a count that does not exceed 100 percent. OMB's stated goals are to provide the most accurate and comprehensive body of racial/ethnic data, while at the same time ensuring that such data conform to legislative and statistical needs. The Voting Rights Act and other key civil rights legislation demand data that are consistent with, or at least intelligible in terms of, its goals.[8] Federal statistical agencies require data that are technically manageable, amply informative, and greatly consistent with past statistical data and analysis.

The issue of how to count again raised the issue of the assumptions and the logic of racial categorization in U.S. census-taking. Attempting to understand the categories according to some type of objective criterion is to disregard the history of racial thought and politics that have fundamentally shaped census-taking from the start. The dismantling of formal racial segregation, the enforcement of civil rights legislation, and significant increases in immigration to the United States have all introduced new political and social agendas based on the logic of racial categorization that has governed census-taking and, at the same time, are at odds with it. Contemporary contention, first over categorization and now over tabulation, reflects this tension: the competing purposes of racial enumeration necessarily problematize the logic of racial categorization. For 170 years, the Census Bureau's mission in regard to the race question was clear: define and then distinguish who was "white" from who was "nonwhite" and especially from who was "black." The logic reflected in enumerators' instructions corresponded to this paramount mission.

Today, census-taking is called upon to serve several objectives, all laudable but often at odds. Enforcing civil rights legislation requires the use of past methods of racial categorization, on the assumption that past constructions of race are still salient—socially, politically, and economically. Yet another goal, however hard it might be to attain, is to measure the racial and ethnic diversity of the United States accurately. OMB's review of Statistical Directive

No. 15 was prompted by concern that existing categories were incapable of capturing America's growing diversity and increases in interracial marriage. Although in many ways past racial categorization seems stable and serves as common sense, there are clear signs that Americans have begun to view race differently and want census categories to reflect these new perceptions. This objective of capturing diversity calls historical methods of categorization into question, since past methods were never merely, if at all, about measuring diversity. A final objective is to develop broad, statistically useful and manageable categories whose significance is separate from legislative needs and popular mobilization. Demographers and statisticians still hold out for objective or at least neutral categories, but they do not identify a source for this objectivity and neutrality. In its review of Statistical Directive No. 15, OMB was called upon to satisfy these competing objectives.

To Alter or Remove the Race Question?

The place of the race question in the census appears secure, although the emerging consensus is that current racial categorization is illogical, politically divisive, and scientifically indefensible. Critics demand that the term *race*, if not the concept itself, be replaced by *ethnicity*, or that the question be dropped from the census altogether. Although the reasons for this consensus vary, they converge on the symbolic power of the race question, which is itself a reminder and a register of the place of race in American politics and society. Both the liberal proposal to alter the question's terminology and the conservative proposal to remove the question altogether promise to strike a larger symbolic blow than either would likely produce politically or socially. Replacing the word *race* with *ethnicity* would neither require nor produce any changes in thinking about groups or in their treatment. Racial groups could easily be termed ethnic groups, and the data used in the ways in which racial data are currently used. Eliminating the race question altogether would certainly throw basic demographic research into crisis, forcing public policies that rely on racial data to use proxies, such as class, region, or language, whenever possible. The claim that census categories may exacerbate political divisions is partly true precisely because contentious legislation and public policy depend on census data. Census categorization serves as a lightning rod for opposition or support. That both sides still disagree on civil rights law and public policies is central to their particular criticism of the census question. Although color-blind and color-conscious remedies are debated in terms of constitutional law and public policy, they bear directly, if understatedly, on the census. A strong commitment to color blindness would demand the elimination of the question, and a strong commitment to color consciousness that the question be kept, but in a different form.

As in the past, the whys and hows of the race question today rest as much on the thoughts and decisions of (social) scientists, politicians, administrators, and organized groups as on the thoughts and decisions of demographers and statisticians. However unsatisfying and discomforting, whether a race question should be asked (and if so how) is inextricably linked to larger political and philosophical questions about citizenship, justice, and democracy, whose answers are best provided through political argument and deliberation. The issue is not simply, or only, one of keeping politics at bay; it is to determine the kind of politics census-taking should support and engender. For most of its history, it has supported a politics of racial segregation and subordination. Today, it supports a politics of remedy, civil rights, and minority representation. The real power of census methods, however, has been to present the process of categorization as a technical procedure, and not a political decision. Producing racial data for a politically "neutral" purpose seems straightforward enough—except that the categories are not simple or transparent. Devised by those with the power to do so, they are infused with the assumptions about race prevalent in the larger political and institutional context, which both validate and constrain the thoughts and actions of census officials and politicians.

What Will IBGE Decide?

IBGE has not yet reached a final decision about the 2000 census color question or its categories, but unlike with past censuses, there is no doubt that the color question will be included. Although the terminology remains in doubt, significant changes seem unlikely, meaning that the term *pardo* (brown or gray) will be retained. Since the 1991 census campaign, however, there has been growing support for replacing *pardo* with *moreno* (brown), which is widely used in popular parlance, while *pardo* is not. As we have seen, the "brown" or "mixed" category, in the census and in society, has been the key to Brazilian distinctiveness. Until the mid twentieth century, it was simultaneously a marker of racial degeneration and a step up on the ladder to whiteness. Since then it has been regarded as a symbol of true Brazilianness. At present, brownness or mixture carries a positive value in certain cultural representations and a negative one in others. Census data show that the economic and educational well-being of *pardos* is only slightly better than that of blacks and far below that of whites.[9]

Many remain critical of the *moreno* option. For black activists, the term is too expansive, but also too deeply implicated in Gilberto Freyre's racial democracy idea to be added to the census, especially at this historical moment. Demographers also recognize its particular ideological baggage and remain skeptical of its adoption. And research has shown significant regional differences in the use of *moreno* that also render it an undesirable option. Using data from the 1976 Household Survey (PNAD), which included both open-ended and closed color questions, the demographer Nelson do Valle Silva found that individuals from the northeast and central-west regions of Brazil were more likely to self-identify as *moreno* or *moreno claro* (light brown) in response to the open-ended question than were individuals from the more southern regions of São Paulo and Rio.[10] He also found that in response to the closed question (i.e., the standard census question), those who had self-identified as *moreno claro* in response to the open-ended question most often reclassified themselves as white, and those who had self-identified as *moreno* reclassified themselves as *pardo*. Such findings led Silva to suggest that *pardo* is an acceptable proxy for *moreno* in the census.

Whether IBGE keeps *pardo* or replaces it with *moreno* is of considerable concern to black activists, but it also sidesteps their point. Their ultimate goal is to subsume "brown" or "mixed" under "black," and if possible, to eliminate "brown" altogether. As they see it, IBGE should choose a term or set of terms explicitly anchored in the notion of African ancestry. Activists have asked IBGE to consider a formulation that keeps *pardo*, but includes the optional subidentifier of "African ancestry." This option would allow Brazilians to say that their color is brown and that the ancestry that they choose to claim is primarily (if not exclusively) African. At bottom, however, activists would prefer to replace *preto* (black) and *pardo* (brown) with one term, *negro* (black).

The term *negro*, however, carries political connotations and implications IBGE does not want to advance. Replacing *preto* and *pardo* with the all-encompassing *negro*, would flatten and reshape the meaning of both, but especially of *pardo*. Plainly stated, *pardo* is not currently viewed as a subset of *negro;* rather, it is treated as a discrete category, with meanings and applications quite separate from blackness. Indeed, *pardo* has signified Brazil's uniqueness, and subsuming *pardo* under *negro* would be a decision of profound consequence, having political and social meaning beyond the issue of census terminology. One obvious result would be that the Brazilian census schedule would virtually duplicate U.S. census schedules insofar as the categories "white" and "black" are concerned. For this reason, among others, an all-encompassing *negro* category will surely not be adopted. Planting his feet in both camps, President Cardoso called for IBGE "to consider the *mulatos*, browns and blacks as part of the black population," which would allow it to keep the separate categories of black and brown, even while urging it to group them together.

As for IBGE, the methods employed in the November 1997 pilot census tests are an artful synthesis of competing demands and suggestions.[11] The tests of the short form kept the same color/race question used on the 1991 long form ("What is your color or race?"), with the same options: white, black, yellow, indigenous, and brown (or mixed).[12] On its two long forms, IBGE also tested an entirely new question on "origins," asking: "Which words best define your origin?" The options were: "Brazilian, African, Portuguese, Italian, Japanese, Jewish, Arab, Indigenous, Latin-American, and Other (specify)."[13] The color question and the origins question were asked sequentially, each of the long forms presenting them in reverse order: on the first, the origins question came first (inquiry #9), followed by the color question (inquiry #10). On the second, the order was reversed.

In another important development, IBGE included the color question on the basic schedule distributed to every household. If IBGE decides to retain the question on the basic schedule for the 2000 census, its decision ensures that color data will be processed more rapidly and distributed more widely than in the past. Color data from the 1991 census were not released until late 1995, although preliminary data derived from the short form were available by mid 1992. If finalized for the 2000 census, the placement of the color question on the basic schedule and the origins question would appear to be significant, if uncertain, victories for the black movement. It remains to be seen how Brazilians will answer them, and then how the data will be interpreted.

IBGE officials and black activists have already expressed their concern that the Brazilian public has misunderstood the origins question and its purpose. Not surprisingly, many chose the "Brazilian" option. For black activists, the outcome was entirely predictable and strongly suggests that Brazilian should not be one of the choices, given IBGE's stated reasons for the origins question itself.[14] As IBGE President Simon Schwartzman explained, the question was intended "to more clearly differentiate the various ethnic and cultural groups that form the Brazilian nationality and that still maintain a distinct identity."[15] At bottom, however, the origins question was a potential vehicle for introducing a new racial discourse, that of a racially and culturally "plural" but not (necessarily) assimilated society.

As in the United States, public discussion in Brazil has focused as much on political meanings and purposes as on census terminology and methodology. In early 1998, Federal Senator Benedita da Silva (PT) introduced a bill proposing that a color identification be placed on the state identification cards that all Brazilians are required to have. The bill also proposed that such identification appear on all employment, educational, hospital, and police registries. Da Silva, the first black woman elected to the Brazilian Senate, insisted that such measures were needed to assess the color composition of Brazil's population and to evaluate how fairly public goods and penalties are currently distributed. Such record-keeping would also create greater consciousness of Brazilian society's "plurality."[16] Her proposal set off a firestorm of criticism.

IBGE's president replied publicly and negatively to Da Silva's bill and its underlying rationale. In *Jornal do Brasil*, Schwartzman argued that Da Silva's proposal was counterproductive, unnecessary, and dangerous.[17] It was counterproductive, because it confronted the same difficulties IBGE has faced in measuring the racial composition of Brazil's population. "The racial identity of the Brazilian is in fact diffuse," Schwartzman wrote. Color is an imperfect marker of and proxy for race. Da Silva's proposal that such an imprecise marker be widely used by public institutions would only reproduce and amplify inaccuracy. Socioeconomic data pegged to color already exist and are produced by IBGE. Schwartzman argued, finally, that the Brazilian state's role is not to define "in authoritarian fashion" the identities of its citizens, "no matter how noble the ideas of research and knowledge are," and that bloodshed and civil strife have been known to result from such attempts.

Da Silva's bill was intended to undercut the relative plasticity of color identification, both self-ascribed and ascribed by others, by assigning one official color. As numerous studies have shown, an individual's color identification is contingent on who is doing the classifying (self or other) and on class background, educational level, and the meaning of the color categories themselves. The terms *white, brown,* and *black,* are charged with positive and negative meaning that can deeply inform whether a person chooses to self-identify as white, brown, black, or any of the numerous color terms in between. Not only are color categories relatively fluid, but most Brazilians have every reason to choose or assign themselves "lighter" colors.

Assigning individuals an official color identification, as Da Silva proposed, would effectively have destroyed the social mechanism allowing individuals to move upward symbolically and to do so in socially and politically nondisruptive ways. At present, most Brazilians appear content to self-identify as "light," "white," or "nonblack" without automatically demanding the economic and political privileges that "whiteness" and "lightness" confer. As we have seen, the census campaign attempted to introduce another identity calculus, according to which "black" is positively valued and considered deserving of the material benefits of Brazilian citizenship. Da Silva's bill, however, neither depended on individual self-identification nor clearly identified who would make the final determination, the state or the individual. Leaving the determination to the individual would have worked at cross-purposes to the bill's stated goals. Indeed, the bill was an attempt to circumvent the proclivities of Brazilians to pick and choose color identifications by assigning them one. But if forced to choose one, what would prevent them from choosing "lighter" colors over "darker" ones? Or from choosing *moreno,* a term that is broadly accommodating yet closely connected to Freyre's notion of racial democracy. The potential for the bill to backfire was evident and real.

In obvious ways, proposing a fixed color classification on identification cards as a positive remedy for racial discrimination seems counterintuitive, but it was understandable in the Brazilian context. Da Silva's proposal reflected an underlying commitment to Brazilian insularity and exceptionalism. It possessed a characteristically Brazilian optimism that a racial/ethnic fraternity exists in the country, which identification cards and redistributive public policies presumably cannot disrupt. Similarly, Schwartzman's reaction was in keeping with the well-worn rhetoric about the ambiguous and hence inconsequential nature of color categorization. Like other IBGE officials before him, Schwartzman bemoaned the scientific imprecision of color categorization, questioning the value and usefulness of such data. Although acknowledging the evident importance of color identification in the distribution of public goods and in the texture of social life, he cast doubt on the ability of the census to measure the material significance of color, even imperfectly. Defending IBGE's methods as the best possible, he discounted any alternative significance that might be imputed to color data. By claiming that all color statistics prove is that color identification in Brazilian society is complex, Schwartzman thus rendered suspect the positive public policies that might be based upon them.

Much of the public reaction to Da Silva's proposal, whether for or against, quickly moved from the specifics of her bill to the main questions that have shaped Brazilian census-taking throughout this century: is Brazil a white, a black, or a *mestiço* nation, what does it all mean, and what distinguishes Brazil from the United States? For black activists aiming to uncover what they claim to be Brazil's true national identity, the answer depends on the question and the terminology used on the census.[18] In the past, census questions, terms, and interpretations have been used to "whiten" the population; they may now be used to "blacken" (or some would say, "re-blacken") it. IBGE's willingness to consider changes in its methods have provoked warnings that such decisions would assist in turning Brazil into another United States, with its rigid racial classifications.[19] Critics argue, too, that such rigid classifications would lay the groundwork for affirmative action policies, an idea that generates both support and opposition. Today, as in the past, the national story of Brazilian identity and the nature of Brazilian social relations is told through the census. A prevailing concern, in certain quarters at least, is that the Brazilian story retain its distinctiveness and not become some pale version of the American one. Brazilian distinctiveness has been rooted in the fluidity of color categorization, the mooted salience of such categories in the distribution of economic goods and political power, and the apparent absence of racial animus.

A Century-Long Conversation Between Americans and Brazilians

The historian Thomas Skidmore recently asked whether the contrast between "biracial" America and "multiracial" Brazil is still valid.[20] Earlier, the historian Carl Degler predicted that the United States would become less racially divided while Brazil would become more so. He hastened to emphasize, however, that Brazilian racial politics would not assume the rigidly segregating and often violent character of those in the United States. Rather, in Brazil, "[racial] friction will be on a low level of violence and Negroes will remain at the bottom of the social and economic pyramid."[21] Their comments are part of a "century-long conversation"[22] between and among scholars of both countries on the topic of race, or more precisely, on the topic of the "Negro's fate."

Until the mid twentieth century, most American observers viewed Brazil favorably. After visiting Brazil in the fall of 1913, ex-President Theodore Roosevelt wrote that in contrast to the United States, in Brazil, "any Negro or mulatto who shows himself fit is without question given the place to which his abilities entitle him."[23] Black American newspapers described the opportunities that Brazilian Negroes seemed to enjoy and that American Negroes most certainly did not.[24] Gilberto Freyre's formulation of racial democracy was deeply informed by the time he spent in the United States in the first two decades of the century. He traveled through the South and even witnessed a lynching while a student at Baylor University in Texas.[25] UNESCO studies of the 1950s began to question Brazil's status as a racial democracy just as the U.S. Civil Rights Movement began to successfully challenge southern segregation. Since the 1960s, a restrained optimism has characterized U.S. public and scholarly discourse on racial politics, while gnawing doubt has characterized that of Brazil. Yet even with these important shifts in thinking, the images of American racial tyranny and Brazilian racial democracy still serve as a powerful shorthand for describing the two countries. These contrasting images have endured because they are believed to correspond to truths about the histories of these two societies.

This book, however, has sought to advance another understanding of race and American and Brazilian politics. In both countries, racial discourse has provided a language of political and national membership. In the United States, to be a member of the white race was to be fully American and enjoy access to the rights and entitlements that U.S. citizenship conferred. To be a member of a "nonwhite" or black race was to be not fully American and denied full access to citizenship. Racial discourse and its corresponding racial categories have been constructed and reconstructed in complex and interrelated ways by science, by political and economic processes, by courts, and in more subtle ways, by the census. In Brazil, likewise, all are members of the ever-evolving Brazilian race, although certain Brazilians have enjoyed the full benefits and privileges of such membership in ways that many more have not. In significant measure, these differences in experience have turned on skin color and other physical features presumed to represent Brazil's three founding races. In both countries, racial membership has pertained to everyone, but certain racial memberships have conferred privilege and served as a standard for full citizenship, and others have denied and then restricted citizenship.

Today, as racial categorization in both countries undergoes unmistakable, if uncertain changes, the basic function of racial discourse in shaping citizenship has become clearer. For American multiracial advocates, being an American, and the experience of U.S. citizenship, is either enhanced or diminished by the availability of a proper racial category and a corresponding multiracial discourse. That a racial category would be required at all usually goes without saying. In Brazil, black activists have attempted to offer another version of who Brazilians are racially. Their efforts challenge the dominant representation of Brazil's national identity as a "meta-race," itself unintelligible without references to race. In both countries, it is the census that provides the occasion and the arena for public debate about issues of individual and group identity, of rights, of national identity, and of fair public policies. Yet the census itself is neither inconsequential nor epiphenomenal to an understanding of these issues. In both the United States and Brazil, the census has contributed directly to the development of ideas about race itself, as well as to state policies that give citizenship its material meanings and the political discourse that gives citizenship its symbolic ones.

Other Categories and Other National Experiences: Are Comparisons Possible?

The American and Brazilian experiences raise two central questions: Is counting by race different from counting by other social categories? Are the United States and Brazil unique cases of racial enumeration? The answer to the first is necessarily equivocal. Other cultural or social categories, such as "ethnicity," "nationality," or "language," also reflect political and social cleavages. Racial categories have always been assigned a natural status, but the categorical rigidity commonly associated with race has not been limited to race. Ethnicity and nationality have also been viewed as rigid categories. Thus, counting by race may in fact be quite similar to counting by nationality or ethnicity, insofar as all three possess overriding social and political salience and are perceived to capture enduring similarities and differences between and among individuals and groups. At the same time, however, the supposed naturalness of racial categories distinguishes them from others, obscuring their origins in politics and society and concealing the political dimensions of scientific thought on the subject.

To the question of whether the United States and Brazil are unique cases, the answer is largely yes. Although several other countries have, at key historical junctures, counted by race, few have developed similarly enduring and pervasive racial discourses that have permeated national life *and* undergirded census-taking. For example, the 1991 British census was the first to ask an ethnicity question; although it was not the first census for which such a question had been considered.[26] The question was introduced for one clear reason: to comply more effectively with the Race Relations Act of 1981, which required racial data in order to measure racial disadvantage. Moreover, the racial discourses of most Latin American societies closely resemble that of Brazil: they are racially mixed populations. Yet, unlike Brazil, few of these discourses have been fully manifested in or advanced by the census. Instead, most other countries have chosen not to count by race (or color) at all. For example, no Venezuelan census since 1854, the year of slavery's abolition, has included race or color questions.[27] Similarly, neither Colombian, Cuban, nor Dominican Republic censuses count by race or color.[28]

The obvious exceptions to this overall pattern are Nazi Germany and apartheid South Africa. It should come as little surprise that in these two cases, the census contained a race question, and that such data served the policies of the regimes.[29] However, the extraordinary nature of these regimes and the centrality of racial thought to them have given counting by race in the United States and Brazil, paradoxically, an illusion of ordinariness. The U.S. Bureau of the Census has long been regarded as one of the most professional in the world. Brazil has been seen as a happy land of racial mixture and racial democracy, as shown by its color data and described in its census texts. Yet, despite the appearance of professionalism and political detachment of their census agencies, the United States and Brazil share company with apartheid South Africa and Nazi Germany precisely because of the fundamental and enduring role racial ideas play in national politics, the economy, and society.

Census Politics in Comparative Perspective

Census-taking is now considered an indispensable element of modern governance. But censuses not only count a population, they also organize it through categorization. The political impulses behind census categories—racial and ethnic categories in particular—vary across national settings and even within national settings across time.[30] Whether the terms *race* or *ethnicity* are used is largely contingent upon historical circumstance. What these terms mean, to whom they apply, and how they are applied are most intelligible in terms of a specific national experience. Once collected, racial and ethnic data are the raw materials for a wide range of policies and laws, both negative and positive. Racial census data have been used to advance race science in the United States and Brazil; to construct apartheid in South Africa, and to detain Japanese Americans during World War II. Racial data have also been used for affirmative action policies and positive laws aimed at counteracting deeply entrenched discrimination and disadvantage, and for seemingly benign, if not positive purposes, such as demographic and social research. The applications may vary, but the point remains: reliance on such data at once sustains and often increases their salience, even as it further obscures their origins. That the categories and their data exist is all that matters. How they came to exist appears insignificant. Of late, however, organized efforts to have categories changed, added, or maintained invite a reexamination of their origins and their purposes. While mobilization around the census process may not result in all that organizers desire, it most certainly demands that census bureaus account for their methods. In so doing, they necessarily reveal themselves as the political insiders they really are, not the detached registers they purport to be.

The power of censuses to shape and to reshape political and social realities has long been recognized by political and intellectual elites, even when they claim that censuses only "count." The United States and Brazil are not the only cases. Past and current events in a range of countries provide ample evidence of how political elites have consciously looked to the census to advance certain aims and to undermine others. Under European colonial regimes in Asia and Africa, for example, censuses were a means of imposing, reinforcing, and extending the colonizers' racial and ethnic perceptions through categorization. After independence, emerging regimes interested in conducting a census had to decide whether former categories would be kept or discarded in keeping with their new nation-building aims. The experience of India is illustrative. By the mid nineteenth century, British officials were convinced that caste and religion, both of which were part of larger racial and ethnic identities, were key to understanding the Indian people.[31] The 1871–72 census was the first to include a caste question, yet the complexities of the caste system at once demanded and defied broad census categories. By the 1931 census, the British had removed the caste question, partly in response to the rise of caste associations, which instructed persons on how to answer it. Indian censuses since independence in 1948 have not included a complete caste inquiry, although there is one for "untouchable" status. Indian state officials, however, have proposed the reintroduction of caste to the 2001 census. Indian social scientists have reacted ambivalently.[32] Proponents argue that the census requires a caste inquiry because of recent legislation requiring quotas for the "other backward classes" (obc). They argue that caste is an evidently central social category, and that without caste census data, knowledge of Indian society is impoverished. For opponents, it is the very salience of caste that argues against inclusion of such a question, which, they argue, would fan caste consciousness, hamper modernization, and undermine national unity.

Although they have far less direct access to census apparatus than political and intellectual elites, ordinary citizens have also enlisted the census in advancing their goals. The U.S. Census Bureau opened itself up to public review and organized involvement beginning in the late 1960s, in the wake of the Civil Rights Movement. In Brazil, democratization has been the catalyst for public accessibility to IBGE. The particular historical and political circumstances under which organized groups approach state census bureaus varies nationally, but in all cases, these groups view census-taking as a far-reaching way of redefining and of fortifying group boundaries. At stake are not only the group's numbers, and even its existence, but also the accompanying political claims that attach to "groupness." The 1994 census of the former Yugoslav republic of Macedonia provides a a recent example of how high the stakes are and how deadly they can become. The 1994 census was needed because that of 1991 was largely discredited. Conducted during the waning days of the Socialist Federal Republic of Yugoslavia, the census was undermined by widespread political animosity and distrust, amid Yugoslavia's impending political disintegration. Albanians throughout the country boycotted the census, because Albanian party leaders claimed that Yugoslav officials would deliberately undercount them.[33] The European Union and Council of Europe, financial supporters of the 1994 census, hoped that it would, in the words of one diplomat, "settle the numbers once and for all."[34]

The 1994 census settled nothing, least of all numbers. Instead, it added fuel to an already explosive political situation. Albanians, Macedonians Slavs, and Serbs all claimed higher proportions of the population than official estimates. Each group's claims to numerical superiority undergirded its claims to rightful political dominance and to ownership of the disputed territory.

Another grim example is Rwanda, where the first comprehensive national "door-to-door" census was conducted in 1978, sixteen years after independence, and the second in 1991. Although demographers consider the actual population figures from these censuses accurate, they distrust the ethnic percentages. Hutu officials deliberately kept the percentage of Rwandan Tutsis slightly below 10 percent, masking anti-Tutsi violence and consequent Tutsi flight, the anthropologist Peter Uvin argues.[35]

In deeply and violently divided societies such as the former Yugoslavia and Rwanda, just as in relatively peaceful societies, census categories and data insinuate themselves throughout larger political struggles. In the end, official census categories and counts, however maligned and mistrusted, continue to be invested with power and authority. Censuses derive their power from their competing sources: statistical methods and the political agendas of state bureaucracies. The crucial point is that political imperatives and, in certain cases, racial ideas infuse the census-taking process. They are not extracted from the process, magically producing a distilled statistical truth. Indeed, it is the tension between the imputed statistical objectivity of censuses and their grounding in political life that generates confusion and ambivalence among the counted. Our expectation that Census Bureaus simply count by race requires that they do what they have never done simply. Nor will they and nor can they.

Reference Matter

Appendix

Race Categories and Instructions to Census Enumerators of U.S.
Population Censuses, 1850–1960

Year of Census	U.S. Census Race Categories	Instructions to Enumerators
1850	^aBlack, Mulatto	On the slave population schedule, the instructions read: "Under heading 5 entitled '*Color*,' insert in all cases, when the slave is black, the letter B; when he or she is a mulatto, insert M. The color of all slaves should be noted." For the free population schedule (schedule #1), enumerators were instructed slightly differently: "Under heading 6, entitled "*Color*," in all cases where the person is white, leave the space black; in all cases where the person is black, insert the letter B; if mulatto, insert M. It is very desirable that these particulars be carefully regarded" (italics in original).
1860	^aBlack, Mulatto, (Indian)	On both the slave and the free population schedules, under "*Color*" the instructions stated: "in all cases where the person is white leave the space blank; in all cases where the person is black without admixture insert the letter 'B'; if a mulatto, or of mixed blood, write 'M'; if an Indian, write 'Ind.' It is very desirable to have these directions carefully observed."
1870	White, Black, Mulatto, Chinese, Indian	The "Color" instructions read: "It must be assumed that, where nothing is written in this column, 'White' is to be understood. The column is always to be filled. Be particularly careful in reporting the class *Mulatto*. The word is here generic, and includes quadroons, octoroons, and all persons having any perceptible trace of African blood. Important scientific results depend upon the correct determination of this class in schedules 1 and 2" (italics in original).
1880	White, Black, Mulatto, Chinese, Indian	The "Color" instructions read: "It must be assumed that, where nothing is written in this column, 'White' is to be understood. The column is always to be filled.

Year of Census	U.S. Census Race Categories	Instructions to Enumerators
(1880, cont.)		Be particularly careful in reporting the class *Mulatto*. The word is here generic, and includes quadroons, octoroons, and all persons having any perceptible trace of African blood. Important scientific results depend upon the correct determination of this class in schedules 1 and 5" (italics in original).
1890	White, Black, Mulatto, Quadroon, Octoroon, Chinese, Japanese, Indian	"Write *white, black, mulatto, quadroon, octoroon, Chinese, Japanese, or Indian,* according to the color or race of the person enumerated. Be particularly careful to distinguish between blacks, mulattoes, quadroons, and octoroons. The word 'black' should be used to describe those persons who have three-fourths or more black blood; 'mulatto,' those persons who have from three-eighths to five-eighths black blood; 'quadroon,' those persons who have one-fourth black blood; and 'octoroons,' those persons who have one-eighth or any trace of black blood" (italics in original).
1900	White, Black, Chinese, Japanese, Indian	"Write 'W' for white; 'B' for black (negro or of negro descent); 'Ch' for Chinese; 'Jp' for Japanese, and 'In' for Indian, as the case may be."
1910	White, Black, Mulatto, Chinese, Japanese, Indian, Other (+ write in)	"Write 'W' for white; 'B' for black; 'Mu' for mulatto; 'Ch' for Chinese; 'Jp for Japanese; 'In' for Indian. For all persons not falling within one of these classes, write 'Ot' (for other), and write on the left-hand margin of the schedule the race of the person so indicated. For census purposes, the term 'black' (B) includes all persons who are evidently full-blooded negroes, while the term 'mulatto' (Mu) includes all persons having some proportion or perceptible trace of negro blood."
1920	White, Black, Mulatto, Indian, Chinese, Japanese, Filipino, Hindu, Korean, Other (+ write in)	"Write 'W' for white; 'B' for black; 'Mu' for mulatto; 'Ch' for Chinese; 'Jp for Japanese; 'In' for Indian; 'Fil' for Filipino; 'Hin' for Hindu; 'Kor' for Korean. For all persons not falling within one of these classes, write 'Ot' (for other), and write on the left-hand margin of the schedule the race of the person so indicated. For census purposes, the term 'black' (B) includes all persons who are evidently full-blooded negroes, while the term 'mulatto' (Mu) includes all persons having some proportion or perceptible trace of negro blood."
1930	White, Negro, Mexican, Indian, Chinese, Japanese, Filipino, Hindu, Korean, (Other races, spell out in full)	1. Negroes.—A person of mixed white and Negro blood should be returned as a Negro, no matter how small the percentage of Negro blood. Both black and mulatto persons are to be returned as Negroes, without distinction. A person of mixed Indian and Negro blood should be returned a Negro, unless the Indian blood predominates and the status of an Indian is generally accepted in the community.

Year of Census	U.S. Census Race Categories	Instructions to Enumerators

2. Indians.—A person of mixed white and Indian blood should be returned as Indian, except where the percentage of Indian blood is very small, or where he is regarded as a white person by those in the community where he lives.

3. Mexicans.—Practically all Mexican laborers are of a racial mixture difficult to classify, though usually well recognized in the localities where they are found. In order to obtain separate figures for this racial group, it has been decided that all persons born in Mexico, or having parents born in Mexico, who are definitely not white, Negro, Indian, Chinese, or Japanese, should be returned as Mexican ('Mex').

4. Other mixed races.—Any mixture of white and nonwhite should be reported according to the nonwhite parent. Mixtures of colored races should be reported according to the race of the father, except Negro-Indian.

1940 White, Negro, Indian, Chinese, Japanese, Filipino, Hindu, Korean, (Other race, spell out in full)

1. Negroes.—A person of mixed white and Negro blood should be returned as a Negro, no matter how small the percentage of Negro blood. Both black and mulatto persons are to be returned as Negroes, without distinction. A person of mixed Indian and Negro blood should be returned a Negro, unless the Indian blood predominates and the status of an Indian is generally accepted in the community.

2. Indians.—A person of mixed white and Indian blood should be returned as Indian, except where the percentage of Indian blood is very small, or where he is regarded as a white person by those in the community where he lives.

3. Other mixed races.—Any mixture of white and nonwhite should be reported according to the nonwhite parent. Mixtures of colored races should be reported according to the race of the father, except Negro-Indian.

1950 White, Negro, Indian, Japanese, Chinese, Filipino, (Other race, —spell out)

1. Negroes.—A person of mixed white and Negro blood should be returned as a Negro, no matter how small the percentage of Negro blood. Both black and mulatto persons are to be returned as Negroes, without distinction. A person of mixed Indian and Negro blood should be returned a Negro, unless the Indian blood predominates and the status of an Indian is generally accepted in the community.

2. Indians.—A person of mixed white and Indian blood should be returned as Indian, except where the percentage of Indian blood is very small, or where he is regarded as a white person by those in the community where he lives.

Year of Census	U.S. Census Race Categories	Instructions to Enumerators
(1950, cont.)		3. Other mixed races.—Any mixture of white and non-white should be reported according to the nonwhite parent. Mixtures of colored races should be reported according to the race of the father, except Negro-Indian.
1960	White, Negro, American Indian, Japanese, Chinese, Filipino, Hawaiian, Part Hawaiian, Aleut, Eskimo, (etc.)	a. Mark the appropriate circle for White, Negro, American Indian, Japanese, Chinese, or Filipino. If the person is of some other race, mark the circle for "Other" and write in the specific entry, such as Korean, Hindu, or Eskimo. Do not mark "Other" for persons reported as Mexicans, Portuguese, etc. (see par. 192).

Definitions for Color or Race

a. *Puerto Ricans, Mexicans, and other persons of Latin-American descent*—These are not racial descriptions. Mark "White" for such persons unless they are definitely of Negro, Indian, or other nonwhite race.

b. *Italians, Portuguese, Poles, Syrians, Lebanese, and other European and Near Eastern nationalities*—These are not racial descriptions; mark "White" for such persons.

c. *Negroes*—Mark "Negro" for Negroes and for persons of mixed white and Negro parentage. A person of mixed Indian and Negro blood should be marked "Negro," unless you know that the Indian blood very definitely predominates and that he is regarded in the community as an Indian.

d. *American Indians*—Mark "American Indian" for fullblooded Indians and for persons of mixed white and Indian blood if you know the proportion of Indian blood is one-fourth or more, or that they are regarded as Indian in the community where they live.

e. *Indians*—For persons originating in India (except those of European stock), mark "Other" and specify as "Hindu." If there is an entry of "Indian" on the Advance Census Report be sure you know whether the person is an American Indian or an Asian Indian.

Mixed Parentage

For persons of mixed white and nonwhite races, report race of nonwhite parent. Other mixtures of nonwhite races should be reported according to the race of the father. However, note exceptions in previous paragraphs.

SOURCE: United States Bureau of the Census.
[a]". . . in all cases where the person is white leave the space blank" (1850 and 1860 censuses).

Notes

Chapter 1: Race, Censuses, and Citizenship

1. Goldstein and Keohane 1993, ch. 1, makes similar arguments in regard to the role of ideas in explaining foreign policy outcomes.

2. Here I draw on the insights of the "new institutionalism" (see Steinmo, Thelen, and Longstreth 1992), which asserts that institutions structure political action and thus influence political outcomes. At the same time, institutions are influenced by the broader political context. Institutions are defined as both "formal organizations and informal rules and procedures that structure conduct" (ibid., p. 2).

3. Here I use the term *statistics* in the generic sense of large numbers manipulated by prevailing methods. The development of statistics as a mathematical science has been a long and involved one. For a useful summary, see Feinberg 1992. See also Porter 1986; Stigler 1990; and Hacking 1990.

4. I borrow the phrase "trust in numbers" from Porter 1995, which argues and demonstrates that quantification is powerfully credible largely because of its claims to objectivity.

5. Woolf 1989; Patriarca 1996; Hacking 1991; and Scott 1998.

6. Stepan 1982, p. xvii.

7. Horsman 1981, ch. 3; Gould 1996; Jordan 1968.

8. See, e.g., "Race: What Is It Good For?," *Discover*, Nov. 1994; Wheeler 1995; Goodman 1997; Lowontin, Rose, and Kamin 1984; Cavalli-Sforza, Menozzi, and Piazza 1994; American Anthropological Association 1997; Cartmill 1998; and Templeton 1998.

9. See Marshall and Bottomore 1992; Somers 1993; and Skhlar 1991.

10. "Yet as long as slaves could be viewed in some sense as property, judges could avoid fitting them into established categories of membership or non-membership. As chattels, slaves were neither aliens nor citizens: 'Persons in the status of slavery are, in contemplation of law, slaves,'" observes James H. Kettner (1978, p. 301).

11. Ibid., p. 315.

12. Under the apartheid regime, ten separate African "homelands" were created, and as these became "self-governing" and "independent," their citizens were deprived of their South African citizenship (Thompson 1995, p. 191). According to the Reich Citizenship Law of 1935, German Jews were redefined as "subjects," not citizens (Burleigh and Wipperman 1991, p. 45).

13. Klein 1986, ch. 6.

14. This number comes from Fogel 1989, p. 18. There is still considerable debate about the size of the slave trade. See Osborne 1998 for a recent discussion.

15. Kolchin 1993, pp. 22–23.

16. See, e.g., Hartz 1964.

17. Horsman 1981; Jordan 1968.

18. See Morse 1964.

19. David Brion Davis 1975; Kettner 1978.

20. Tannenbaum 1947. This thesis came to be known as the "Tannenbaum" thesis and motivated a generation of scholars to disprove it. Elkins 1959 drew conclusions similar to Tannenbaum's.

21. Freyre 1986. See also Hanchard 1994, pp. 52–53.

22. See, e.g., Degler 1971; Bastide 1965; Dzidzienyo 1971; and Florestan Fernandes 1978.

23. See, e.g., Hasenbalg 1979; Fontaine 1985; and Reichmann 1999.

24. Skidmore 1993.

25. See, e.g., Telles and Lim 1998, which begins: "Brazil, with the largest African origin population outside Nigeria, has substantial racial inequality. . . ." The sociologist Peggy Lovell (1994, p. 7) writes: "Today Brazil is home to the world's largest population of African descent except for Nigeria."

26. For example, Hanchard 1994 attributes the lack of an Afro-Brazilian corporate identity to white hegemony. But there lurks a presumption that it would be there were it not for this hegemony. Similarly, Marx 1988 discusses the weakness of Afro-Brazilians in advancing group demands, without fully acknowledging that the question is precisely, who can be called Afro-Brazilians?

27. Hirschman 1987.

28. Mosse 1978.

29. Hirschman 1986; Jordan 1968.

30. Dikötter 1992 and 1997.

31. Omi and Winant 1994, p. 55.

32. Higginbotham 1992, pp. 251–56.

33. Goldberg 1992, p. 563 (italics in original).

34. Haney-Lopez 1996, p. 10.

35. Gates 1986, p. 5.

36. See, e.g., Jordan 1968; Horsman 1981; Gould 1981; Barkan 1992); and Skidmore 1993. It is important to note that many of the more influential works (in the United States at least) have not surprisingly focused on American ideas about race, and more specifically on the enduring preoccupation with "whiteness" and "blackness."

37. Recent work on the law is an important exception to this trend.

38. Mosse 1978; Gossett 1963.

39. Stepan 1982, p. x.

40. See, e.g., Horowitz 1985, esp. ch. 2; Isaacs 1975; and Weber 1968.

41. Wilson 1989; Starr 1987.

42. Goyer and Domschke 1983, pp. 6–7.

43. Merridale 1996.

44. Starr 1987, pp. 38–39.

45. I borrow the phrase "behavorial imperative" from Young 1994, ch. 2.

46. Eckler 1972.

47. Mendonca 1979; Alves 1988.

48. Lawrence Wright 1994, p. 54 (italics in original).

49. Turra and Venturi 1995, p. 35.

50. See, e.g., Crenshaw 1988; Gotanda 1991; Haney-Lopez 1996.

51. Horowitz 1985, pp. 194–96.

52. Hollinger 1995; Hartman 1997.

53. Tarrow 1994, p. 72.

54. Ibid., pp. 17–18.

55. Ibid., p. 18. See also Doug McAdam's "political process" approach (McAdam 1982).

56. Ibid. p. 18. Similarly, McAdam 1996 identifies four elements of political opportunity structures: extent of political opening; elite alignments; presence of elite allies; and the state's capacity and propensity to employ violence.

57. Edmonston and Schultze 1995, p. 148.

58. Directive No. 15's racial and ethnic classifications prior to its October 1997 changes were: "American Indian or Alaskan Native," "Asian or Pacific Islander," "Black," and "White." The ethnic classifications were "Hispanic Origin" and "Not of Hispanic Origin."

Chapter 2: *"The Tables present plain matters of fact"*

1. Although the term *color* actually appeared on nineteenth-century census schedules, it was synonymous with *race* in meaning.

2. Finkelman 1996, pp. 7–18.

3. Jordan 1968, p. 323.
4. Ibid.
5. Horsman 1981, p. 98.
6. Kettner 1978, p. 314.
7. Litwack 1992, p. 276.
8. Patricia Cline Cohen 1982, p. 159.
9. Ibid.
10. Ibid., p. 163.
11. Horsman 1981, p. 2.
12. Fredrickson 1971, ch. 3.
13. Robert C. Davis 1972, p. 158. On *De Bow's Review*, see Paskoff and Wilson 1982.
14. Litwack 1992, p. 315.
15. Ibid.
16. Ibid., p. 316.
17. Stanton 1968, p. 58.
18. Litwack 1981, p. 317.
19. Stanton 1968, p. 61.
20. Ibid.
21. Ibid., p. 62.
22. Ibid., p. 64.
23. Litwack 1981, p. 320.
24. "James McCune Smith to Horace Greeley, 29 June 1844," in Ripley 1991, pp. 430–41; Robert C. Davis 1972, p. 162.
25. Litwack 1981, p. 319.
26. Margo Anderson 1988, pp. 36–37.
27. Wright and Hunt 1900, p. 46.
28. Thornton 1987, p. 212. The clause read: "And it shall be the duty of the different agents and subagents to take a census and to obtain such other statistical information of the several tribes of Indians among whom they respectively reside as may be required by the Secretary of War, and in such form as he shall prescribe."
29. *Congressional Globe* 1850, p. 809.
30. For example, Williamson 1995 is a history of racial miscegenation, which supposedly increased over time. By the 1850s, there was a "grand changeover" under way during which the ever-increasing number of free mulattoes were rejected by whites and came to be explicitly allied with blacks (pp. 61–63). Just as important, many slaves were mulattoes, according to Williamson. He bases his claims on 1850 and 1860 census data. Yet his argument also suggests that the mulatto census data are evidence of an important demographic shift. Williamson does not mention that the 1850 census was the first to contain a mulatto inquiry, thereby making it

impossible to determine whether the 1850s marked such a grand change-over.

31. Stocking 1968, p. 57.
32. Fredrickson 1971, ch. 3; Gould 1981; Stanton 1968.
33. Haller 1971, p. 72.
34. Stocking 1968, p. 48.
35. Nott 1843; Horsman 1987, p. 86; Krieger 1987.
36. Nott 1843, p. 254.
37. Nott 1847, p. 280.
38. "A Bill Providing for the Taking of the Seventh Census of the United States," 31st Cong., 1st sess., Jan. 28, 1850, S. 76.
39. Margo Anderson 1988, pp. 38–39.
40. Ibid., p. 39.
41. Ibid., p. 40.
42. The census historian Margo Anderson also identifies Josiah Nott as the physician to whom Senator Underwood refers (Anderson 1988, p. 40).
43. *Congressional Globe* 1850, p. 672.
44. Ibid., p. 674.
45. Ibid.
46. Ibid.
47. Nott 1847.
48. *Congressional Globe* 1950, p. 674.
49. Ibid., p. 675.
50. Ibid., p. 676.
51. Ibid., p. 677.
52. U.S. Bureau of the Census 1989b, p. 23.
53. Ibid., p. 22.
54. Margo Anderson 1988, p. 53.
55. Grob 1978, p. 143.
56. Wright and Hunt 1900, pp. 50–51.
57. Edmondston and Schultze 1995.
58. Ibid.
59. Grob 1978, p. 186.
60. Margo Anderson 1988, p. 64.
61. Fredrickson 1971, p. 150.
62. *Report on Emancipation and Colonization*, 37 Cong., 2d sess., House Exec. Doc. No. 148, p. 16, quoted in Fredrickson 1971, p. 146.
63. U.S. Bureau of the Census 1864, p. ix.
64. Ibid., p. xi.
65. Ibid.
66. Ibid., p. xii.
67. Grob 1978, p. 187.

68. Ibid., p. 188.
69. Ibid.
70. Bardaglio 1995, p. 179.
71. Ibid.
72. Ibid., p. 182.
73. Smith 1997, ch. 10.
74. Ibid. See also Du Bois 1985; Foner 1988; Woodward 1951.
75. Gossett 1963, ch. 11; Smith 1997, ch. 10; Fredrickson 1971, ch. 6.
76. Gossett 1963, p. 253.
77. Joan Bryant, "Rethinking Race in African-American History," unpublished paper.
78. Grob 1978, p. 196.
79. Ibid., p. 195.
80. Report of the Ninth Census, U.S. House of Representatives, 41st Cong., 2d sess., Jan. 18, 1870, p. 51.
81. Margo Anderson 1988, p. 77.
82. Ibid., pp. 77–78; Grob 1978, pp. 197–98.
83. Wright and Hunt 1900, p. 157.
84. Ibid.
85. Fredrickson 1971, p. 232.
86. Haller 1971, pp. 80–81.
87. Stocking 1968, pp. 48–49.
88. Logan 1997, ch. 6.
89. Lofgren 1987.
90. H.R. 11036, July 30, 1888, 50th Cong., 1st sess., p. 1.
91. *Congressional Record* 1889, , p. 2246.
92. Ibid.
93. Ibid.
94. Ibid., p. 2244.
95. U.S. Census Bureau 1989b, p. 38.
96. Davidson and Ashby 1964, p. 37; Wright and Hunt 1900, pp. 98–99.
97. U.S. Congress 1890, p. 17.
98. Billings 1896.
99. Hoffman 1896, pp. v, 37, 182.
100. Davis and Graham 1995, p. 24.
101. Lofgren 1987, p. 29.
102. Ibid., p. 29.
103. A. Leon Higginbotham, Jr., 1996.
104. Bernstein 1992, pp. 2–11.
105. Russett 1976.
106. Mencke 1979, ch. 2.

107. On the development of American anthropology, see Stocking 1968. On the development of American social science generally, see Ross 1991.

108. Haller 1963; Kevles 1985; Larson 1995.

109. Stocking 1968, p. 266.

110. Applebaum 1964.

111. Cohen 1948; Pascoe 1996.

112. U.S. Bureau of the Census, *Supplementary Analysis and Derivative Tables* (1906), p. 189.

113. U.S. Census Bureau 1989b, p. 50.

114. Even earlier, Willcox was interested in mulatto enumeration. In a private letter to Carroll Wright, commissioner of labor, in 1902, Willcox conveyed his interest in conducting "an anthropological study of the American Negro, in the effort to get more light upon the degree of admixture of white blood." He hoped to receive support from a committee within the Carnegie Institution, of which Wright was a member. Personal Correspondence, Apr. 8, 1902. Carroll D. Wright 1902.

115. Willcox wrote widely and frequently about Negroes, believing them to be natural criminals heading toward extinction and unfit for full inclusion in the civic community. As a consultant to the Census Bureau in its early years, in 1906 Willcox successfully opposed the addition of a "lynching" inquiry to census mortality schedules. Aldrich 1979.

116. Saks 1988.

117. U.S. Bureau of the Census 1928.

118. See, e.g., Le Espiritu 1992, p. 118.

119. Salyer 1995, p. 133.

120. See Haney-Lopez 1996, pp. 42–47.

121. Ibid., p. 6.

122. Murray 1951. This text is the most complete compilation (to date) on state laws prior to the *Brown v. Board of Education* case of 1954, which signaled the beginning of the demise of de jure segregation.

123. As Ian Haney-Lopez writes: "[N]o court offered a complete typology listing the characteristics of Whiteness against which to compare the petitioner. Instead, the courts defined 'white' through a process of negation" (Haney-Lopez 1996, p. 27).

124. Burma 1946; Eckard 1947.

125. Gossett 1963, esp. chs. 15 and 16; Smedley 1993.

126. Gould 1996, ch. 5; Jacobson 1998, ch. 2.

127. Jacobson 1998, ch. 3.

128. U.S. Bureau of the Census 1930, p. 26.

129. U.S. Bureau of the Census 1931.

130. Balderrama and Rodriguez 1995, p. 7.

131. This point is supported by the wider societal views about the racial origins of Mexican identity. For example, an Arizona judge deciding the racial classification of a ligitant in a 1921 miscegenation law case reasoned that: "Mexicans are classed of the Caucasian Race. They are descendants, supposed to be, at least of the Spanish conquerors of that country, and unless it can be shown that they are mixed up with some other races, why the presumption is that they are descendants of the Caucasian race." Pascoe 1996, p. 51.

132. U.S. Bureau of the Census n.d.

133. U.S. Bureau of the Census 1939.

134. Choldin 1996, p. 408.

135. I have found no direct evidence in either primary or secondary sources that the category was added in the service of forced removal.

136. The Hispanic Origins question is *separate* from the race question. Therefore, a person can identify as "white" on the race question and "Mexican" on the Hispanic Origins question.

137. Stocking 1968, chs. 9 and 11; Smedley 1993, chs. 12 and 13; Pascoe 1996.

138. Pascoe 1996, p. 54.

139. Montagu 1972, p. x.

140. Ballentine 1983; Ford 1994; Evinger 1995.

141. The multiracial movement is examined closely in Chapter 4. The Arab-American Institute called for the reclassification of persons of the Middle East from "white" to a new "Middle-Eastern" category. Helen Hatab Samhan, prepared written statement before the House Subcommittee on Census, Statistics, and Postal Personnel, 30 June 1993. The Celtic Coalition recommended that "white" be subdivided into three subcategories: a person having origins in either (1) "the original peoples of Europe," (2) "the original peoples of North Africa," or (3) "the original peoples of Southwest Asia (Middle East)." From Document #11 in Public Comments about Statistical Directive No. 15, Binder #1 (Public Documents Room, New Executive Office Building, Washington, D.C.). The Society for German-American Studies recommended a "German-American" category that would subsume nine German ethnic groups. From Document #2 in ibid.

142. For liberal views, see, e.g., Hollinger 1995; Patterson 1997; American Anthropological Association 1997; Denton 1997. For conservative views, see D'Souza 1996.

143. The discussion here of Directive No. 15 is necessarily general; it does not provide a detailed administrative history of the directive or subsequent reviews. This discussion also relies heavily on available official sources. A full administrative history and analysis of the directive remains to be written.

144. Federal Interagency Committee on Education, "Report of the Ad Hoc Committee on Racial and Ethnic Standards"; U.S. Congress 1997a, p. 17.

145. U.S. Congress 1997a.

146. Ibid., p. 19.

147. Le Espiritu 1992, pp. 124–26.

148. Ibid., ch. 5.

149. Choldin 1986; Hernàndez, Estrada, and Alvirez 1973.

150. Edmonston et al. 1996. See also Edmonston and Schultze 1995.

151. U.S. Bureau of the Census 1996 and 1997; Tucker 1996.

152. U.S. OMB 1997a.

153. Ibid., p. 396937.

Chapter 3: With "time . . . , they will be white"

1. Kelsey 1940.

2. I use "Brazilian Statistical Institute" to refer both to the modern Instituto Brasileiro de Geográfia e Estatística (IBGE), established in 1938, and to its predecessor, the Directoria Geral de Estatística.

3. In the 1950s, Brazilian sociologist Oracy Nogueira postulated that the mark of "origin" (U.S.) versus the mark of "color" (Brazil) was the key difference between prejudice in the United States and Brazil.

4. See Conrad 1994, esp. ch. 7.

5. Klein 1986, ch. 2; Conrad 1986; Skidmore 1993a, ch. 1.

6. Skidmore 1993a, p. 23.

7. Conrad 1994.

8. Skidmore 1993a, pp. 22–23.

9. Schwartzman 1991a.

10. Piza and Rosemberg 1999.

11. See Skidmore 1993a, which remains a definitive text on Brazilian thought.

12. Stepan 1982, pp. 105–6.

13. Skidmore 1993a, pp. 27–32.

14. Stepan 1991, p. 45.

15. See Schwarcz 1993, which does not, however, discuss census-taking. See also Borges 1993; Skidmore 1993a.

16. Costa 1982; Andrews 1991.

17. Holloway 1977, p. 163.

18. Holloway 1980, p. 179.

19. Ibid., p. 42.

20. According to the historian George Reid Andrews, freed slaves were pushed out of coffee cultivation, Brazil's most productive economic sector,

because many decided to resist employers' demands and attempted to bargain over the terms of employment. However, the planters' ability to import workers gave them the upper hand. See Andrews 1991, ch. 3.

21. Celia Maria Marinho de Azevedo 1987, p. 252.

22. Emília Viotti da Costa 1988.

23. Andrews 1991; Levine n.d.; Butler 1998.

24. Pickel 1993, pp. 19–22.

25. Eakin 1985, p. 163.

26. Burns 1993, ch. 6; Roett 1992, pp. 21–22.

27. Mendonca 1979.

28. Goyer and Domschke 1983.

29. Ibid., p. 84.

30. Mendonca and Dias Alves 1988.

31. Vianna 1956.

32. Giralda Seiferth, Federal University of Rio de Janeiro, in conversation with the author, Rio de Janeiro, Apr. 27, 1998.

33. Maram 1977 and 1979.

34. Andrews 1991, p. 87.

35. See Stepan 1991.

36. Neo-Lamarckian biological theories, as opposed to Mendelian theories, posited that acquired characteristics could be inherited. Improving the social and physical environment through better public sanitation, hygiene, and general moral uplift would, in turn, affect the physiology of reproductive cells. However, although Brazilian eugenics had its intellectual origins in France, many of its Brazilian practitioners were neither geneticists nor well read in the scientific literature on genetics. See Stepan 1990.

37. The text's author, Oliviera Vianna, explained that there were no absolutely inferior races, but races that became inferior owing to their contact with races richer in "eugenics." Invariably, the "eugenically stronger" race was "white" and the "eugenically weaker" races were "black" and "red."

38. Skidmore 1993a, pp. 200–203. Stepan 1990 offers one of the most comprehensive examinations of Brazilian eugenic associations but does not identify Vianna as an active participant.

39. Vieira 1976 observes that the "analysis of the composition and behavior" of the Brazilian people is a "permanent theme" of Vianna's writings (p. 105). Needell 1995 argues that the scholarly tendency to separate Vianna's political views from his racial views is wrong.

40. Schwartzman 1991b, p. 245.

41. Indeed, this discrepancy in tone between his other writings and the census text suggests that the 1920 section was intended to alter elite thinking about the desirability of European immigrants.

42. Needell 1995a, p. 12. Vianna's comments appeared in the introduction to the second edition of *Populações meridionais* (Vianna 1973–74).

43. Medeiros 1978, pp. 190–91.

44. On black activism, see Butler 1998. On reaction to the Modernist movement, see Burns, pp. 326–31.

45. Figueira 1990, pp. 63–72.

46. Subervi-Velez and Oliveira 1991; Pinto 1987; Fórum Estadual 1991.

47. More precisely, IBGE was finally established in 1938 when two separate government councils, O Conselho de Estatística (created in 1936) and O Conselho de Geográfia (created in 1937), were consolidated. Penha 1993, p. 66.

48. Freyre extended his ideas, justifying and defending Portuguese colonialism in Africa. His idea of "luso-tropicalism," which posited the comfort of Catholicism and the Portuguese with "darker-skinned" people, accounted for the supposed benignancy of Portuguese rule. In fact, Portuguese colonialism was far more rapacious than French or British, if less developed and less rigidly stratified. Subsequent scholarship on Portuguese colonialism has diminished significantly the explanatory power of these factors by showing that, while they account for the apparent differences between Portuguese and British colonialism, they did not produce a less brutal system. On the critical reexamination of Portuguese colonialism, see Bender 1978; Perry Anderson 1962.

49. For a useful discussion of the myth of racial democracy and national identity, see Denise Ferreira da Silva 1989.

50. Mitchell 1997; Andrews 1991 and 1996.

51. Andrews 1992a, pp. 158–59.

52. Skidmore 1993a, p. 206.

53. Levine 1970, p. 21.

54. Lesser 1995, p. 58.

55. Skidmore 1993a, p. 205.

56. Ibid., p. 206.

57. Ibid.

58. Skidmore 1963, p. 31.

59. IBGE 1950, p. 8.

60. Ibid., p. 9.

61. IBGE 1969, the report of the National Census Commission's deliberations on the color question of the 1970 census, provides a brief history of past IBGE decisions on color questions. The information on the 1940 census in the report was taken from a summary by Afranio de Carvalho, "Observations about the Organization and Execution of the General Census of Brazil."

62. Italian-born Giorgio Mortara was an influential statistician and policymaker within the IBGE in the 1940s and 1950s. He returned to Italy in 1956. He was the author of numerous articles and IBGE documents. In 1995, the IBGE published a commemorative volume. *Giorgio Mortara: Publicação comemorativa do centenário de nascimento* (IBGE 1995).

63. IBGE 1969, p. 2.

64. IBGE 1950, p. 10.

65. Skidmore 1993a, p. 208.

66. Fernando de Azevedo 1950. The original census text was published in 1943.

67. Fernando de Azevedo 1950, p. 31.

68. Ibid., p. 33.

69. Ibid., p. 41.

70. Hanchard 1994, pp. 104–9; Andrews 1992a, pp. 147–71.

71. Levine 1970, pp. 20–21.

72. Ibid., p. 21.

73. This report was reprinted in IBGE 1970a, p. 169.

74. Ibid.

75. IBGE 1969, pp. 2–3.

76. Inter-American Statistical Institute 1953.

77. Andrews 1991, p. 184.

78. Ibid., p. 159.

79. Ibid., p. 185.

80. Ibid., p. 184.

81. Racusen 1996, p. 5. Racusen takes the passage from Freyre 1966.

82. Eccles 1991.

83. Gordon 1951, p. 5.

84. Ibid., p. 6.

85. Banton 1996, p. 139.

86. Bastide and Fernandes 1959.

87. Wagley 1963; Thales de Azevedo 1966.

88. Skidmore 1992, p. 2.

89. Roett 1992, p. 165.

90. Ibid., p. 164.

91. Keck 1987.

92. Maria Alves 1985.

93. Andrews 1996, p. 491.

94. Winant 1994, pp. 132–35.

95. IBGE 1969.

96. Note that he used *ethnic*, not *racial*. These terms appear as synonyms throughout his testimony.

97. IBGE 1969, p. 8.

98. In Portuguese, *"alva-escura," "branca suja," "morena bem chegada," "meio morena," "meio preta,"* and *"retinha."* See IBGE 1976.

99. Oliveira et al. 1985, p. 10.

100. Tereza Cristina N. Araújo Costa 1974.

101. Ibid., p. 100.

102. Tereza Cristina N. Araújo Costa 1987.

103. Roett 1992, p. 150.

104. Keck 1992.

105. Roett 1992, p. 150.

106. Hanchard 1994, pp. 109–29; Andrews 1992a, pp. 163–68.

107. Turner 1985; Mitchell 1985.

108. Brazil, Federal Republic, 1979.

109. "Censo–80 vai pesquisar côr, decide o IBGE," *A Folha de São Paulo,* Nov. 9, 1979, p. 6. The meeting's attendees were Olavo Brasil de Lima, the executive secretary of the National Association of Post-Graduate Education; Orlando Fernandes and Olimpio Marques dos Santos, the president and vice-president of the Institute for the Study of Black Culture; Giralda Seiferth of the Association of the National Museum, and Carlos Hasenbalg of the Institute of University Research of Rio de Janeiro.

110. *Latin America Regional Report* 1980.

111. Freyre 1979.

112. Berquó 1988; Lovell 1991; Hasenbalg and Silva 1988; Hasenbalg 1979; Wood and Lovell 1992.

113. Skidmore 1992, p. 12.

114. *Veja,* Aug. 28, 1985.

115. Oliveira et al. 1985.

116. Ibid.

117. Ibid., p. 11.

118. Ibid., p. 12.

119. Ibid.

120. Roett 1992, p. 177.

121. "Reforma administrativa compremete censo de 90," *Jornal do Brasil* (Rio de Janeiro), June 29, 1990, p. 4; "IBGE confirma adiamento do Censo por falta de Funcionarios," *Folha de São Paulo,* Aug. 11, 1990; "Presidente do IBGE culpa a burocracia," *Folha de São Paulo,* Aug. 31, 1990, p. 9; "Funcionarios criticam adiamento do Censo 90," *Jornal do Brasil* (Rio de Janeiro), Aug. 16, 1990, p. 6.

122. "Indios serão contados," *O Dia* (Rio de Janeiro), May 13, 1990, p. 5.

123. Gondim 1991.

124. Parada 1992.

125. Purcell and Roett 1997, p. 74.

126. Fry 1996.
127. Moffett 1996.
128. This number is based on the official 1991 census figure of 146,813 million Brazilians.
129. Schemo 1996.
130. Turra and Venturi 1995.
131. Ibid., p. 5.
132. *Datafolha* refers to the Folha de São Paulo reporters and other outside experts and researchers who contributed to the project.
133. Turra and Venturi 1995, p. 36.
134. Ibid., p. 32.
135. Marvin Harris et al. 1993.
136. Roberto Pompeu de Toledo, "The Blacks, According to the President: President Cardoso Discusses Race Relations in Brazil," *Veja*, May 6, 1998. An article drawn from interviews published in Toledo 1998.
137. Lovell and Wood 1998.

Chapter 4: Identities in Search of Bodies

1. Appiah 1997.
2. Fernandez 1993.
3. Association of Multiethnic Americans, leaflet distributed at Multiracial/Multiethnic Solidarity March, Washington, D.C., July 20, 1996.
4. Grosz 1997. The *Interracial Voice* website address is http://www.webcom.com/~intvoice/.
5. Payson 1996; Gilanshah 1993; Lyncott-Haims 1994.
6. Root 1995.
7. Henkin 1990; Kymlicka 1995.
8. Root 1996, p. 7.
9. Byrd 1996a. Nearly all of the *IV* editorials (Sept. 1995–Dec. 1997) argue against black leadership, often at great length.
10. Byrd 1996c.
11. Douglas 1996.
12. Written statement submitted by G. Reginald Daniel, Professor of Sociology, University of California at Santa Barbara, to the Subcommittee on Government Management and Technology, U.S. House of Representatives, 22 May 1997, p. 2.
13. Written testimony of Ramona E. Douglass, president of the Association of Multiethnic Americans (AMEA), before the Subcommittee on Government Management and Technology, U.S. House of Representatives, 22 May 1997, p. 2.
14. Daniel (cited n. 12 above), p. 2.
15. Project RACE web page, "About Project RACE."

16. Marvin Harris 1980, p. 56.

17. Byrd 1997a.

18. Root 1992, p. 385.

19. U.S. Congress 1994, p. 127.

20. Taylor 1992, p. 25.

21. Lynn Sanders, "Objectivity in Black and White," unpublished paper, May 1998.

22. Hernández 1988, p. 103.

23. Prewitt 1987.

24. U.S. OMB 1997a, p. 36906; Project RACE web page, "State Legislative Updates" link.

25. U.S. OMB 1997a, p. 36906.

26. Ibid., p. 36903.

27. U.S. Congress 1994, p. 101.

28. Fletcher 1997. *Cablinasian* is the term Woods himself invented to describe his racial makeup. According to Woods, he is one-eighth Caucasian, one-fourth black, one-eighth American Indian, and one-half Asian (one-quarter Thai, one-quarter Chinese).

29. With the 1994 election of the Republican Congress, the former Committee on Post Office and Civil Service and its Subcommittee on Census, Statistics, and Postal Personnel were abolished. Their responsibilities were reconstituted within a committee dedicated to downsizing government, the Committee on Government Reform and Oversight.

30. U.S. Bureau of the Census 1996.

31. U.S. Bureau of the Census 1997.

32. Author's notes.

33. For example, Susan Graham of Project RACE appeared on *Our Voices*, Black Entertainment Television (BET), Dec. 4, 1994, and on National Public Radio's *Talk of the Nation*, Apr. 8, 1997; Charles Byrd appeared on PBS's *NewsHour*, July 16, 1997.

34. See, e.g., Poe 1993; Rosin 1994; Pressley 1994; Gross 1996; Mathews 1996; Younge 1996; Marriot 1996; Fletcher 1997; White 1997.

35. This author attended the march. Various news reports, CNN for example, put the number at between 100 and 200. Multiracial activists put the number at 500.

36. Fernandez 1997. A letter from Carlos Fernandez, coordinator for law and civil rights for the Association of Multiethnic Americans, to Representative Tom Petri (R-WI), sponsor of H.R. 830 (the "Tiger Woods" Bill) reveals the AMEA's compromising posture. In the letter, Fernandez states unequivocally that he is against a stand-alone multiracial category for several reasons. The two most important for our purposes are: (1) the category would do nothing to challenge the "one-drop rule," and (2) it

would pose a threat to other minority groups. A multiracial category with subidentifiers, however, "does not necessarily alienate people of goodwill in the civil rights community whose backing for any proposal to count multiracial/ethnic people we believe is essential if it is to gain bipartisan support and have any reasonable chance of succeeding." This letter was posted on the *Interracial Voice* webpage, May–June 1997 edition.

37. Douglas 1997, "Leaving the Scene of a Crime." The "crime" Douglas refers to is Petri's "betrayal" of the multiracial movement in withdrawing the "Tiger Woods" Bill.

38. Ramona E. Douglass, "Report on the Census 2000 Ad Campaign from a Multiracial Perspective," May 5, 1999. AMEA webpage.

39. Brooke 1994.

40. The most comprehensive study of the black movement to date is Hanchard 1994; see esp. ch. 5. See also Mitchell 1977; Andrews 1991.

41. For example, Diva Moreira, "The Black Brazilian Movement," talk delivered on Mar. 22, 1994.

42. "Uma nova tomada de consciencia," *O Dia* (Rio de Janeiro), May 13, 1990, p. 5.

43. Hanchard 1994, ch. 6.

44. Alvarez 1990; Mainwaring 1989.

45. Andrews 1992a, p. 166; Valente 1986.

46. Soares and Silva 1987.

47. O Conselho de Participação e Desenvolvimento da Comunidade (The Council of Black Community Participation and Development).

48. Johnson 1998.

49. For example, Johnson paraphrases Federal Deputy Chico Vigilante's explanation for the absence of a black political caucus. In addition to ideological and partisan divisions, Vigilante noted, in Johnson's words, "a hesitancy among some black representatives to accept their blackness; that is, their racial identity as blacks and their political responsibility as privileged blacks to work to improve the situation of the black masses" (ibid., p. 113).

50. "Uma nova tomada de consciencia," *O Dia* (Rio de Janeiro), May 13, 1990, p. 5.

51. Ibid., p. 5.

52. In Portuguese: Instituto de Pesquisa das Culturas Negras (IPCN); Instituto Palmares de Direitos Humanos (IPDH); Centro de Articulações Marginalizadas (CEAP); Centro de Referência Negromestiça (CERNE); Agentes de Pastoral Negros (APN); Instituto de Estudos da Religião (ISER); Centro de Estudos Afro-Asiáticos (CEAA), and Núcleo da Cor—IFCS/UFRJ.

53. Hanchard 1994, p. 119.

54. Wania Sant'Anna, interview by author, tape recording, Rio de Janeiro, July 10, 1992.

55. Ibid.

56. Andrews 1996, p. 495.

57. Januario Garcia, interview by author, tape recording, Rio de Janeiro, July 20, 1992.

58. Regina Domingues, interview by author, tape recording, Rio de Janeiro, July 5, 1992.

59. "Negros querem sua côr assumida no censo 91," *Jornal do Brasil* (Rio de Janeiro), Sept. 24, 1991, p. 3.

60. Tereza Cristina N. Araújo Costa 1987.

61. Piza and Rosemberg 1999.

62. Nelson do Valle Silva 1994.

63. Wood and Magno de Carvalho 1995.

64. Harris and Kotak 1963; Harris 1970; Pacheco 1987.

65. "Mandela atraí 40 mil a Praça da Apoteose," *Jornal do Brasil* (Rio de Janeiro), Aug. 2, 1991, p. 1.

66. "Mandela agradece ao Brasil apoio na luta anti-apartheid," *Jornal do Commercio,* Aug. 2, 1991, p. 1.

67. "Mandela contradiz lideres negros do Brasil," *Folha de São Paulo,* Aug. 2, 1991, p. 7.

68. "Mandela agradece apoio dos brasileiros," *O Estado de São Paulo,* Aug. 4 1991, p. 11; "Mandela elogia Igreja na luta contra racismo," *Jornal do Commercio,* Aug. 5, 1991.

69. "Igualdade ilusoria," *Folha de São Paulo,* Aug. 2, 1991.

70. "Grito contra o Racismo," *Jornal do Brasil,* Aug. 7, 1991, p. 3.

71. "Movimentos negros veem discriminação," *Jornal do Commercio,* Aug. 2, 1991, p. 2.

72. "Movimento negro protesta," *Folha de São Paulo,* Aug. 2, 1991, p. 7.

73. "Benedita dedica seu discurso a 'irma de luta,'" *O Globo* (Rio de Janeiro), Aug. 6, 1991, p. 3.

74. "Presidente lembra as raizes comuns," *O Globo* (Rio de Janeiro), Aug. 6, 1991, p. 3.

75. "Apartheid no Brasil é pior que na Africa, diz secretario," *Folha de São Paulo,* Aug. 2, 1991.

76. "Lider nota amargura do negro," *Jornal do Brasil* (Rio de Janeiro), Aug. 6, 1991, p. 5.

77. Aquino 1991.

78. Instituto Brasileiro de Análises Sociais e Econômicas 1991.

79. *Folha de São Paulo*, Nov. 16, 1998 as cited in the "News from Brazil" electronic mail service, supplied by SEJUP (Serviço Brasileiro de Justice e Paz). Web page: http: //www.oneworld.org/sejup/.

80. Lovell and Wood 1998, p. 98.

81. Ibid., pp. 99–106.

82. Fry 1996; Movimento Nacional de Meninos e Meninas de Rua [MNMMR], Instituto Brasileiro de Analises Sociais e Econômicas [IBASE], and Nucleo de Estudos de Violencia de Universidade de São Paulo [NEV-USP] 1992.

Chapter 5: Counting by Race

1. U.S. OMB 1997b: 58788.

2. Tabulation Working Group of the Interagency Committee for the Review of Standards for Data on Race and Ethnicity, "Provisional Guidance on the Implementation of the 1997 Standards for Federal Data on Race and Ethnicity" (Washington, D.C.: Office of Management and Budget), Feb. 17, 1999.

3. Ibid. pp. 21–22, 25.

4. Ibid. pp. 22, 26–27.

5. U.S. Bureau of the Census 1997; Pinal 1998; U.S. OMB 1999.

6. Pinal 1998, p. 12.

7. Ibid., p. 14.

8. U.S. OMB 1997b, p. 58788.

9. Nelson do Valle Silva 1995.

10. Nelson do Valle Silva 1996.

11. The pilot tests for the 2000 census were conducted in two cities in the states of Rio de Janeiro and Mato Grosso.

12. In Portuguese the question read: "Qual a sua côr ou raça? Branca, preta, amarela, indígena, parda" ("I prova piloto do censo demográfico 2000, questionàrio básico," IBGE form).

13. Two separate long forms were tested and the wording of the question was slightly different on each. Long form #1 read: "Qual(is) a (as) palavra(s) que melhor define(m) a sua origem? (Assinalar todos itens correspondentes à resposta da pessoa)." Long form #2 said the same, without the parenthetical instructions. "I prova piloto do censo demográfico 2000, questionário da amostra 1 and questionário da amostra 2," IBGE, 1997.

14. Wania Sant'Anna, "População negra em destaque," unpublished paper, CEBRAP, São Paulo, 1998.

15. Schwartzman 1998a.

16. Schwartzman 1998b quotes from Da Silva's bill.

17. Ibid.

18. Dos Santos 1998; Motta and de Oliveira 1998.

19. "Identidades sociais," *Jornal do Brasil* (Rio de Janeiro), Apr. 26, 1998, p. 10. In its view, the denunciation of Brazilian racial democracy does not mean that Brazilian racism, such as it is, is in any way equivalent to American racism. Brazilian society continues to be distinguished by the cordiality of its social relations and the richness and complexity of its social identities. Current attempts to reduce the many social categories that connote "racial mixture" into one or two distorts Brazilian culture. More important, such attempts sacrifice the richness of Brazilian ways in order to implement the American-style civil rights strategies aggressively advocated by domestic black activists.

20. Skidmore 1993b.

21. Degler 1971, p. 285.

22. Andrews 1996, p. 484.

23. Ibid., p. 497.

24. Hellwig 1992. For a useful summary article of the book's findings, see Hellwig 1990.

25. Needell 1995b.

26. Booth 1985; Bhrolcháin 1990.

27. Winthrop R. Wright 1990.

28. Oviedo 1992.

29. For Nazi German censuses, see Hughes 1958; Seltzer 1998. For South African censuses, see Ford 1994.

30. Hirschman 1987; Rafael 1993; Hirsch 1997.

31. Cohn 1987; Dirks 1992.

32. Deshpande and Sundar 1998.

33. Friedman 1996.

34. Roger Cohen 1994.

35. Uvin forthcoming.

Bibliography

NOTE: Anonymous Portuguese-language newspaper and magazine articles are listed in a separate subsection at the end of this Bibliography.

Adams, Mark B., ed. 1990. *The Wellborn Science: Eugenics in Germany, France, Brazil, and Russia.* New York: Oxford University Press.

Aldrich, Mark. 1979. "Progressive Economists and Scientific Racism: Walter Willcox and Black Americans, 1895–1910." *Phylon* 40, no. 1 (Spring): 11–13.

Alonso, William, and Paul Starr, eds. 1987. *The Politics of Numbers.* New York: Russell Sage Foundation.

Aluko, S. A. 1963. "How Many Nigerians? An Analysis of Nigeria's Census Problems, 1901–63." *Journal of Modern African Studies* 3: 371–92.

Alvarez, Sonia E. 1990. *Engendering Democracy in Brazil: Women's Movements in Transition Politics.* New Haven, Conn.: Yale University Press.

Alves, Maria Helena Moreira, 1985. *State and Opposition in Military Brazil.* Austin: University of Texas Press.

Alves, Marilda Dias. 1988. "O desenvolvimento do sistema estatístico nacional." Rio de Janeiro: Fundação IBGE.

American Anthropological Association. 1997. "Press Release/OMB 15." AAA web page, Oct.

Anderson, Benedict R. [1983] 1991. *Imagined Communities: Reflections on the Origin and Spread of Nationalism.* New York: Verso.

Anderson, Margo. 1988. *The American Census: A Social History.* New Haven, Conn.: Yale University Press.

Anderson, Margo, and Stephen E. Fienberg. 1999. *Who Counts?: The Politics of Census-Taking in Contemporary America.* New York: Russell Sage Foundation.

Anderson, Perry. 1962. "Portugal and the End of Ultra-Colonialism." Three-part article. *New Left Review,* May–June, July–Aug., Nov.–Dec.

Andrews, George Reid. 1991. *Blacks and Whites in São Paulo, Brazil, 1888–1988.* Madison: University of Wisconsin Press.

———. 1992a. "Black Political Protest in São Paulo, 1888–1988." *Journal of Latin American Studies* 24, no. 1 (Feb.): 147–71.

———. 1992b. "Racial Inequality in Brazil and the United States: A Statistical Comparison." *Journal of Social History* 26, no. 2: 230–62.

———. 1996. "Brazilian Racial Democracy, 1900–1990: An American Counterpoint." *Journal of Contemporary History* 31, no. 3 (July): 483–507.

———. 1997. "Black Workers in the Export Years: Latin America, 1880–1930." *International Labor and Working-Class History* 51 (Spring): 7–29.

Andrews, George Reid, and Herrick Chapman, eds. 1995. *The Social Construction of Democracy, 1870–1990.* New York: New York University Press.

Appadurai, Arjun. 1993. "Number in the Colonial Imagination." In *Orientalism and the Post-Colonial Predicament,* ed. Carol A. Breckenridge and Peter van der Veer, pp. 314–39. Philadelphia: University of Pennsylvania Press.

Appiah, K. Anthony. 1992. *In My Father's House: Africa in the Philosophy of Culture.* New York: Oxford University Press.

———. 1997. "The Multicultural Misunderstanding." *New York Review of Books,* Oct. 9, pp. 30–36.

Applebaum, Harvey M. 1964. "Miscegenation Statutes: A Constitutional and Social Problem." *Georgetown Law Journal* 53 (Fall): 49–91.

Aquino, Ruth de. 1991. "Lembranças do Brasil: Entrevista/Nelson Mandela." *O Dia* [Rio de Janeiro], Aug. 8.

Azevedo, Cecilia Maria Marinho de. 1987. *Onda negra, medo branco: o negro no imaginário das elites—século XIX.* São Paulo: Paz e Terra.

Azevedo, Fernando de. 1950. *Brazilian Culture: An Introduction to the Study of Culture in Brazil.* Translated by William Rex Crawford. New York: Macmillan.

Azevedo, Thales de. 1966. *Cultura e situação racial no Brasil.* Rio de Janeiro.

Balderrama, Francisco E., and Raymond Rodriguez. 1995. *Decade of Betrayal: Mexican Repatriation in the 1930s.* Albuquerque: University of New Mexico Press, 1995.

Ballentine, Chris. 1983. "'Who Is a Negro?' Revisited: Determining Individual Racial Status for Purposes of Affirmative Action." *University of Florida Law Review* 35, no. 4 (Fall): 683–700.

Banton, Michael. 1987. *Racial Theories.* New York: Cambridge University Press.

———. 1996. *International Action Against Racial Discrimination*. Oxford: Clarendon Press.

Bardaglio, Peter W. 1995. *Reconstructing the Household: Families, Sex, and the Law in the Nineteenth-Century South*. Chapel Hill: University of North Carolina Press.

Barkan, Elazar. 1992. *The Retreat of Scientific Racism*. New York: Cambridge University Press.

Bastide, Roger. 1965. "The Development of Race Relations in Brazil." In *Industrialization and Race Relations: A Symposium*, ed. Guy Hunter, pp. 9–29. New York: Oxford University Press.

Bastide, Roger, and Florestan Fernandes. 1959. *Brancos e negros em São Paulo*. São Paulo: Companhia Editora Nacional.

Beiner, Ronald, ed. 1995. *Theorizing Citizenship*. Albany: State University of New York Press.

Bender, Gerald J. 1978. *Angola under the Portuguese: The Myth and the Reality*. Berkeley and Los Angeles: University of California Press.

Bernstein, Barton J. 1992. "*Plessy v. Ferguson*: Conservative Sociological Jurisprudence." In *The Age of Jim Crow: Segregation from the End of Reconstruction to the Great Depression*, vol 4. of *Race, Law, and American History, 1700–1990*, ed. Paul Finkelman, pp. 2–11. New York: Garland.

Berquó, Elza. 1988. "Demografia da desigualdade: Algumas considerações sobre os negros no Brasil." *Novos Estudos CEBRAP* 21: 74–84.

Bhrolcháin, Máire Ní. 1990. "The Ethnicity Question for the 1991 Census: Background and Issues." *Ethnic and Racial Studies* 13, no. 4 (Oct.): 544.

Bieder, Robert E. 1982. *Science Encounters the Indian, 1820–1880: The Early Years of American Ethnology*. Norman: University of Oklahoma Press.

Bittencourt, Angelo. 1946. "A nossa gente de côr." *Boletim Geográfico* 45: 1145–46.

Booth, Heather. 1985. "Which 'Ethnic Question'? The Development of Questions Identifying Ethnic Origin in Official Statistics." *Sociological Review* 23, no. 2 (May).

Borges, Dain. 1993. "'Puffy, Ugly, Slothful and Inert': Degeneration in Brazilian Social Thought, 1880–1940." *Journal of Latin American Studies* 25, no. 2 (May): 235–56.

Brooke, James. 1994. "From Brazil's Misty Past, a Black Hero Emerges." *New York Times*, Nov. 30, p. A-4.

Burchell, Graham, Colin Gordon, and Peter Millers, eds. 1991. *The Foucault Effect: Studies in Governmentality*. Chicago: University of Chicago Press.

Burleigh, Michael, and Wolfgang Wipperman. 1991. *The Racial State: Germany, 1933–1945.* New York: Cambridge University Press.

Burma, John H. 1946. "The Measurement of Negro 'Passing.'" *American Journal of Sociology* 52, no. 1 (July): 18–22.

Burns, E. Bradford. 1970. *A History of Brazil.* New York: Columbia University Press.

Butler, Kim D. 1998. *Freedoms Given, Freedoms Won: Afro-Brazilians in Post-Abolition São Paulo and Salvador.* New Brunswick, N.J.: Rutgers University Press.

Butz, William P. 1985. "Data Confidentiality and Public Perceptions: The Case of the European Censuses." Paper presented at the Annual Meeting of the American Statistical Association, Las Vegas, Nevada, Aug. 5–8.

Byrd, Charles Michael. 1995. "From the Editor: About Race: The Census' One-Drop Rule." *Interracial Voice* web page, Sept.–Oct.

———. 1996a. "From the Editor: Kweisi Mfume: Perpetuating White 'Racial Purity'?" *Interracial Voice* web page, Mar.–Apr.

———. 1996b. "From the Editor: Why the Multiracial Community Must March on July 20th!" *Interracial Voice* web page, July.

———. 1996c. "Charles Byrd Speech at Multiracial Solidarity March." *Interracial Voice* web page, July.

———. 1997a. "From the Editor: Kweisi Mfume Just Doesn't Get It!" *Interracial Voice* web page, Mar.–Apr.

———. 1997b. "From the Editor: Leftist Socialism or Multiracial Libertarianism: Our Community's Two Choices?" *Interracial Voice* web page, Nov.–Dec.

———. 2000a. "Census 2000 Protest: Check American Indian." *Interracial Voice* web page, Jan.–Feb.

———. 2000b. "From the Editor: The Third Wave: Mediations on a New-Era Synthesis." *Interracial Voice* web page, Jan.–Feb.

Cartmill, Matt. 1998. "The Status of the Race Concept in Physical Anthropology." *American Anthropologist* 100, no.3 (Sept.): 651–60.

Cavalli-Sforza, L. Luca, Paolo Menozzi, and Alberto Piazza. 1994. *The History and Geography of Human Genes.* Princeton, N.J.: Princeton University Press.

Choldin, Harvey M. 1994. *Looking for the Last Percent: The Controversy over Census Undercounts.* New Brunswick, N.J.: Rutgers University Press.

———. 1986. "Statistics and Politics: The 'Hispanic Issue' in the 1980 Census." *Demography* 23, no. 3 (Aug.): 403–18.

Choldin, Harvey M., José Hernàndez, Leo Estrada, and David Alvirez. 1973. "Census Data and the Problem of Conceptually Defining the

Mexican American Population." *Social Science Quarterly* 53, no. 4 (Mar.): 671–87.

Cohen, Harold. 1948. "An Appraisal of the Legal Tests Used to Determine Who Is a Negro." *Cornell Law Quarterly* 34: 246–55.

Cohen, Jean L. 1985. "Strategy or Identity: New Theoretical Paradigms and Contemporary Social Movements." *Social Research* 52, no. 4: 663–716.

Cohen, Patricia Cline. 1982. *A Calculating People: The Spread of Numeracy in Early America.* Chicago: University of Chicago Press.

Cohen, Roger. 1994. "Macedonia Census Just Inflames the Dispute." *New York Times,* July 17, p. A-8.

Cohn, Bernard S. 1987. *An Anthropologist Among the Historians and Other Essays.* Oxford: Oxford University Press.

Colker, Ruth. 1996. *Hybrid: Bisexuals, Multiracials and Other Misfits under American Law.* New York: New York University Press.

Congressional Globe. 1950. 31st Cong., 1st sess.

Congressional Record. 1889. 50th Cong., 2d sess. Vol. 20.

Conrad, Robert. 1972. *The Destruction of Brazilian Slavery, 1850–1888.* Berkeley and Los Angeles: University of California Press.

———. 1983. *Children of God's Fire: A Documentary History of Brazilian Slavery: A Documentary History of Black Slavery in Brazil.* Princeton, N.J.: Princeton University Press.

Costa, Emília Viotti da. [1966] 1982. *Da senzala à colônia.* São Paulo: Livraria Editora Ciências Humanas.

———. [1985] 1988a. *The Brazilian Empire: Myths and Histories.* Chicago: Dorsey Press.

———. 1988b. "The Policy of Neglect or the Neglect of Policies?" Unpublished paper, Yale University, History Department.

Costa, Tereza Cristina N. Araújo. 1974. "O princípio classificatório 'côr,' sua complexidade e implicações para un estudo censitário." *Revista Brasileira de Geografia* 36, no. 3: 91–103.

———. 1987. "A classificação de 'côr' nas pesquisas do IBGE: Notas para uma discussão." *Cadernos de Pesquisas* 63 (Nov.): 14–16.

Cox, Oliver C. 1942. *Caste, Class and Race.* New York: Monthly Review Press.

Crenshaw, Kimberlé. 1988. "Race, Reform, and Retrenchment: Transformation and Legitimation in Antidiscrimination Law." *Harvard Law Review* 101, no. 7 (May): 1331–87.

Daniels, George, ed. 1972. *Nineteenth-Century American Science: A Reappraisal.* Evanston, Ill.: Northwestern University Press.

Daniels, Roger. 1982. "The Bureau of the Census and the Relocation of the

Japanese Americans: A Note and a Document." *Amerasia* 9, no. 1: 101–5.

Davidson, Katherine H., and Charlotte M. Ashby. 1964. *Preliminary Inventories: Records of the Bureau of the Census.* Washington, D.C.: National Archives and Records Service.

Davis, Abraham L., and Barbara Luck Graham. 1995. *The Supreme Court, Race, and Civil Rights.* London: Sage Publications.

Davis, David Brion. 1975. *The Problem of Slavery in the Age of Revolution, 1770–1823.* Ithaca, N.Y.: Cornell University Press.

Davis, Robert C. 1972. "The Beginning of American Social Research." In *Nineteenth-Century American Science: A Reappraisal,* ed. George Daniels, pp. 152–78. Evanston, Ill.: Northwestern University Press.

Degler, Carl N. 1971. *Neither Black nor White: Slavery and Race Relations in Brazil and the United States.* New York: Macmillan.

Denton, Nancy A. 1997. "Racial Identity and Census Categories: Can Incorrect Categories Yield Correct Information?" *Law and Inequality* 15, no. 1: 83–97.

Deshpande, Satish, and Nandini Sundar. 1998. "Caste and the Census: Implications for Society and the Social Sciences." *Economic and Political Weekly,* Aug. 8, pp. 2157–59.

Dikötter, Frank. 1992. *The Discourse of Race in Modern China.* Stanford: Stanford University Press.

———. 1997. *The Construction of Racial Identities in China and Japan.* Honolulu: University of Hawai'i Press.

Dippie, Brian. 1982. *The Vanishing American: White Attitudes and U.S. Indian Policy.* Middletown, Conn.: Wesleyan University Press.

Dirks, Nicholas B. 1992. "Castes of Mind." *Representations* 37 (Winter 1992): 56–78.

Dos Santos, Ivanir. 1998. "Quantos somos?" *Jornal do Brasil* [Rio de Janeiro], Apr. 22.

Douglas, Nathan. 1996. "Semantic Equality." Speech delivered at the Multiracial Solidarity March, Washington, D.C., July 20. *Interracial Voice* web page, July.

———. 1997. "Leaving the Scene of a Crime." Guest editorial, *Interracial Voice* web page, July–Aug.

Drescher, Seymour. 1988. "Brazilian Abolition in Comparative Perspective." *Hispanic American Historical Review* 68, no. 3 (Aug.): 440.

Dreyfus, Hubert L., and Paul Rabinow. 1982. *Michel Foucault: Beyond Structuralism and Hermeneutics.* Chicago: University of Chicago Press.

D'Souza, Dinesh. 1996. "The 'One-Drop-of-Blood' Rule." *Forbes,* Dec. 2.

Du Bois, W. E. B. [1935] 1985. *Black Reconstruction in America: An Essay*

Toward a History of the Part Which Black Folk Played in the Attempt to Reconstruct Democracy in America, 1860–1880. New York: Atheneum.

Durão, Vera Saavedra. 1991. "Pesquisador devera ser treinado." *Gazeta Mercantil,* Mar. 21, 1991, p. 3.

Dzidzienyo, Anani. 1971. "The Position of Blacks in Brazilian Society." *Minority Rights Group Report* 7: 2–11.

Eakin, Marshall C. 1985. Eakin, "Race and Identity: Sílvio Romero, Science, and Social Thought in Late Nineteenth-Century Brazil." *Luso-Brazilian Review* 22, no. 2: 151–74.

Eccles, Peter R. 1991. "Culpados atè prova em contràrio: Os negros, a lei e os direitos humanos no Brasil." *Estudos Afro-Asiáticos,* 135–63.

Eckard, E. W. 1947. "How Many Negros 'Pass'?" *American Journal of Sociology* 52, no. 6 (May): 498–500.

Eckler, A. Ross. 1972. *The Bureau of the Census.* New York: Praeger.

Eckstein, Susan, ed. 1989. *Power and Popular Protest: Latin American Social Movements.* Berkeley and Los Angeles: University of California Press.

Edmonston, Barry, and Charles Schultze, eds. 1995. *Modernizing the U.S. Census.* Washington, D.C.: National Academy Press.

Edmonston, Barry, Joshua Goldstein, and Juanita Tamayo Lott, eds. 1996. *Spotlight on Heterogeneity: The Federal Standards for Racial and Ethnic Classification.* Washington, D.C.: National Academy Press.

Elkins, Stanley. 1959. *Slavery: A Problem in American Institutional and Intellectual Life.* Chicago: University of Chicago Press.

Escobar, Arturo, and Sonia E. Alvarez, eds. 1992. *The Making of Social Movements in Latin America.* Boulder, Colo.: Westview Press.

Evinger, Suzann. 1995. "How Shall We Measure Our Nation's Diversity?" *Chance* 8, no. 1: 7–14.

Farley, Reynolds. 1991. "The New Census Question about Ancestry: What Did It Tell Us?" *Demography* 28, no. 3: 411–29.

Fehrenbacher, Don E. 1981. *Slavery, Law and Politics.* New York: Oxford University Press.

Feinberg, Stephen E. 1992. "A Brief History of Statistics in Three and One-Half Chapters: A Review Essay." *Statistical Science* 7, no. 2: 208–25.

Fernandes, Adriana. 1991. "Censo vem com um ano de atraso e muita polêmica." *Jornal do Commercio,* Aug. 18–19, p. 25.

Fernandes, Florestan. [1965] 1978. *A integração do negro na sociedade de classes.* 3d ed. 2 vols. São Paulo: Ática. Translated by Jacqueline D. Skiles, A. Brunel, and Arthur Rothwell, ed. Phyllis B. Eveleth, as *The Negro in Brazilian Society* (New York: Columbia University Press, 1969).

Ferretti, Mundicarmo M. R. 1986. "Côr e identidade social." *Cadernos de Pesquisas: São Luis* 2, no. 2: 156–60.

Fields, Barbara Jeanne. 1982. "Race and Ideology in American History." In *Region, Race, and Reconstruction*, ed. J. Morgan Kousser and James M. McPherson, pp. 143–77. New York: Oxford University Press.

———. 1990. "Slavery, Race, and Ideology in the United States of America." *New Left Review* 181 (May–June): 95–118.

Figueira, Vera Moreira. 1990. "O preconceito racial na escola." *Estudos Afro-Asiáticos* 18: 63–72.

Finkelman, Paul. 1986. "Prelude to the Fourteenth Amendment: Black Legal Rights in the Antebellum North." *Rutgers Law Journal* 17: 415–82.

———, ed. 1992a. *Race and Law Before Emancipation*. Vol. 2 of *Race, Law, and American History, 1700–1990*. New York: Garland.

———, ed. 1992b. *The Age of Jim Crow: Segregation from the End of Reconstruction to the Great Depression*. Vol. 4 of *Race, Law, and American History, 1700–1990*. New York: Garland.

———. 1993a. "The Color of Law." *Northwestern University Law Review* 87.

———. 1993b. "The Crime of Color." *Tulane Law Review* 67: 2075.

———. 1996. *Slavery and the Founders: Race and Liberty in the Age of Jefferson*. New York: M. E. Sharpe.

Fletcher, Michael A. 1997. "Woods Put Personal Focus on Mixed-Race Identity." *Washington Post*, Apr. 23, p. A-1.

Flynn, Peter. 1978. *Brazil: A Political Analysis*. Boulder, Colo.: Westview Press.

Fogel, William. 1989. *Without Consent or Contract: The Rise and Fall of American Slavery*. New York: Norton.

Foner, Eric. 1988. *Reconstruction: America's Unfinished Revolution, 1863–1877*. New York: Harper & Row.

Fontaine, Pierre Michel, ed. 1985. *Race, Class and Power in Brazil*. Los Angeles: UCLA Center for Afro-American Studies.

Ford, Christopher A. 1994. "Administering Identity: The Determination of 'Race' in Race-Conscious Law." *California Law Review* 82: 1231–85.

Fórum Estadual sobre o Ensino da História das Civilizações Africanas no Escola Pública. 1991. *A Africa na escola brasileira: Relatório do 1° Fórum estadual sobre o ensino da história das civilizações africanas na escola pública, Rio de Janeiro, junho–agosto de 1991*. Rio de Janeiro: Governo do Estado do Rio de Janeiro.

Foucault, Michel. 1979. *Discipline and Punish: The Birth of the Prison*. Translated by Alan Sheridan. New York: Random House, Vintage Books.

Fredrickson, George M. 1971. *The Black Image in the White Mind: The Debate on Afro-American Character and Destiny, 1817–1914.* New York: Harper & Row.

Freyre, Gilberto. [1950] 1966. *Quase política: 9 discursos e 1 conferência, mandados publicar por um grupo de amigos.* Rio de Janeiro: José Olympio.

———. 1978. "O Brasileiro como uma além-raça." *Folha de São Paulo,* May 21.

———. 1979. "Brasileiro—sua côr?" *Folha de São Paulo,* Dec. 5, p. 3.

———. [1946] 1986a. *The Masters and the Slaves: A Study in the Development of Brazilian Civilization.* Translated by Samuel Putnam. Berkeley and Los Angeles: University of California Press. Originally published as *Casa-grande & senzala: Formação da família brasileira sob o regimen de economia patriarchal* (Rio de Janeiro: Maia & Schmidt, 1933).

———. [1970] 1986b. *Order and Progress: Brazil from Monarchy to Republic.* Translated by Rod W. Horton. Berkeley and Los Angeles: University of California Press. Originally published as *Ordem e progresso* (Rio de Janeiro: José Olympio, 1959).

Friedman, Victor A. 1996. "Observing the Observers: Language, Ethnicity and Power in the 1994 Macedonian Census and Beyond." In *Toward Comprehensive Peace in Southeast Europe: Conflict Prevention in the South Balkans,* ed. Barnett R. Rubin, pp. 81–105. New York: Twentieth Century Fund Press.

Fry, Peter. 1996. "Color and the Rule of Law in Brazil." Paper presented at conference on The Rule of Law and the Underprivileged in Latin America, University of Notre Dame, Nov. 9–10.

Galanter, Marc. 1984. *Competing Equalities: Law and the Backward Classes in India.* Berkeley and Los Angeles: University of California Press.

Gates, Henry Louis, Jr. 1986. "Introduction: Writing 'Race' and the Difference It Makes." In *Race, Writing, and Difference,* ed. Henry Louis Gates, pp. 1–20. Chicago: University of Chicago Press.

———. 1996. "White Like Me." *New Yorker,* June 17, pp. 66–81.

Gilanshah, Bijan. 1993. "Multiracial Minorities: Erasing the Color Line." *Law and Inequality* 12: 183–204.

Glazer, Nathan. 1996. "Race for the Cure." *New Republic,* Oct. 7, p. 29.

Glèlè-Ahanhanzo, Maurice (Special Rapporteur on Contemporary Forms of Racism, Racial Discrimination, Xenopbobia and Related Intolerance). 1995. "Implementation of the Programme of Action for the Third Decade to Combat Racism and Racial Discrimination." Commission on

Human Rights, United Nations Economic and Social Council, 23 January, New York.

Goldberg, David Theo, ed. 1990. *Anatomy of Racism*. Minneapolis: University of Minnesota Press.

———. 1992. "The Semantics of Race." *Ethnic and Racial Studies* 15, no. 4 (Oct.): 543–69.

Goldstein, Judith, and Robert Keohane. 1993. *Ideas and Foreign Policy: Beliefs, Institutions, and Political Change*. Ithaca, N.Y.: Cornell University Press.

Gondim, Abnor. 1991. "Indios Caiapó barram recenseadores no Pará: Cacique diz que censo ajuda a reduzir reservas." *Folha de São Paulo*, Nov. 14, p. 9.

Goodman, Alan H. 1997. "Bred in the Bone?" *The Sciences*, Mar.–Apr.

Gordon, Eugene. 1951. *An Essay on Race Amalgamation*. Ministry of Foreign Relations booklet. Rio de Janeiro: Service of Publications.

Gossett, Thomas. 1963. *Race: The History of an Idea in America*. Dallas: Methodist University Press.

Gotanda, Neil. 1991. "A Critique of 'Our Constitution is Color-Blind.'" *Stanford Law Review* 44, no. 1 (Nov.): 1–68.

Gould, Stephen Jay. [1981] 1996. *The Mismeasure of Man*. New York: Norton.

Goyer, Doreen S., and Elaine Domschke. 1983. *The Handbook of National Population Censuses: Latin America and the Caribbean, North America and Oceania*. Westport, Conn.: Greenwood Press.

Graham, Richard, ed. 1990. *The Idea of Race in Latin America, 1870–1940*. Austin: University of Texas Press.

Graham, Susan. 1997. "From the Executive Director." Project RACE web page, Oct. 29.

Greenberg, Stanley. 1982. *Race and State in Capitalist Development*. New Haven, Conn.: Yale University Press.

Grob, Gerald N. 1978. *Edward Jarvis and the Medical World of Nineteenth-Century America*. Knoxville: University of Tennessee Press.

Gross, Jane. 1996. "UC Berkeley at Crux of New Multiracial Consciousness and Diversity." *Los Angeles Times*, Jan. 9, p. A-1.

Grosz, Gabe. 1997. "In the News—Interview with Charles Michael Byrd." *Interrace Magazine* 37: 12.

Guilhermino, Luiz. 1991. "IBGE encontra dificuldades para contratar as pessoas que iniciarão no próximo semestre o censo." *O Estado de São Paulo*, Apr. 9, p. 14.

———. 1991. "IBGE vai gastar U.S.$ 250 milhões para fazer censo." *O Estado de São Paulo*, July 13, p. 8.

Hacking, Ian. 1986. "Making Up People." In *Reconstructing Individualism: Autonomy, Individuality, and the Self in Western Thought*, ed. Thomas Heller, Morton Susna, and David Wellberg, pp. 222–36. Stanford: Stanford University Press.

———. 1990. *The Taming of Chance*. Cambridge: Cambridge University Press.

———. 1991. "How Should We Do the History of Statistics?" In *The Foucault Effect: Studies in Governmentality*, ed. Graham Burchell, Colin Gordon, and Peter Miller, pp. 181–95. Chicago: University of Chicago Press.

Haller, John S., Jr. 1971. *Outcasts from Evolution: Scientific Attitudes of Racial Inferiority, 1859–1900*. Urbana: University of Illinois Press.

Hanchard, Michael G. 1994. *Orpheus and Power: The "Movimento Negro" Rio de Janiero and São Paulo, Brazil*. Princeton, N.J.: Princeton University Press.

Haney-Lopez, Ian. 1996. *White by Law: The Legal Construction of Race*. New York: New York University Press.

Harris, Cheryl. 1993. "Whiteness as Property." *Harvard Law Review* 106, no. 8: 1709–91.

Harris, Marvin. 1970. "Referential Ambiguity in the Calculus of Brazilian Racial Identity." *Southwestern Journal of Anthropology* 26: 1–14.

———. [1964] 1980. *Patterns of Race in the Americas*. Westport, Conn.: Greenwood Publishers.

Harris, Marvin, and Conrad Kotak. 1963. "The Structural Significance of Brazilian Categories." *Sociologia* 25, no. 3 (1963): 203–8.

Harris, Marvin, Josildeth Gomes Consorte, Joseph Lang, and Bryan Byrne. 1993. "Who Are the Whites? Imposed Census Categories and the Racial Demography of Brazil." *Social Forces* 72, no. 2 (Dec.): 451–62

Hartman, Chester. 1997. *Double Exposure: Poverty and Race in America*. New York: M. E. Sharpe.

Hartz, Louis, ed. 1964. *The Founding of New Societies*. New York: Harcourt, Brace & World.

Hasenbalg, Carlos. 1979. *Discriminação e desigualdades raciais no Brasil*. Rio de Janeiro: Graal.

Hasenbalg, Carlos, and Nelson do Valle Silva. 1988. *Estructura social, mobilidade e raça*. Rio de Janeiro: Vertice and IUPERJ.

Hasenbalg, Carlos, Nelson do Valle Silva, and Luiz Claudio Barcelos. 1989. "Notas sobre miscigenação racial no Brasil." *Estudos Afro-Asiáticos* 16: 188–97.

Hellwig, David J. 1990. "Racial Paradise or Run-Around? Afro-North American Views of Race Relations in Brazil." *American Studies* 31, no. 2: 43–60.

———, ed. 1992. *African-American Reflections on Brazil's Racial Paradise*. Philadelphia: Temple University Press.

Henkin, Louis. 1990. *The Age of Rights*. New York: Columbia University Press, 1990.

Hernàndez, Jose, Leo Estrada, and David Alvírez. 1973. "Census Data and the Problem of Conceptually Defining the Mexican American Population." *Social Science Quarterly* 53, no. 4 (Mar.): 671–87.

Hernández, Tanya Katerí. 1988. "'Multiracial' Discourse: Racial Classifications in an Era of Color-Blind Jurisprudence." *Maryland Law Review* 57, no. 1: 98–173.

Hickman, Christine B. 1997. "The Devil and the One Drop Rule: Racial Categories, African Americans, and the U.S. Census." *Michigan Law Review* 95, no. 5: 1161–1265.

Higginbotham, A. Leon, Jr. 1978. *In the Matter of Color: Race and the American Legal Process*. New York: Oxford University Press.

———. 1996. *Shades of Freedom: Racial Politics and the Presumptions of the American Legal Process*. New York: Oxford University Press.

Higginbotham, Evelyn Brooks. 1992. "African-American Women's History and the Metalanguage of Race." *Signs: Journal of Women in Culture and Society* 17, no. 2: 251–74.

Hirsch, Francine. 1997. "The Soviet Union as a Work-in-Progress: Ethnographers and the Category *Nationality* in the 1926, 1937, and 1939 Censuses." *Slavic Review* 56, no.2: 251–78.

Hirschman, Charles. 1986. "The Making of Race in Colonial Malaya: Political Economy and Racial Ideology." *Sociological Forum* 1, no. 2: 330–61.

———. 1987. "The Meaning and Measurement of Ethnicity in Malaysia: An Analysis of Census Classifications." *Journal of Asian Studies* 46, no. 3 (Aug.): 555–82.

Hoffman, Frederick L. 1896. *Race Traits and Tendencies of the American Negro*. New York: American Economic Association and Macmillan Co.

Hollinger, David. 1995. *Postethnic America: Beyond Multiculturalism*. New York: Basic Books.

Holloway, Thomas P. 1977. "Immigration and Abolition: The Transition from Slave to Free Labor in the São Paulo Coffee Zone." In *Essays Concerning the Socioeconomic History of Brazil and Portuguese India*, ed. Dauril Alden and Warren Dean. Gainesville: University Presses of Florida.

———. 1980. *Immigrants on the Land: Coffee and Society in São Paulo, 1886–1934*. Chapel Hill: University of North Carolina Press.

Horowitz, Donald L. 1985. *Ethnic Groups in Conflict*. Berkeley and Los Angeles: University of California Press.

Horsman, Reginald. 1981. *Race and Manifest Destiny: The Origins of American Racial Anglo-Saxonism.* Cambridge, Mass.: Harvard University Press.

———. 1987. *Josiah Nott of Mobile: Southerner, Physician, and Racial Theorist.* Baton Rouge: Louisiana State University Press.

Hughes, Everett C. 1958. "Census Problems of Racial Enumeration." In *Race: Individual and Collective Behavior,* ed. Edgar T. Thompson and Everett C. Hughes, pp. 544–49. Glencoe, Ill.: Free Press.

Instituto Brasileiro de Análises Sociais e Econômicas. 1991. "Temas relevantes para produção de novos indicadores socio-econômicos sobre a população negra e mestiça." Typewritten transcript of seminar proceedings. Rio de Janeiro, Sept. 28.

Instituto Brasileiro de Geográfia e Estatística [IBGE]. 1950. "Estudos sobre a composição da população do Brasil segundo a côr." In *Estudos de Estatística Teórica e Aplicada, Estatística Demográfica.* Rio de Janeiro: Fundação IBGE.

———. 1969. "Ata dos trabalhos: A quesito côr no censo de 1970." 6a Sessão Ordinária [Sept. 9], Comissão Censitária Nacional.

———. 1970a. *Estudos de estatística teórica e aplicada, contribuições para o estudo da demográfica do Brasil.* 2d ed. Rio de Janiero: Fundação IBGE.

———. 1976. Departamento de Estatísticas de População e Sociais. "Resultados da apuração de Boletim Especial l.02 da PNAD 76." Vol. 1. Rio de Janeiro: Fundação IBGE.

———. 1980. "Considerações sobre os censos nacionais." Rio de Janeiro: Fundação IBGE.

———. 1995. *Giorgio Mortara: Publicação Comemorativa do Centenario de Nascimento.* Rio de Janeiro: Fundação IBGE.

Instituto de Pesquisa das Culturas Negras. 1990. "Racismo e machismo de todo dia"[Everyday Racism and Sexism].

Inter-American Statistical Institute. 1953. *The Story of the 1950 Census of the Americas.* Washington, D.C.: Inter-American Statistical Institute.

Jackson, Walter A. 1990. *Gunnar Myrdal and America's Conscience: Social Engineering and Racial Liberalism, 1938–1987.* Chapel Hill: University of North Carolina Press.

Jacobson, Matthew Frye. 1998. *Whiteness of a Different Color: European Immigrants and the Alchemy of Race.* Cambridge, Mass.: Harvard University Press.

Johnson, Ollie A., III. 1998. "Racial Representation and Brazilian Politics: Black Members of the National Congress, 1983–1999." *Journal of Interamerican Studies and World Affairs* 40, no. 4 (Winter): 97–117.

Joint Canada–United States Conference on the Measurement of Ethnicity.

1993. *Challenges of Measuring an Ethnic World: Science, Politics and Reality. Proceedings of the Joint Canada–United States Conference on the Measurement of Ethnicity, April 1–3, 1992.* Ottawa: Statistics Canada; Washington, D.C.: U.S. Dept. of Commerce, Economics and Statistics Administration, Bureau of the Census.

Jordan, Winthrop D. 1968. *White over Black: American Attitudes Toward the Negro, 1550–1812.* Chapel Hill: University of North Carolina Press.

Keck, Margaret. 1987. "The New Unionism in the Brazilian Transition." In *Democratizing Brazil: Problems of Transition and Consolidation,* ed. Alfred Stepan, pp. 252–96. New York: Oxford University Press.

———. 1992. *The Workers' Party and Democratization in Brazil.* New Haven, Conn.: Yale University Press.

Kelsey, Vera. 1940. *Seven Keys to Brazil.* New York: Funk & Wagnalls.

Kettner, James H. 1978. *The Development of American Citizenship, 1608–1870.* Chapel Hill: University of North Carolina Press.

King, Desmond. 1995. *Separate and Unequal: Black Americans and the U.S. Federal Government.* New York: Oxford University Press.

Klein, Herbert S. 1986. *African Slavery in Latin America and the Caribbean.* New York: Oxford University Press.

Kolchin, Peter. 1993. *American Slavery, 1619–1877.* New York: Hill & Wang.

Kousser, J. Morgan, and James M. McPherson, eds. 1982. *Region, Race, and Reconstruction.* New York: Oxford University Press.

Krieger, Nancy. 1987. "Shades of Difference: Theoretical Underpinnings of the Medical Controversy on Black/White Differences in the United States, 1830–1870." *International Journal of Health Services* 17, no. 2: 259–78.

Kymlicka, Will. 1995. *Multicultural Citizenship.* New York: Oxford University Press.

Lamounier, Bolívar. 1973. "Côr." *Cadernos CEBRAP* 15: 27–37.

———. 1989. "Brazil: Inequality Against Democracy." In *Democracy in Developing Countries: Latin America,* ed. Larry Diamond, Juan J. Linz, and Seymour Martin Lipset, pp. 111–57. Boulder, Colo.: Lynne Rienner.

Larson, Edward J. 1995. *Sex, Race, and Science: Eugenics in the Deep South.* Baltimore: Johns Hopkins University Press.

Lauren, Paul Gordon. 1988. *Power and Prejudice: The Politics and Diplomacy of Racial Discrimination.* Boulder, Colo.: Westview Press.

Lavin, Michael R. 1996. *Understanding the Census.* Kenmore, N.Y.: Epoch Books.

Leal, Luciana Nunes. 1990. "Brasil: 150 milhões em 90." *Jornal do Brasil* [Rio de Janeiro], Jan. 20, p. 5.

Le Espiritu, Yen. 1992. *Asian-American Panethnicity: Bridging Institutions and Identities.* Philadelphia: Temple University Press.

Lee, Sharon M. 1993. "Racial Classification in the U.S. Census, 1890–1990." *Racial and Ethnic Studies* 16, no. 1: 75–88.

Lesser, Jeffrey. 1995. *Welcoming the Undesirables: Brazil and the Jewish Question.* Berkeley and Los Angeles: University of California Press.

Levine, Robert M. 1970. *The Vargas Regime: The Critical Years, 1934–1938.* New York: Columbia University Press.

———. N.d. "Urban Workers under the Brazilian Republic, 1889–1937." Unpublished paper.

Lewontin, R. C., Steven Rose, and Leon J. Kamin. 1984. *Not in Our Genes: Biology, Ideology, and Human Nature.* New York: Pantheon Books.

Lieberson, Stanley, and Mary C. Waters. 1988. *From Many Strands: Ethnic and Racial Groups in Contemporary America.* New York: Russell Sage Foundation.

Litwack, Leon F. 1992. "The Federal Government and the Free Negro." In *Race, Law, and American History 1700–1990,* ed. Paul Finkelman, vol. 2: *Race and Law Before Emancipation,* pp. 313–30. New York: Garland.

———. 1967. *North of Slavery: The Negro in the Free States, 1790–1860.* Chicago: University of Chicago Press.

Lofgren, Charles A. 1987. *The Plessy Case: A Legal-Historical Interpretation.* New York: Oxford University Press.

Logan, Rayford. 1997. *The Betrayal of the Negro: From Rutherford B. Hayes to Woodrow Wilson.* New York: Da Capo Press. Originally published as *The Negro in American Life and Thought: The Nadir, 1877–1981* (New York: Dial Press, 1954).

Lombardo, Paul A. 1988. "Miscegenation, Eugenics, and Racism: Historical Footnotes to *Loving v. Virginia.*" *Davis Law Review* 21: 421–52, 444.

Lovell, Peggy. 1991. *Desigualidade racial no Brasil contemporâneo.* Belo Horizonte: MGSP Editores.

———. 1994. "Race, Gender, and Development in Brazil." *Latin American Research Review* 29, no. 3: 7–35.

Lovell, Peggy A., and Charles H. Wood. 1998. "Skin Color, Racial Identity, and Life Chances in Brazil." *Latin American Perspectives* 25, no. 3 (May): 90–109.

Lovell, W. George, and Christopher H. Lutz. 1994. "Conquest and Population: Maya Demography in Historical Perspective." *Latin American Research Review* 29, no. 2: 137.

Lowry, Ira S. 1982. "The Science and Politics of Ethnic Enumeration." In *Ethnicity and Public Policy*, ed. Winston A. van Horne, pp. 42–61. Milwaukee: University of Wisconsin System, American Ethnic Studies Coordinating Committee/Urban Corridor Consortium.

Lyncott-Haims, Julie C. 1994. "Where Do Mixed Babies Belong? Racial Classification in America and Its Implications for Transracial Adoption." *Harvard Civil Rights–Civil Liberties Law Review* 29, no. 2 (Summer): 531–58.

Mackenzie, Donald A. 1981. *Statistics in Britain, 1865–1930: The Social Construction of Scientific Knowledge*. Edinburgh: Edinburgh University Press.

Magocsi, Paul Robert. 1987. "Are the Armenians Really Russians?—Or How the U.S. Census Bureau Classifies America's Ethnic Groups." *Government Publications Review* 14: 133–68.

Mainwaring, Scott. 1989. "Grassroots Popular Movements and the Struggle for Democracy: Nova Iguaçu." In *Democratizing Brazil*, ed. Alfred Stepan, pp. 168–204. New York: Oxford University Press.

Mangum, Charles S. 1940. *The Legal Status of the Negro*. Chapel Hill: University of North Carolina Press.

Maram, Sheldon L. 1979. "Urban Labor and Social Change in the 1920s." *Luzo-Brazilian Review* 16, no. 2: 215–23.

———. 1977. "Labor and the Left in Brazil, 1890–1921: A Movement Aborted." *Hispanic American Historical Review* 57, no. 2: 254–72.

March, James G., and Johan P. Olsen. 1984. "The New Institutionalism: Organizational Factors in Political Life." *American Political Science Review* 78: 734–49.

Marriot, Michel. 1996. "Multiracial Americans Ready to Claim Their Own Identity." *New York Times,* July 20, p. A-1.

Marshall, T. H., and Tom Bottomore. [1950] 1992. *Citizenship and Social Class*. Concord, Mass.: Pluto Press.

Marx, Anthony. 1998. *Making Race and Nation: A Comparison of the United States, South Africa and Brazil*. New York: Cambridge University Press.

Matta, Roberto da. 1981. *Relativizando: Uma introdução à antropologia social*. Petrópolis: Vozes.

Matthews, Linda. 1996. "More than Identity Rides on a New Racial Category." *New York Times,* July 6, pp. A-1, 7, col. 3.

McAdam, Doug. 1982. *Political Process and the Development of Black Insurgency, 1930–1970*. Chicago: University of Chicago Press.

———. 1996. "Conceptual Origins, Current Problems, Future Directions." In *Comparative Perspectives on Social Movements: Political*

Opportunities, Mobilizing Structures, and Cultural Framings, ed. Doug McAdam, John D. McCarthy, and Mayer N. Zald, pp. 23–40. Cambridge: Cambridge University Press.

McNeil, Donald G. 1996. "Who Counts in South Africa? Finally, Everyone." *New York Times,* Oct. 30, p. A4.

Medeiros, Jarbas. 1978. *Ideologia autoritária no Brasil, 1930–1945.* Rio de Janeiro: Editora da Fundação Getúlio Vargas.

Mencke, John G. 1979. *Mulattoes and Race Mixture: American Attitudes and Images, 1865–1918.* Ann Arbor, Mich.: UMI Research Press.

Mendonca, Yedda Borges de. 1979. "Roteiro para uma monografia sobre a história do I.B.G.E." Rio de Janeiro: IBGE Central Library.

Mendonca, Yedda Borges de, and Marilda Dias Alves. 1988. "O desenvolvimento do sistema estatístico nacional." Rio de Janeiro: Fundação IBGE.

Merridale, Catherine. 1996. "The 1937 Census and the Limits of Stalinist Rule." *Historical Journal* 39, no. 1: 225–40.

Mitchell, Michael. 1977. "Racial Consciousness and the Political Attitudes of Blacks in São Paulo, Brazil." Ph.D. diss., Indiana University.

———. 1983. "Race, Legitimacy and the State in Brazil." Paper presented at the Latin American Studies Association Meetings, Mexico City, Sept. 29–Oct. 1, 1983.

———. 1985. "Blacks and the Abertura Democrática." In *Race, Class, and Power in Brazil,* ed. Pierre Michel-Fontaine, pp. 95–119. Los Angeles: Center for Afro-American Studies.

Mitroff, Ian I., Richard O. Mason, and Vincent P. Barabba. 1983. *The 1980 Census: Policymaking amid Turbulence.* Lexington, Mass.: Lexington Books.

Moffett, Matt. 1996. "Seeking Equality: A Racial 'Democracy' Begins Painful Debate on Affirmative Action." *Wall Street Journal,* Aug. 6, p. A-4.

Montagu, Ashley. 1964. *The Concept of Race.* New York: Free Press.

———. 1965. *The Idea of Race.* Lincoln: University of Nebraska Press.

———. 1972. *Statement on Race: An Annotated Elaboration and Exposition of the Four Statements on Race Issued by the United Nations Educational, Scientific, and Cultural Organization.* 3d ed. New York: Oxford University Press.

Morganthau, Tom. 1995. "What Color Is Black?" *Newsweek,* Feb. 13, pp. 63–72.

Morin, Richard. 1995. "A Distorted Image of Minorities." *Washington Post,* Oct. 8, p. A-1.

Morris, Thomas D. 1996. *Southern Slavery and the Law, 1619–1860.* Chapel Hill: University of North Carolina Press.

Mosse, George L. 1978. *Toward the Final Solution: A History of European Racism.* New York: Howard Fertig.

Mota, Carlos Guilherme. 1990. *Ideologia da cultura brasileira, 1933–1974.* São Paulo: Ática.

Motta, Athayde, and Eduardo H. P. de Oliveira. 1998. "Raça, côr e informação." *Jornal do Brasil* [Rio de Janeiro], May 1.

Moura, Clovis. 1988. *Sociologia do negro brasileiro.* São Paulo: Ática.

Movimento Nacional de Meninos e Meninas de Rua [MNMMR], Instituto Brasileiro de Análises Sociais e Econômicas [IBASE], [e] Núcleo de Estudos da Violência da Universidade de São Paulo [NEV-USP]. 1992. *Vidas em risco: Assassinatos de crianças e adolescentes no Brasil.* Rio de Janeiro: IBASE and MNMMR; São Paulo: NEV-USP.

Murray, Pauli, ed. 1951. *States' Laws on Race and Color.* Cincinnati, Ohio: Women's Division of Christian Service, 1951.

Nascimento, Abdias do. 1979. *Mixture or Massacre? Essays in the Genocide of a Black People.* New York: Afrodiaspora.

Needell, Jeffrey D. 1995a. "History, Race, and the State in the Thought of Oliveira Viana." *Hispanic American Historical Review* 75, no. 1: 3.

————. 1995b. "Identity, Race, Gender, and Modernity in the Origins of Gilberto Freyre's *Oeuvre*." *American Historical Review* 100, no. 1: 51–77.

Newby, I. A., ed. 1968. *The Development of Segregationist Thought.* Homewood, Ill.: Dorsey Press.

Noble, Kenneth B. 1992a. "After Nigeria's Census, Skeptic Count Is High." *New York Times,* June 4, p. A-13.

————. 1992b. "Nigeria Reveals Census' Total, 88.5 Million, and Little More." *New York Times,* Mar. 25, p. A-10.

Nobre, Carlos. 1990. "Negro quer declarar côr no censo." *O Dia* [Rio de Janeiro], May 13, p. 5.

Nogueira, Oracy. 1985. *Tanto preto quanto branco: Estudos de relações raciais.* São Paulo: T. A. Queiroz.

Nott, Josiah C. 1843. "The Mulatto a Hybrid—Probable Extermination of the Two Races if the Whites and Blacks Are Allowed to Intermarry." *American Journal of the Medical Sciences* 11 (July): 252–56.

————. 1847. "Statistics of Southern Slave Population." *Commercial Review* [De Bow's Review] 4, no. 3 (Nov.): 275–87.

Okamura, Raymond Y. 1981. "The Myth of Census Confidentiality." *Amerasia* 8, no. 2: 111–20.

Oliveira, Lúcia Elena Garcia de, Rosa Maria Porcaro, and Tereza Cristina N. Araújo. 1985. *O lugar do negro na força de trabalho.* Rio de Janeiro: IBGE.

Olusanya, P. O. 1983. *Nigeria's Demographic Delusion: A Critical Examination of the Census Controversy.* Lagos: Lagos University Press.

Omi, Michael. 1997. "Racial Identity and the State: The Dilemmas of Classification." *Law and Inequality* 15, no. 7: 7–23.

Omi, Michael, and Howard Winant. [1986] 1994. *Racial Formation in the United States: From the 1960s to the 1980s.* 2d ed. New York: Routledge.

Osborne, Lawrence. 1998. "The Numbers Game." *Lingua Franca*, Sept., pp. 49–58.

Ortiz, Renato. 1985. *Cultura brasileira e identidade nacional.* São Paulo: Editora Brasiliense.

Oviedo, Rodolfo Monge. 1992. "Are We or Aren't We?" *NACLA: Report on the Americas* 4: 19.

Pacheco, Moema do Poli T. 1987. "A questão da côr nas relações de um grupo de Baixa Renda." *Estudos Afro-Asiáticos* 14: 85–97.

Parada, Marcelo. 1992. "País faz de Conta." *Isto É Senhor,* Jan. 15, pp. 12–18.

Pascoe, Peggy. 1996. "Miscegenation Law, Court Cases, and the Ideologies of 'Race' in Twentieth-Century America." *Journal of American History* (June): 44–69.

Paskoff, Paul F., and Daniel J. Wilson, eds. 1982. *The Cause of the South: Selections from De Bow's Review, 1846–1867.* Baton Rouge: Louisiana State University Press.

Patterson, Orlando. 1997. "The Race Trap." *New York Times,* July 11, p. A-25.

Patriarca, Silvana. 1996. *Numbers and Nationhood: Writing Statistics in Nineteenth-Century Italy.* Cambridge: Cambridge University Press.

Payson, Kenneth E. 1996. "Check One Box: Reconsidering Directive No. 15 and the Classification of Mixed-Race People." *California Law Review* 84: 1233–91.

Penha, Eli Alves. 1993. *A criação do IBGE no contexto da centralização política do estado nôvo.* Rio de Janeiro: Fundação IBGE.

Perin, Kátia. 1991. "Censo 91, o Brasil se perde na mulditão." *Jornal da Tarde,* Dec. 10, p. 32.

Persons, Stow. 1987. *Ethnic Studies at Chicago, 1905–45.* Urbana: University of Illinois Press.

Petersen, William. 1997. *Ethnicity Counts.* New Brunswick, N.J.: Transaction Press.

Pickel, Mary Louise. 1993. "Race, Nationalism, and Domestic Politics in the 1934 Brazilian Constituent Assembly: The Debate on Japanese Immigration." M.A. thesis, University of Texas at Austin.

Pierson, Donald. 1967. *Negroes in Brazil.* Carbondale: Southern Illinois University Press.

Pinal, Jorge del. 1998. "Approaches for Developing Tabulations of Race Data from the 2000 Census." Paper presented at the Joint Meeting of the Commerce Secretary's 2000 Census Advisory Committee, the Census Advisory Committee of Professional Associations, and the Census Advisory Committees on the African American Population, on the American Indian and Alaska Native Populations, on the Asian and Pacific Islander Populations, and on the Hispanic Population. Alexandria, Va., June 3.

Pinto, Regina Pahim. 1987. "A representação do negro em livros didaticos de leitura." *Cadernos de Pesquisa: São Paulo* 63: 88–92.

———. 1996. "Problemas subjacentes ao processo de classificação da côr da população no Brasil." *IV Conferencia Nacional de Estatística: Textos Para Disçussão* 3 (May 27–31). Rio de Janeiro: Fundação IBGE.

Piza, Edith, and Fulvia Rosemberg. 1999. "Color in the Brazilian Census." In *From Indifference to Inequality: Race in Contemporary Brazil,* ed. Rebecca Reichmann, pp. 37–52. University Park, Pa.: Pennsylvania State University Press.

Podesta, Don. 1993a. "Black Slums Belie Brazil's Self-Image." *Washington Post,* Aug. 17, p. A-9.

———. 1993b. "In Much of South America, Descendants of Africans Are Getting Hard to Find." *Washington Post,* Aug. 17, p. A-13.

Poe, Janita. 1993. "Multiracial People Want a Single Name That Fits." *Chicago Tribune,* May 3, News-Section, p. 1.

Pompeu de Toledo, Roberto. 1998. *O presidente segundo o sociologo: Entrevista de Fernando Henrique Cardoso a Roberto Pompeu de Toledo.* São Paulo: Companhia das Letras.

Porter, Theodore M. 1986. *The Rise of Statistical Thinking.* Princeton, N.J.: Princeton University Press.

———. 1995. *Trust in Numbers: The Pursuit of Objectivity in Science and Public Life.* Princeton, N.J.: Princeton University Press.

Pressley, Sue Anne. 1994. "The Color of Love: In a Country Transfixed by Race, Black-White Couples Turn to Each Other for Support." *Washington Post,* Aug. 22, p. B-1.

Prewitt, Kenneth. 1987. "Public Statistics and Democratic Politics." In *The Politics of Numbers,* ed. William Alonso and Paul Starr, pp. 261–74. New York: Russell Sage Foundation.

Public Comments about Statistical Directive No. 15. 1994. Binders 1–4. Public Documents Room, New Executive Office Building, Washington, D.C.

Purcell, Susan Kaufman, and Riordan Roett, eds. 1997. *Brazil under Cardoso*. Boulder, Colo.: Lynne Rienner.

"Race: What Is It Good For?" 1994. *Discover Magazine*, special issue on "The Science of Race" (Nov.).

Racusen, Seth. 1996. "Public and Private Representations of Racial Discrimination: Contemporary Handling of Non-White Citizenship Claims in Sao Paulo, Brazil, 1993–1995." Paper presented at the Northeastern Political Science Association Meeting, Nov.

Rafael, Vincente L. 1993. "White Love: Surveillance and Nationalist Resistance in the U.S. Colonization of the Philippines." In *Cultures of United States Imperialism*, ed. Amy Kaplan and Donald Pease, pp. 185–228. Durham, N.C.: Duke University Press.

Reichmann, Rebecca. 1995. "Brazil's Denial of Race." *NACLA Report on the Americas* 23, no. 6 (May–June): 35–45.

———, ed. 1999. *From Indifference to Inequality: Race in Contemporary Brazil*. University Park, Pa.: Pennsylvania State University Press.

Reuter, Edward Byron. [1918] 1969. *The Mulatto in the United States: Including a Study of the Role of Mixed-Blood Races Throughout the World*. New York: New American Library.

Ricupero, Rubens. 1993. "Racial Harmony in Brazil." Letter to the editor. *Washington Post*, Aug. 30.

Ripley, C. Peter, ed. 1991. *Black Abolitionist Papers*. Vol. 3: *The United States, 1830–1846*. Chapel Hill: University of North Carolina Press.

Rodriguez, Clara E., and Hector Cordero-Guzman. 1992. "Placing Race in Context." *Ethnic and Racial Studies* 15, no. 4 (Oct.): 523–41.

Roett, Riordan. [1972] 1992. *Brazil: Politics in a Patrimonial Society*. 4th ed. Westport, Conn.: Praeger.

Root, Maria P. P., ed. 1992. *Racially Mixed People in America*. Newbury Park, Calif.: Sage Publications.

———. 1995. "The Multiracial Contribution to the Psychological Browning of America." In *American Mixed Race: The Culture of Microdiversity*, ed. Naomi Zack, pp. 231–36. Lanham, Md.: Rowman & Littlefield.

———. 1996. "A Bill of Rights for Racially Mixed People." In *The Multiracial Experience: Racial Borders as the New Frontier*, ed. id., pp. 3–14. Thousand Oaks, Calif.: Sage Publications, 1996.

Rosenwaike, Ira. 1993. "Ancestry in the United States Census, 1980–1990." *Social Science Research* 22: 383–90.

Rosin, Hanna. 1994. "Boxed In." *New Republic*, Jan. 3, p. 12.

Ross, Dorothy. 1991. *The Origins of American Social Science*. New York: Cambridge University Press.

Rufino, Joel. 1985. "O movimento negro e a crise brasileira." Unpublished paper.

Russett, Cynthia Eagle. 1976. *Darwin in America: The Intellectual Response, 1865–1912*. San Francisco: W. H. Freeman.

Saks, Eva. 1988. "Representing Miscegenation Law." *Raritan* 8, no. 2 (Fall): 39–69.

Salyer, Lucy E. 1995. *Laws Harsh as Tigers: Chinese Immigrants and the Shaping of Modern Immigration Law*. Chapel Hill: University of North Carolina Press.

Salzano, Francisco M. 1986. "Em busca das raizes." *Ciência Hoje* 5, no. 25: 48–53.

Salzano, Francisco M., and N. Freire-Maia. 1967. *Populações brasileiras: Aspectos demográficos, genéticos e antropológicos*. São Paulo: Companhia Editora Nacional.

Saunders, John. 1972. "Class, Color, and Prejudice: A Brazilian Counterpoint." In *Racial Tensions and National Identity*, ed. Ernest Q. Campbell, pp. 141–65. Nashville, Tenn.: Vanderbilt University Press.

Schemo, Diana Jean. 1996. "Among Glossy Blondes, a Showcase for Brazil's Black Faces." *New York Times*, Oct. 18, p. A-13.

Schiesel, Seth, and Robert L. Turner. 1996. "Is Race Obsolete?" *Boston Globe Magazine*, Sept. 22, p. 13.

Schwarcz, Lilia Moritz. 1999. *The Spectacle of the Races: Scientists, Institutions, and the Race Question in Brazil, 1870-1930*. Translated by Leland Guyer. New York: Hill and Wang. Originally published as *O espetáculo das raças: Cientistas, instituições, e questão racial no Brasil, 1870–1930*. São Paulo: Companhia das Letras, 1993.

Schwartzman, Simon. 1991a. *A Space for Science: The Development of the Scientific Community in Brazil*. University Park, Pa.: Pennsylvania State University Press. Originally published as *Formação da comunidade científica no Brasil* (Rio de Janeiro: Financiadora de Estudos e Projetos; São Paulo: Companhia Editora Nacional, 1979).

———. 1991b. "Changing Roles of New Knowledge: Research Institutions and Societal Transformations in Brazil." In *Social Sciences and Modern States: National Experiences and Theoretical Crossroads*, ed. Peter Wagner et al. New York: Cambridge University Press.

———. 1998a. "Estatísticas e identidades." *Jornal do Brasil* [Rio de Janeiro], May 5.

———. 1998b. "Cor discriminação e identidade social." *Jornal do Brasil* [Rio de Janeiro], Apr. 12.

Scott, James C. 1998. *Seeing Like a State: How Certain Schemes to Improve the Human Condition Have Failed*. New Haven, Conn.: Yale University Press.

Seiferth, Giralda. 1986. "A estrategia do branqueamento." *Ciência Hoje* 5, no. 25: 54–56.

Seltzer, William. 1998, "Population Statistics, the Holocaust, and the Nuremberg Trials." *Population and Development Review* 24, no. 3: 511–52.

Shklar, Judith N. 1991. *American Citizenship: The Quest for Inclusion.* Cambridge, Mass.: Harvard University Press.

Silva, Denise Ferreira da. 1989. "Revisitando a 'democracia racial': Raça e identidade nacional no pensamento brasileiro." *Estudos Afro-Asiáticos* 16: 157–70.

Silva, Jorge da. 1994. *Direitos civis e relações raciais no Brasil.* Rio de Janeiro: Luam Editora.

Silva, Nelson do Valle. 1994. "Uma nota sobre 'raça social.'" *Estudos Afro-Asiáticos* 26 (Sept.): 67–80.

———. 1985. "Updating the Cost of Not Being White in Brazil." In *Race, Class and Power in Brazil,* ed. Pierre-Michel Fontaine, pp. 42–55. Los Angeles: UCLA Center for Afro-American Studies.

———. 1996. "Morenidade: Modo de usar." *Estudos Afro-Asiáticos* 30 (Dec.): 79–95.

Simoneau, Karin. 1990. *South American Population Censuses since Independence: An Annotated Bibliography of Secondary Sources.* Madison: University of Wisconsin, Memorial Library.

Skidmore, Thomas. [1967] 1986. *Politics in Brazil 1930–1964: An Experiment in Democracy.* New York: Oxford University Press.

———. 1988. *The Politics of Military Rule in Brazil, 1964–1985.* New York: Oxford University Press.

———. 1992. "Fact and Myth: Discovering a Racial Problem in Brazil." Helen Kellogg Institute for International Studies Working Paper No. 173. Notre Dame, Ind.: University of Notre Dame.

———. [1974] 1993a. *Black into White: Race and Nationality in Brazilian Thought.* Durham, N.C.: Duke University Press.

———. 1993b. "Bi-racial U.S.A./Multi-racial Brazil: Is the Contrast Still Valid?" *Journal of Latin American Studies* 25 (1993): 373–86.

Smedley, Audrey. 1993. *Race in North America: Origin and Evolution of a Worldview.* Boulder, Colo.: Westview Press.

Smith, Rogers. 1997. *Civic Ideals: Conflicting Visions of Citizenship in U.S. History.* New Haven, Conn.: Yale University Press.

Snipp, Matthew C. 1986. "Who Are American Indians? Some Observations about the Perils and Pitfalls of Data for Race and Ethnicity." *Population Research and Policy Review* 5: 237–52.

Soares, Glaucio Ary Dillon, and Nelson do Valle Silva. 1987. "Urbanization, Race, and Class in Brazilian Politics." *Latin American Research Review* 22, no. 2: 155–76.

Somers, Margaret R. 1993. "Citizenship and the Place of the Public Sphere: Law, Community, and Political Culture in the Transition to Democracy." *American Sociological Review* 58 (Oct.): 587–620.

Stanton, William. 1968. *The Leopard's Spots: Scientific Attitudes Towards Race in America, 1815–59*. Chicago: University of Chicago Press.

Steinmo, Sven, Kathleen Thelen, and Frank Longstreth, eds. 1992. *Structuring Politics: Historical Institutionalism in Comparative Analysis*. New York: Cambridge University Press.

Stepan, Nancy Leys. 1982. *The Idea of Race in Science: Great Britain, 1800–1960*. Hamden, Conn.: Archon Books.

———. 1990. "Eugenics in Brazil: 1917–1940." In *The Wellborn Science: Eugenics in Germany, France, Brazil, and Russia*, ed. Mark Adams. New York: Oxford University Press.

———. 1991. *The Hour of Eugenics: Race, Gender, and Nation in Latin America*. Ithaca, N.Y.: Cornell University Press.

Stephenson, Gilbert Thomas. [1910] 1970. *Race Distinctions in American Law*. New York: Johnson Reprint Corp.

Stigler, Stephen M. 1990. *The History of Statistics: The Measurement of Uncertainty Before 1900*. Cambridge, Mass.: Harvard University Press.

Stocking, George. 1968. *Race, Culture and Evolution*. New York: Free Press.

Subervi-Velez, Federico, and Omar Souki Oliveira. 1991. "Negros (e outras etnias) em comerciais da televisão brasileira: Uma investigação exploratória." *Comunicação e Sociedade: Revista Semestral de Estudos de Comunicação* 17: 79–101.

Takaki, Ronald. 1989. *Strangers from a Different Shore: A History of Asian-Americans*. New York: Penguin Books.

Tannenbaum, Frank. 1947. *Slave and Citizen: The Negro in the Americas*. New York: Knopf.

Tarrow, Sidney. 1994. *Power in Movement: Social Movements, Collective Action, and Politics*. New York: Cambridge University Press.

Taylor, Charles. 1992. "The Politics of Recognition." In *Multiculturalism and the Politics of Recognition*, ed. Charles Taylor and Amy Gutmann, pp. 25–73. Princeton, N.J.: Princeton University Press.

Telles, Edward E., and Nelson Lim. 1998. "Does It Matter Who Answers the Race Question? Racial Classification and Income Inequality in Brazil." *Demography* 35, no. 4 (Nov.): 465–74.

Templeton, Alan R. "Human Races: A Genetic and Evolutionary Perspective." *American Anthropologist* 100, no. 3 (Sept.): 632–50.

Thernstrom, Stephan. 1992. "American Ethnic Statistics." In *Immigrants in Two Democracies: French and American Experience*, ed. Donald L. Horowitz and Gerard Noiriel. New York: New York University Press.

Thompson, Leonard. [1990] 1995. *A History of South Africa*. Rev. ed. New Haven, Conn.: Yale University Press.

Thornton, Russell. 1987. *American Indian Holocaust and Survival: A Population History since 1492*. Norman: University of Oklahoma Press.

Tienda, Maria, and Vilma Ortiz. 1986. "'Hispanicity' and the 1980 Census." *Social Science Quarterly* 67, no. 1 (Mar.): 3–20.

Tolnay, Stewart E., and E. M. Beck. 1995. *A Festival of Violence: An Analysis of Southern Lynchings, 1882–1930*. Urbana: University of Illinois Press.

Tucker, Clyde, et al. 1996. "Testing Methods of Collecting Racial and Ethnic Information: Results of the Current Population Survey Supplement." *Bureau of Labor Statistics Statistical Notes*, no. 40.

Tucker, William H. 1994. *The Science and Politics of Racial Research*. Urbana: University of Illinois Press.

Turner, J. Michael. 1985. "Brown into Black: Changing Racial Attitudes of Afro-Brazilian University Students." In *Race, Class, and Power in Brazil*, ed. Pierre Michel-Fontaine, pp. 73–94. Los Angeles: Center for Afro-American Studies.

Turra, Cleusa, and Gustavo Venturi. 1995. *Racismo cordial: A mais completa análise sobre preconceito de côr no Brasil*. São Paulo: Ática.

UNESCO. 1983. *Racism, Science, and Pseudo-Science: Proceedings of the Symposium to Examine Pseudo-Scientific Theories Invoked to Justify Racism and Racial Discrimination, Athens, 30 March to 3 April 1981*. Paris: UNESCO.

Urla, Jacqueline. 1993. "Cultural Politics in an Age of Statistics: Numbers, Nations, and the Making of Basque Identity." *American Ethnologist* 20: 818–43.

U.S. Bureau of the Census. 1864. *Population of the United States in 1860: Compiled from the Original Returns of the Eighth Census*. Washington, D.C.: GPO.

———. 1872. *A Compendium of the Ninth Census*. Washington, D.C.: GPO.

———. 1906. *Supplementary Analysis and Derivative Tables*. Washington, D.C.: GPO.

———. [1918] 1968. "Color—Black and Mulatto Elements." In *Negro Population in the United States, 1790–1915*. New York: Arno Press and the New York Times.

———. 1928. "Resolutions Adopted by the Advisory Committee, December 14–18, 1928." RG 29. Box "Advisory Committee Meetings, Apr. 16–17, 1926 to Oct. 1932." File "Advisory Committee Minutes Dec. 14–15, 1928." National Archives, Washington, D.C.

———. 1930. "Instructions to Enumerators." RG 29. Scrapbooks, vol. 2, p. 26. National Archives, Washington, D.C.

———. 1931. "Population of the United States by Color or Race." RG 29. Form 15–927. National Archives, Washington, D.C.

———. 1939. "Memorandum for the Director." RG 29. Advisory Committee Minutes, Feb. 6. National Archives, Washington, D.C.

———. 1940a. "Editing Instructions—Individual Card, Fourteenth Census of the U.S." RG 29. Scrapbooks Relating to the Censuses of Population, 1920–1940, vol. 1. Washington, D.C.: National Archives.

———. 1940b. "Key for Population Test I." RG 29. Scrapbooks Relating to the Censuses of Population, 1920–1940, vol. 4, p. 87. National Archives, Washington, D.C.

———. 1940c. "Sixteenth Census of the United States: 1940, TEST I, Based on Abridged Instructions to Enumerators for Population Schedule." RG 29. Scrapbooks Relating to the Censuses of Population, 1920–1940, vol. 4, p. 86. National Archives, Washington, D.C.

———. 1940d. "Special Notice to Enumerators." Form 9–305. RG 29. Scrapbooks Relating to the Censuses of Population, 1920–1940, vol. 1, p. 81. National Archives, Washington, D.C.

———. 1960. *Historical Statistics of the United States: Colonial Times to 1957.* Washington, D.C.: GPO.

———. 1980. *Questionnaire Reference Book—20th Decennial Census—1980.* Form D-561.

———. 1989a. *Questionnaire Reference Book—21st Decennial Census—1990.* Form D-561 (May).

———. 1989b. *200 Years of U.S. Census Taking: Population and Housing Questions, 1790–1990.* Washington, D.C.: GPO.

———. 1996. *Findings on Questions on Race and Hispanic Origin Tested in the 1996 National Content Survey.* Population Division Working Paper No. 16. Washington, D.C.: Bureau of the Census.

———. 1997. *Results of the 1996 Race and Ethnic Targeted Test.* Population Division Working Paper No. 18 (May). Washington, D.C.: Bureau of the Census.

———. N.d. "General Memorandum on Changes under Consideration for the 1940 Census of Population." RG 29. Advisory Committee Minutes. National Archives, Washington, D.C.

U.S. Congress. 1849. Senate. Letters Addressed to the Hon. John Davis, Concerning the Census of 1849, by Nahum Capen and Jesse Chickering. Miscellaneous Document. 30 Cong., 2d sess., 1849, no. 64, serial 533.

———. 1850. "A Bill Providing for the Taking of the Seventh Census of the United States." S. 76. 31st Cong., 1st sess., Jan. 28, 1850.

———. 1870. House. Report of the Ninth Census. 41st Cong., 2d sess., Jan. 18, 1870.

———. 1888. House. H.R. 11036. 50th Cong., 1st sess., July 30, 1888.

———. 1890. House. *The Executive Documents of the House of Representatives.* 51st Cong., 1st sess., 1889–1890. Washington, D.C.: GPO, 1890.

———. 1994. House. Subcommittee on Census, Statistics and Postal Personnel. *Review of Federal Measurements of Race and Ethnicity.* Serial No. 103–7 (Apr. 14; June 30; July 29; Nov. 3, 1993). Washington, D.C.: GPO.

———. 1997a. House. Subcommittee on Government Management, Information, and Technology. "Hearing on Federal Measures of Race and Ethnicity and the Implications for the 2000 Census" (April 23, 1997).

———. 1997b. House. Subcommittee on Government Management, Information, and Technology. "Hearing on Federal Measures of Race and Ethnicity and the Implications for the 2000 Census" (May 22, 1997).

———. 1997c. House. Subcommittee on Government Management, Information, and Technology. "Hearing on Federal Measures of Race and Ethnicity and the Implications for the 2000 Census" (July 25, 1997).

U.S. Department of the Interior, Census Office. 1896. *Report on Vital and Social Statistics in the United States at the Eleventh Census, 1890.* Part I. Analysis and Rate Tables. 52nd Congress, 1st sess., misc. doc. no. 340, pt. 28. Washington, D.C.: GPO.

U.S. General Accounting Office. 1992. *Federal Data Collection: Agencies' Use of Consistent Race and Ethnic Definitions.* Washington, D.C.: General Accounting Office.

———. 1993. *Census Reform: Early Outreach and Decisions Needed on Race and Ethnic Questions.* Washington, D.C.: General Accounting Office.

U.S. Office of Management and Budget. 1997a. "Recommendations from the Interagency Committee for the Review of the Racial and Ethnic Standards to the Office of Management and Budget Concerning Changes to the Standards for the Classification of Federal Data on Race and Ethnicity." *Federal Register,* July 9.

———. 1997b. "Revisions to the Standards for the Classification of Federal Data on Race and Ethnicity." *Federal Register* 62, no. 210 (Oct. 30).

———. 1999. "Draft Provisional Guidance on the Implementation of the 1997 Standards for the Collection of Federal Data on Race and Ethnicity." OMB web page, Feb. 17.

Uvin, Peter. Forthcoming. "On Counting and Categorizing in Burundi and Rwanda: The Creation of Ethnicity and Power as Instruments of Power." In *Categorizing Citizens: The Use of Race, Ethnicity and Language in National Censuses,* ed. David I. Kertzer and Dominique Arel.

Valente, Ana Lúcia E. F. 1986. *Política e relações raciais: Os negros e as eleições paulistas de 1982.* São Paulo: FFLCH–Universidade de São Paulo.

Van den Berghe, Pierre L. [1967] 1978. *Race and Racism: A Comparative Perspective.* New York: John Wiley.

Vianna, Oliveira. [1923] 1956. *Evolução do povo brasileiro.* 4th ed. Rio de Janeiro: José Olympio.

———. [1920] 1973–74. *Populações meridionais do Brasil.* 2 vols. Rio de Janeiro: Paz e Terra.

———. [1932] 1959. *Raça e assimilação.* 4th ed. Rio de Janeiro: José Olympio.

Vieira, Evaldo Amaro. 1976. *Oliveira Vianna e o estado corporativo: Um estudo sobre corporativismo e autoritarismo.* São Paulo: Editorial Grijalbo.

Wade, Peter. 1993. *Blackness and Race Mixture: The Dynamics of Racial Identity in Colombia.* Baltimore: Johns Hopkins University Press.

Wagley, Charles. 1963. *Race and Class in Rural Brazil.* New York: Columbia University Press.

Wagner, Peter, Björn Wittrock, and Richard Whitley. 1991. *Social Sciences and Modern States: National Experiences and Theoretical Crossroads.* New York: Cambridge University Press.

Watkins, Susan Cotts, ed. 1994. *After Ellis Island: Newcomers and Natives in the 1910 Census.* New York: Russell Sage Foundation.

Wheeler, David L. 1995. "A Growing Number of Scientists Reject the Concept of Race." *Chronicle of Higher Education,* Feb. 17, pp. A-8–9, 15.

White, Jack E. 1997. "I'm Just Who I Am." *Time,* May 5.

White, R. M. 1979. "What's in a Name? Problems in Official and Legal Usages of 'Race.'" *New Community: Journal of the Commission for Racial Equality* 7, no. 3 (Winter): 333–49.

Willcox, Walter F. N.d. [c. 1910–20]. "Race Problems of the South." Paper presented to Conference of the Southern Society for the Promotion of the Study of Race Conditions and Problems in the South. Walter Willcox Papers, box 38, folder, "Negro Studies." Manuscript Division, Library of Congress, Washington, D.C.

———. 1902. Personal Correspondence, Apr. 8, 1902. Walter Willcox Papers, box 26, folder, "General Correspondence with Carroll D. Wright, 1890–1904." Manuscript Division, Library of Congress, Washington, D.C.

Williamson, Joel. 1995. *New People: Miscegenation and Mulattoes in the United States.* Baton Rouge: Louisiana State University Press.

Winant, Howard. 1992. "Rethinking Race in Brazil." *Journal of Latin American Studies* 24: 173–92.

————. 1994. *Racial Conditions: Politics, Theory, Comparisons.* Minneapolis: University of Minnesota Press.

Wirth, John D., Edson de Oliveira Nunes, and Thomas E. Bogenschild, eds. 1987. *State and Society in Brazil: Continuity and Change.* Boulder, Colo.: Westview Press.

Wood, Charles H. 1991. "Categorias censitárias e classificações subjetivas de raça no Brasil. In *Desigualdade racial no Brasil contemporâneo,* ed. Peggy Lovell, pp. 93–111. Belo Horizonte: MGSP Editores.

Wood, Charles H., and Peggy A. Lovell. 1992. "Racial Inequality and Child Mortality in Brazil." *Social Forces* 70, no. 3: 703–24.

Wood, Charles H., and José Alberto Magno de Carvalho. 1995. "Census Categories and Racial-Ethnic Identity in Brazil." Paper presented at the Annual Meeting of the Population Association of America, San Francisco, Apr. 6–8.

Wood, Joe. 1994. "Escape from Blackness: Once Upon a Time in Creole America." *Village Voice,* Dec. 6, pp. 25–34.

Woolf, Stuart. 1989. "Statistics and the Modern State." *Comparative Study of Society and History* 31: 588–604.

Wright, Carroll D., and William Hunt. 1900. *The History and Growth of the United States Census.* Washington, D.C.: GPO.

Wright, Lawrence. 1994. "One Drop of Blood." *New Yorker,* July 25, pp. 46–55.

Wright, Winthrop R. 1990. *Café con Leche: Race, Class, and National Image in Venezuela.* Austin: University of Texas Press.

Young, Crawford. 1994. *The African Colonial State in Comparative Perspective.* New Haven, Conn.: Yale University Press.

Younge, Gary. 1996. "Multiracial Citizens Divided on Idea of Separate Census Classification." *Washington Post,* July 19, p. A-3.

*Anonymous Portuguese-Language Newspaper
and Magazine Articles*

"Apartheid no Brasil é pior que na África, diz secretário." *Folha de São Paulo,* Aug. 2, 1991.

"As côres do Brasil." *Veja,* May 30, 1990, pp. 40–44.

"Benedita dedica seu discurso a 'irma de luta.'" *O Globo* [Rio de Janeiro], Aug. 6, 1991, p. 3.

"Censo-80 vai pesquisar côr, decide o IBGE." *A Folha de São Paulo,* Nov. 9, 1979.

"Especialistas atacam falhas do censo de 91." *Folha de São Paulo,* Jan. 5, 1992, p. 4.

240   Bibliography

"Falta de gen*e, material e transporte prejudica o censo em todo o Brasil."
Folha de São Paulo, Sept. 3, 1991, p. 1.

"Funcionários criticam adiamento do Censo 90." *Jornal do Brasil* [Rio de Janeiro], Aug. 16, 1990, p. 6.

"Governo garante Cr$ 5 bilhões para a realização do censo 90." *Jornal do Brasil* [Rio de Janeiro], July 11, 1990, p. 7.

"Grito contra o racismo." *Jornal do Brasil* [Rio de Janeiro], Aug. 7, 1991, p. 3.

"IBGE confirma adiamento do censo por falta de Funcionários." *Folha de São Paulo*, Aug. 11, 1990, p. 4.

"IBGE reconhece que o censo não reflectirá a realidade." *Jornal do Brasil* [Rio de Janeiro], Feb. 3, 1991, p. 3.

"Identidades sociais." *Jornal do Brasil* [Rio de Janeiro], Apr. 26, 1998, Sunday editorial, p. 10.

"Igualdade ilusoria." *Folha de São Paulo*, Aug. 2, 1991, editorial.

"Indios serão contados." *O Dia* [Rio de Janeiro], May 13, 1990, p. 5.

"Lider nota amargura do negro." *Jornal do Brasil* [Rio de Janeiro], Aug. 6, 1991, p. 5.

"Mandela agradece ao Brasil apoio na luta anti-apartheid." *Jornal do Commercio*, Aug. 2, 1991, p. 1.

"Mandela agradece apoio dos brasileiros." *O Estado de São Paulo*, Aug. 4, 1991, p. 11.

"Mandela atrai 40 mil à Praça da Apoteose." *Jornal do Brasil* [Rio de Janeiro], Aug. 2, 1991, p. 1.

"Mandela contradiz lideres negros do Brasil." *Folha de São Paulo*, Aug. 2, 1991, p. 7.

"Mandela elogia Igreja na luta contra racismo." *Jornal do Commercio*, Aug. 5, 1991.

"Movimento negro protesta." *Folha de São Paulo*, Aug. 2, 1991, p. 7.

"Movimentos negros veem discriminação." *Jornal do Commercio*, Aug. 2, 1991, p. 2.

"Negros querem sua côr assumida no censo 91." *Jornal do Brasil* [Rio de Janeiro], Sept. 24, 1991, p. 3.

"Presidente do IBGE culpa a burocracia." *Folha de São Paulo*, Aug. 31, 1991, p. 9.

"Presidente lembra as raízes comuns." *O Globo* [Rio de Janeiro], Aug. 6, 1991, p. 3.

"Reforma administrativa compromete censo de 90." *Jornal do Brasil* [Rio de Janeiro], June 29, 1990, p. 4.

"Uma nova tomada de consciencia." *O Dia* [Rio de Janeiro], May 13, 1990.

Index

242 *Index*

Census bureaus, U.S. (general discussion), 17; as agencies of state governance, 1, 3, 14, 15, 19; political and economic influences of, 1–2, 22; race and, 2, 4, 12, 14–17
Censuses, Brazilian: 1872, 86, 87, 88–89; 1890, 93; 1900, 93; 1920, 92–96, 93, 94, 95, 112; 1940, 98–106; 1950–1960, 106–10, 117; 1970, 110–15; 1980, 115–19, 150; 1991, 100, 120–22, 154, 155–56, 159–62; 2000, 86, 87, 100, 123–26, 171–77; advertising campaign for 1991 census, 155–56, 161; assessment of the 1991 campaign, 159–62; 1997 pilot tests for 2000, 172–73
—(general discussion), 23–24, 85, 96, 153; census-taking process and methods, 5, 16, 89, 91, 147, 154–55, 159, 176; color question on, 110–15, 117–18, 150, 155, 171–77; *movimento negro* and, 146–62; racial ideas/ideology and, 89; scientific standards for, 114–15; texts, 85, 91, 98, 106, 109. *See also* Racial census data, Brazilian
Censuses, U.S.: 1790–1830, 25, 26–31; 1840, 31–35; 1850, 35–38, 38–43, 52, 56, 61; 1860, 43–48, 52, 56; 1870, 50–52, 56; 1880, 52, 56–57; 1890, 54–62, 67; 1900–1930, 65–69; 1910, 70, 137; 1920, 61, 69; 1930–1960, 69–75; 1970, 81; 1980, 81; 2000, 75, 81, 129, 142, 145; 2010, 144
—(general discussion), 1, 24, 63–64; citizenship issues and, 5; civil rights and, 75–84; influences and uses of, 15, 63; politics of, 6, 180–84; post–Civil War, 48–54; public policies and, 18–19; race and, 23, 75–84; race question on, 169–70; racial discourse and, 17, 63, 74, 79, 130–31; role of, 50, 63, 77, 79; slave schedules, 24–27, 35, 36, 38–39, 42, 43, 52; societal uses of, 31–32; U.S./Brazilian comparisons of, 86–87, 88, 177–79. *See also* Enumeration and enumerators, census; Race categories, U.S.; Racial census data, U.S.

Census-taking, process and methods, U.S., 22–23, 34, 51, 78; all-inclusive approach, 165; 2000 census, 145; collapsing categorization approach, 165, 166, 167–68; equal fractional approach, 166; full racial distribution approach, 165, 167; historical (priority reassignment) approach, 165, 167; impartiality issues and, 1, 2, 14, 15, 16, 25; by observation, 61–62; as political process, 15–16; proportional distribution approach, 166, 167; racial discourse and, 25, 77; racial discrimination and, 143; random reassignment approach, 166; reform, 51; schedules, 5–6, 29–30, 35–36, 38, 43; societal applications of, 31–32; standardization of, 15; statistics and, 2–3, 14, 16–17; unequal variant approach, 166; U.S./Brazilian comparisons of, 129–30; vs. law, 55–58; whole reassignment or imputation approach, 166, 167. *See also* Enumeration and enumerators, census
Citizenship, 1, 24, 178, 179; black, 4–5, 13, 29, 37, 48–49, 54–55, 137; in Brazil, 5, 91, 151–53, 175, 178, 179; exclusion from, 6; laws, 48; national, 22; public policies and, 1, 18; race and, 4–6; rights associated with, 4–5, 152–53; status, 28–29
Civil rights, 76, 142, 170; activism/politics, 78, 133, 134, 137; in Brazil, 150; censuses and, 75–84; discourse, 75–76; enforcement, 83; laws, 19, 20, 23, 34, 63, 75, 78, 79, 137, 140, 141, 168, 170; organizations, 78, 134, 137, 140, 141, 143, 167
Civil Rights Acts (1964, 1968), 48, 54, 75
Civil Rights Movement, 20, 75, 78, 117, 129, 130, 134, 138, 177
Committee on the 1950 Census of the Americas (COTA), 107
Congressional Record (previously, *Congressional Globe*), 23, 38

Darwinism, 50, 53–54, 56, 65
Da Silva, Benedita, 157, 174–75, 176

74, 77, 79, 130–31; changes in, 30–
31; decentralization of, 138; multiracial, 132–38, 137, 178; post–Civil
War, 49; race categories and, 75,
130; race science/theory and, 55, 74–
75; scientific thought and, 13, 61;
slavery/slaves and, 32; U.S./Brazilian
comparisons of, 8, 10, 18, 22, 129–
30, 177–78
Racial ideas/ideology, 2, 10–11, 12, 24–
26, 31, 41–42, 89; 1850 census and,
42; census-taking process and, 168;
Darwinism and, 53–54; perception of
blacks as inferior, 48–54, 60, 67, 71;
political, 37, 55; post–Civil War censuses and, 48–54; public policies and,
2, 42–43, 63, 75, 84; racial discourse
and, 55; as rationale for treatment of
blacks, 46–47; scientific, 13, 26, 42,
43, 50, 52–53, 63, 64, 77
Racial identity: in Brazil, 86–87; in
United States, 132–38; U.S./Brazilian
comparisons of, 10, 23. *See also*
National identity, Brazilian
Racial thought, *see* Racial
ideas/ideology
Racism, 13, 20, 50, 75; in Brazil, 99,
101, 105, 106, 108, 121, 124–25,
156, 157–59, 177; in South Africa,
157–58; in United States, 133, 158
Reconstruction, 48, 49, 54
Representation by population, 26–27,
29–31, 51, 76, 89, 164
Rios, José Arthur, 112–13, 114
Romero, Sílvio, 90–91

Schedules, *see* Census-taking, process
and methods, U.S.
Science of race, *see* Race science/theory
Segregation, 7, 23, 43, 48, 54, 61, 64, 71,
75, 105, 170, 177; in Brazil, 177; laws,
18, 19, 61–62, 66, 72, 75, 76, 138
Slavery/slaves, 4, 12, 13, 23, 30; 1840
census and, 31–35; 1850 census and,
35–43; 1860 census and, 42, 43–48;
abolition of, 7, 9, 43–48, 48; abolition of, in Brazil, 87, 88, 146, 147,
155, 180; in Brazil, 87, 88, 90, 97,

98, 102, 146; census data, 45, 46;
children of, 39, 40, 41; colonization
programs for emancipated slaves, 45;
debates, 31–32, 38–43, 42, 43; early
censuses (1790–1830) and, 26–31;
representational apportionment and,
26, 27, 29–30, 51; U.S./Brazilian
comparisons of, 7–9, 10. *See also*
Censuses, U.S. (general discussion):
slave schedules; Free blacks
Social Darwinism, 54–62, 65
Socialism moreno, 148
South Africa, 5, 147, 156, 157, 158,
159, 180; apartheid, 5, 147, 156,
157, 158, 159, 180
Statistical Directive No. 15, *see* Office
of Management and Budget (OMB)
Statistics, 2–3, 14, 16–17, 59; accuracy
of, 34, 37, 39, 47, 67, 68–69; Civil
War, 45; Negro, 37–38, 57, 58, 60;
science of, 31–32, 64; slave, 40; social, 35–36. *See also* Racial census
data
Supreme Court: Dred Scott Decision, 4,
29; race and, 138; segregation decisions, 54–55, 61–62, 66

Taxation, 27, 29; enumeration and, 36,
43
Thirteenth Amendment, 4, 48, 62
Three-fifths clause, 26–27
"Tiger Woods Bill" (H.R. Bill 830),
141, 144

Underwood, Joseph, 25, 38, 39–40, 42,
61
Unions, labor, 94, 103, 116, 157
United Nations, 15, 109, 114; Universal
Declaration of Human Rights, 133
United Nations Educational Scientific
and Cultural Organization
(UNESCO), 74, 110, 111, 156, 177

Vargas, Getúlio, 92, 96–99, 103, 106
Vianna, Francisco José Oliviera, 87, 93,
95–96, 98, 102, 112
Violence against blacks, 54–55
Voting Rights Act, 20, 75, 168